LINUX®
ASSEMBLY LANGUAGE
PROGRAMMING

ISBN 0-13-087940-1

90000

9 780130 879400

PRENTICE HALL PTR
OPEN SOURCE TECHNOLOGY SERIES

LINUX®
ASSEMBLY LANGUAGE
PROGRAMMING

BOB NEVELN

Prentice Hall PTR
Upper Saddle River, New Jersey 07458
www.phptr.com

Editorial/production supervision: *Vincent Janoski*
Acquisitions editor: *Miles Williams*
Marketing manager: *Kate Hargett*
Manufacturing manager: *Alexis Heydt*
Cover design director: *Jerry Votta*
Cover designer: *Nina Scuderi*

Published by Prentice Hall PTR
Prentice-Hall, Inc.
Upper Saddle River, NJ 07458

Prentice Hall books are widely used by corporations and government agencies
for training, marketing, and resale.

The publisher offers discounts on this book when ordered in bulk quantities.
For more information, contact: Corporate Sales Department, Phone: 800-382-3419;
Fax: 201-236-7141; E-mail: corpsales@prenhall.com; or write: Prentice Hall PTR,
Corp. Sales Dept., One Lake Street, Upper Saddle River, NJ 07458.

Printed in the United States of America
10 9 8 7 6 5 4 3 2 1

ISBN   0-13-087940-1

Prentice-Hall International (UK) Limited, *London*
Prentice-Hall of Australia Pty. Limited, *Sydney*
Prentice-Hall Canada Inc., *Toronto*
Prentice-Hall Hispanoamericana, S.A., *Mexico*
Prentice-Hall of India Private Limited, *New Delhi*
Prentice-Hall of Japan, Inc., *Tokyo*
Prentice-Hall Asia Pte. Ltd.
Editora Prentice-Hall do Brasil, Ltda., *Rio de Janeiro*

This book is dedicated to all imprisoned Plowshares activists for attempting to do with iron what also needs to be done with silicon.

CONTENTS

CHAPTER 3

LOGIC CIRCUITS AND COMPUTATION 27

CHAPTER 4

ASSEMBLY LANGUAGE 63

CHAPTER 5

MACHINE LANGUAGE 81

CHAPTER 6

MEMORY 94

CHAPTER 7

THE STACK 111

CHAPTER 8

LINUX USER PROGRAMS 122

CHAPTER 9

INTERRUPTS 145

CHAPTER 10

BIT MANIPULATIONS 164

CHAPTER 11

DEVICE DRIVERS 171

CHAPTER 12

DOS PROGRAMS 212

CHAPTER 13

LINUX BOOT TIME PROGRAMS 228

PREFACE

Assembly language is language which gives the programmer direct control over the computer. That is what appeals to people about assembly language. It is like using a stick shift. Programming with other languages, high-level languages, is like using an automatic.

Many people who use computers simply run programs. To them a program is a canned software package. People who like to write programs like to be able to shape the behavior of the machine the way metalsmiths shape metal into useful mechanical tools. Amongst all the programs on a computer, there is one program which runs the machine: the operating system. It controls everything. It offers "services" to the other programs. Most operating systems force programmers to leave their programming skills behind as they approach the operating system and to use it as they would a canned software package. That is because its source code is a secret. Linux portends the end of secret code in computing. Because the Linux source code and a compiler for it are right there on the computer along with the other source code, it allows programmers to work with the operating system as they do with programs they have written.

Operating systems were once written by programmers employed by computer manufacturers. Revolutions in hardware produced corresponding revolutions in the software. When Linus Torvalds rewrote Linux so that it would run on the Alpha architecture, his goal was not to increase its hardware base from one platform to two, but to make Linux platform-independent. The subsequent ports of Linux, to everything from a Sparc to a PowerPC, demonstrate the success of his rewrite. The chief value of it is that it provides us with confidence that Linux is here to stay. We don't have to fear a PowerPC revolution coming along and forcing us to dump all of our old software.

Assembly code, on the other hand, is intrinsically platform-dependent and is justifiably regarded with caution for just this reason. It will have to be redone when the next hardware revolution takes place. Furthermore, people who compare the machine language of the 386 with other machine languages, both real and ideal, inevitably end up regarding the 386 language as a historical accident. On the other hand, the genetic code is sometimes referred to as a *frozen accident*. The term is based on the idea that the genetic code ceased its evolution when the number of proteins whose code would be "broken" by a mutation in the genetic code became so large that such mutations became lethal, and so the code became fixed. It remains to be seen whether 386 machine code has been "frozen" into place by the size of its software base. The threat of a PowerPC revolution has passed. On the other hand, many Linux enthusiasts anticipate an Alpha revolution.

But the Alpha revolution has not happened and it may not happen. The 386 language has been around for a long time. With many RISC machines now emulating the 386 architecture, isn't it time to consider programming in 386 assembly language? Assembly language is more work but it has its advantages. A very nice feature of assembly language code, which it shares with Linux itself incidentally, is that from a crass performance standpoint, it functions beautifully. Relying on compilers to produce good code is usually justifiable as a time saving measure. But to get the best possible code, there is still no better option than to use assembly language. When high-level languages were still a novelty and referred to as *automatic programming*, many programmers were greatly offended by them. They were convinced that no compiler program could write code as well as they could. They were right of course. Compilers produce cheaper code but not better code. To get the full measure of speed and grace that a machine is capable of, there is no substitute for assembly language.

Furthermore, even if the Alpha revolution arrives on schedule tomorrow, there will remain in the world millions of processors running a 386 language, which work beautifully and need to be put to a socially responsible use.

Computers can be programmed to report on our buying habits or to send off nuclear missiles. But they can also be programmed to communicate with privacy or to support medical research. As siliconsmiths, our job is to shape the behavior of the machine towards a human agenda.

This book assumes that the reader has some knowledge of C, but it makes no other assumptions.

Starred sections of the book are not needed subsequently and may be skipped when they are not of intrinsic interest.

I owe thanks to Dave Felter for writing a partial simulator of the 8080. This simulator got me started writing Edlinas.

I owe thanks to Bruce Grant, Itzick Vatnick, and Kate L'Armand for working with me on the scalex device driver.

I owe thanks to the many students who have found errors in earlier drafts of this book. I owe special thanks to Joe Bissell, Scott Hawkins, Jason Kroll, Nancy Yoshimura, and Joanne Yurchak for their careful, detailed, and thoughtful crititism. Many errors undoubtedly remain. To those readers who notify me of them at *neveln@cs.widener.edu* I shall be grateful.

Linux-Driven Serial Port Input Device

INTRODUCTION

In this chapter some necessary tools and background ideas are reviewed.

1.1 The Fetch-Execute Cycle

One of the earliest electronic computers was the ENIAC. When it was first built it could not store programs. Each new computation required moving plugs and jumper cables. Now, however, nearly all computers store programs. For these computers, doing a computation means running a program. The place where the program is stored is called *memory*. The part of the machine which does the computation is called the *processor*. Computer programs generally take the form of a list of instructions. Computation is performed by the processor using the fetch-execute cycle. The fetch-execute cycle consists of a repeated process that includes these steps:

1. The processor fetches an instruction from memory.

2. The processor executes the instruction.

3. The processor cycles back to step 1.

Computers based on the fetch-execute cycle are sometimes called *Von Neumann* computers. Von Neumann was a well-known mathematician who was also an early computer theorist.

Probably the most important examples of computers which are not based on the fetch-execute cycle are DNA computers and quantum computers. Of course

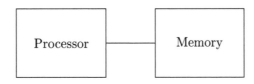

Figure 1-1. A Stored Program Computer

it may be that these computers will reach a point in their development when they
are ready to leave university laboratories and that by that time, they too will run
stored programs.

1.2   The Linux Operating System

Most computers do not simply run one program at a time. They run a program
running program called an *operating system*. It interacts with the user and manages
hardware devices such as the disk drives and printers, and runs other programs. The
earliest operating systems were written by computer vendors. Each computer had
its own operating system. The first vendor-independent operating system was the
Unix operating system. It was developed by a handful of researchers at Bell Labs.

AT&T, the principal owner of Bell Labs, soon made Unix available for a nominal
fee to academic institutions, which in turn developed Unix further. This generous
behavior on the part of AT&T may have been influenced by a consent decree entered in 1956, which restricted commercial activity on the part of AT&T beyond
"furnishing common carrier communications services." This decree was the result
of a complaint in 1949 by the Justice Department against Western Electric and
AT&T, claiming that they were trying to leverage their telephone monopoly into
other sectors.

The version of Unix developed at the University of California at Berkeley became
very widely used. It was designed to be portable, i.e., easy to transfer from one
type of computer to another. It is known as *Berkeley Unix* or *BSD Unix*, (Berkeley
Software Division).

Linux is a non-proprietary variant of Unix, which was created by Linus Torvalds
on a 386-based computer and subsequently developed by an online community of
users. Although several non-PC versions of Linux exist, most existing installations
of Linux are on Intel-compatible hardware.

Many users of Linux have Linux installed along with another operating system.
Having separate disk partitions for Linux and Windows/DOS is common.

1.3   The Gnu C Compiler

The portability of the Unix operating system was partly a consequence of the fact
that by 1973 it had been rewritten in a high-level language, C. The C language was
in turn designed to be a portable language.

The first nonproprietary version of C was developed by Richard Stallman of the
Free Software Foundation. Its name,   *gnu*, which stands for "Gnu's Not Unix,"
proclaims its escape from proprietary copyright restrictions. The gnu C compiler
is widely used, not only because it's free, but because it has set a standard for
reliability. The Linux operating system depends heavily on the gnu C compiler.

A compiler is a program which translates a program such as a C language program into a machine code program that can be stored in a computer's memory and
run. A program that can be stored in memory and run is called an *executable file*

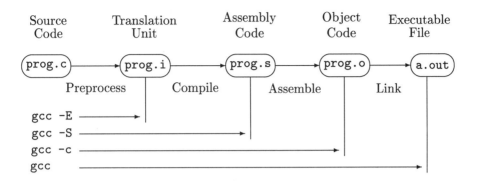

Figure 1-2. Stages of Gnu C Compilation

or sometimes just an *executable*.

The gnu C compiler works in stages. See Figure 1-2. To compile a program such as `prog.c` with the gnu compiler, one can enter the command

        linuxbox$ gcc prog.c

This command takes the translation through all the stages and produces an executable file called `a.out`. To stop at an earlier stage, one can add a *switch* to the gcc command line. For example, to produce an assembly code file, the "-S" switch (upper case) is used. Entering the command

        linuxbox$ gcc -S prog.c

yields an assembly language file, `prog.s`. To finish the compilation, the **gcc** command may be used on the `.s` file

        linuxbox$ gcc prog.s

1.4   The Edlinas Assembler

The assembly language in the `.s` files produced by the gnu compiler is different from the widely used Intel assembly language for the x86 processors. Edlinas assembly language is essentially the Intel assembly language. Its object code files run under x86 Linux. Edlinas is an interactive environment consisting of an editor, an assembler, and a simulator.

1.4.1   Editing

Source code editing uses commands borrowed from EDLIN, a DOS editor. Among the commands are **i** for insert, **d** for delete, **c** for change, **e** for exit, **q** for quit, and **h** for help. Commands affect the *current line*, which is the line that has the asterisk, ∗. The asterisk is moved using the arrow keys. Entered lines are checked by the assembler for syntax errors.

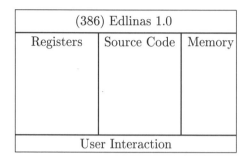

(386) Edlinas 1.0		
Registers	Source Code	Memory
User Interaction		

Figure 1-3. The Edlinas Screen

1.4.2 Assembling

Code is assembled as it is entered or loaded. Assembly code appears in the default window on the right side of the screen. Assembled code can be saved at any time using the **o** command.

1.4.3 Interpreting

Code can be executed either from a loaded program or from a command prompt below.

To step through lines of code, the space bar is used. The line about to be executed is displayed in yellow. It is the line pointed at by the *instruction pointer*. The enter key resets the instruction pointer to the current line. Instructions can therefore be executed in any order by moving the asterisk around.

The escape key brings up a cursor at the command prompt below. Commands here are executed *immediately*. An empty command exits the command line.

To observe the effects of code execution, various areas of the machine may be brought into view in the right panel of the screen. The different choices for the contents of the right panel can be cycled through using the tab key.

The layout of the Edlinas screen, which is adapted from that of an 8080 simulator written by Dave Felter, is shown in Figure 1-3.

Edlinas is a DOS program, EDL.EXE.

1.4.4 Dosemu

The Edlinas assembler is a DOS program. If you have a machine which has a DOS partition, the simplest way of getting to DOS is by rebooting. But it is not necessarily the most convenient. Further, your machine may not have a DOS partition. The dosemu program makes it possible to run DOS programs from Linux. It is available from *www.dosemu.org*.

To run Edlinas, the `$_graphics` variable in `dosemu.conf` should be set to (1).

1.5 NASM

The Netwide Assembler, or NASM, is an open source assembler that runs under Linux as well as DOS. Its use is increasing and has much to recommend it. In particular due to its widespread use, it has been exposed to a very thorough debugging. It also accepts a broader vocabulary of assembly language instructions than does Edlinas. Most of the programs in this book may be assembled using either assembler. Edlinas can be used to step through the example programs in the text, but for the bigger programs such as the interrupt handler in chapter 11, NASM is definitely the better choice. NASM is an industrial-strength assembler.

To unpack the distribution, which comes with this book, use the command

```
linuxbox$ unzip -aL nasm097s.zip
```

after copying it to a suitable directory. To build it, you can then copy the appropriate makefile

```
linuxbox$:  cp makefile.unx Makefile
```

and run

```
linuxbox$:  make
```

1.6 Other Assemblers

MASM and Turbo-Assembler are assemblers that have been very widely used in connection with DOS. The fact that Windows is not so easy to work with using assembly language has led to a decrease in the popularity of these assemblers. Many people have the impression that Linux is not particularly assembler-friendly either. This impression is partly based on the view of assembly language that you get working with gcc. Those accustomed to Intel syntax may understandably find the AT&T syntax awkward. Worse, when assembly language instructions are inserted into C code, the quotation marks required by gcc and the line-jumbling that occurs are pretty repellent. I hope that by chapter 7, readers will be persuaded that interacting with Linux using assembly language can be clean and neat.

There are a few other assemblers around. A brief discussion of them can be found in an Assembly-HOWTO at the Linux Documentation Project's Website, *www.linuxdoc.org/HOWTO*.

Further Reading

Open Sources, Voices from the Open Source Revolution, ed. Chris DiBona et. al., O'Reilly: 1999.

A Quarter Century of Unix, Peter Salus, Addison-Wesley: 1994.

2

PLACEHOLDING NUMERATION

The ENIAC did not use the binary system. Its arithmetic processor used vacuum tubes wired together into rings, which worked like old desktop adding machine wheels. These were base ten contraptions. Since then, however, all electronic computers have done their arithmetic using the binary system (base two). Consequently, descriptions of computer arithmetic are customarily expressed using the binary system or related systems such as hexadecimal (base sixteen) or octal (base eight). An understanding of these number systems is essential. Readers already familiar with them may prefer to skip this chapter.

2.1 The Decimal and Pentimal Systems

Before the invention of placeholding decimal notation in the East, probably in India or China, systems of notation built around powers of ten, which were not placeholding systems, were common. The system used by Archimedes, for example, is shown in Table 2.1. In this system, SPA represents the number *171*. Greek letters of course, not Latin letters, were used. The most apparent disadvantage of

A	1	J	10	S	100
B	2	K	20	T	200
C	3	L	30	U	300
D	4	M	40	V	400
E	5	N	50	W	500
F	6	O	60		
G	7	P	70		
H	8	Q	80		
I	9	R	90		

Table 2.1. Non-Placeholding Decimal System

this kind of system is computational. The notation is no help at all in seeing that

$$B + C = E$$
$$K + L = N \qquad \text{and}$$
$$T + U = W$$

all represent essentially the same basic fact. But this is only a problem when notations themselves are used to do calculations (as we do with pencil and paper). When calculations are done with physical tokens, such as beads on an abacus or with pebbles, this is no longer a problem. In fact, this kind of notation may have served to prevent reading errors. Anyone who has received $20.00 when cashing a $200.00 check will understand this point.

But when the notations themselves are used to do the calculations, it is better to have a notational system which brings out such basic similarities as the following:

$$2 + 3 = 5$$
$$20 + 30 = 50$$
$$200 + 300 = 500$$

Placeholding systems do this. Placeholding numerals, sometimes less sympathetically referred to as "heathen cyphers," were popularized in Europe around the year 1200 by Leonardo of Pisa, also known as Fibonacci. Fibonacci was presumably relying on a work written in Arabic by al-Khwārizmi (whose name we see in the word *algorithm*) around the year 820 in Baghdad. Like all European scholars of the day, Fibonacci was necessarily versed in Arabic.

All the numeration systems discussed in this book, including the decimal system we use every day, are placeholding systems. Before proceeding to nondecimal systems, let us consider the role that base ten plays in the U.S. monetary system.

2.1.1 Purely Decimal Money

The current U.S. monetary system was adopted following the introduction of the metric system in France in the Revolution of 1789. The purpose of both of these extensions of the decimal system was to simplify calculations by bringing monetary and measurement units into harmony with the decimal system used to represent numbers.

To bring the alignment of the monetary and numeral systems into sharp relief, let us imagine a pared down version of the U.S. monetary system that includes only pennies, dimes, $1 bills, $10 dollar bills, $100 dollar bills, $1000 dollar bills, and so on.

$$
\begin{aligned}
\text{1 dime} &= \text{10 pennies} \\
\text{1 dollar bill} &= \text{10 dimes} \\
&= \text{100 pennies} \\
\text{1 ten dollar bill} &= \text{10 dollar bills} \\
&= \text{100 dimes} \\
&= \text{1000 pennies} \\
&\quad\text{and so on}
\end{aligned}
$$

In this purely decimal monetary system, each denomination except pennies is worth exactly ten times the next smaller unit. Denominations correspond to place values in the base ten numeration system, and vice versa. Pennies are ones, dimes are tens, dollars are hundreds, etc.

To carry exact change for any possible transaction in this bare bones monetary system, one would need nine items of each denomination. For example, to make a purchase whose cost was $56.78, or 5,678 cents, would require 5 ten dollar bills, 6 dollar bills, 7 dimes, and 8 pennies.

If we actually used this system, our change purses would need to be bulkier than they are. The existence of nickels, quarters, etc. reduces the amount of change we must carry. To get a less bulky system which was nonetheless based on simple multiples we could imagine a system based on fives instead of tens.

2.1.2 Pentimal Money

Suppose we imagine a monetary system whose denominations are pennies, nickels, quarters, $1.25 bills, $6.25 bills, and so on. In this system, the value of each denomination except pennies is exactly five times the value of the next smaller denomination. Let's call 125 cents a "Big Dollar" and imagine that the currency for it is a bill with a big "1" on it.

$$
\begin{array}{rcl}
\text{1 nickel} & = & \text{5 pennies} \\
\text{1 quarter} & = & \text{5 nickels} \\
& = & \text{25 pennies} \\
\text{1 Big Dollar} & = & \text{5 quarters} \\
& = & \text{25 nickels} \\
& = & \text{125 pennies} \\
& & \text{and so on}
\end{array}
$$

To be prepared to carry out any transaction in this system, we would need to carry only four items of each unit. This would create less bulk in our change purses. But look what would happen to the arithmetic! To make a purchase of $56.78 would require

$$
\begin{array}{rll}
\text{one} & \text{\$31.25 bill} = & \text{\$31.25} \\
\text{four} & \text{\$6.25 bills} = & \text{\$25.00} \\
\text{zero} & \text{\$1.25 bills} = & \text{\$0.00} \\
\text{two} & \text{quarters} = & \text{\$0.50} \\
\text{zero} & \text{nickels} = & \text{\$0.00} \\
\text{three} & \text{pennies} = & \underline{\text{\$0.03}} \\
& = & \text{\$56.78}
\end{array}
$$

This arithmetic is no longer transparently obvious as it is when we have decimal money. This is true despite the fact that this pentimal monetary system is just as simple as the decimal monetary system. The decimal monetary system appears to be simpler because it matches our decimal numeration system. However, if we used a pentimal numeration system as well as pentimal money system, simplicity would return. Every monetary unit would correspond to a place value in the pentimal numeration system, and vice versa.

2.1.3 Pentimal Numerals

The place values in the pentimal numeral system are one, five, twenty-five, one hundred twenty-five, etc. Each value is worth five of the next smaller.

Any number can be represented using at most four of any one place value. So the digits 5, 6, 7, 8, and 9 are not used. All numbers are represented using only the numerals 0, 1, 2, 3, and 4.

The pentimal 24 is the same as the ordinary decimal 14. It means 2 fives and 4 ones, like 2 nickels and 4 pennies. Similarly, 124 is the same as 39 in base ten. In cents it means 1 quarter, 2 nickels and 4 pennies.

Counting goes like this: 1, 2, 3, 4, 10, 11, 12, 13, 14, 20, 21, 22, 23, 24, 30, 31, 32, 33, 34, 40, 41, 42, 43, 44, 100, 101, 102, 103, 104, 110, 111, and so on. Using pentimal numeration to describe pentimal money, we get this table:

$$
\begin{array}{rcll}
\text{1 nickel} & = & \text{10 pennies} & (10 = \text{five}) \\
\text{1 quarter} & = & \text{10 nickels} & \\
& = & \text{100 pennies} & (100 = \text{twenty-five}) \\
\text{1 Big Dollar} & = & \text{10 quarters} & \\
& = & \text{100 nickels} & \\
& = & \text{1000 pennies} & (1000 = \text{one hundred twenty-five})
\end{array}
$$

2.2 Pentimal Arithmetic

Given a base five arithmetic problem:

$$
\begin{array}{r}
423 \\
+\ 334 \\
\end{array}
$$

we have a choice of methods. We can convert these numbers into base ten, do the arithmetic, and then convert back to base five. Or we can do the problem without any conversions using the "native arithmetic."

The first method is easier at first since we are used to base ten. Thinking in terms of monetary units: 423 is four quarters, two nickels and three pennies, i.e., 113 cents in ordinary base ten. Similarly, 334 is 94 cents in ordinary base ten. So we can do the addition using ordinary base ten arithmetic:

$$
\begin{array}{r}
113 \\
+\ 94 \\
\hline
207 \\
\end{array}
$$

One hundred thirteen plus 94 is 207, or $2.07. To convert back, start by taking out one big dollar, a dollar and a quarter, and we have 82 cents left. This is three quarters, one nickel and two pennies. So the answer is 1312.

25s	5s	1s	Pentimal	Decimal
0	0	1	1	1
0	0	2	2	2
0	0	3	3	3
0	0	4	4	4
0	1	0	10	5
0	1	1	11	6
0	1	2	12	7
0	1	3	13	8
0	1	4	14	9
0	2	0	20	10
0	2	1	21	11
0	2	2	22	12
0	2	3	23	13
0	2	4	24	14
0	3	0	30	15
0	3	1	31	16
0	3	2	32	17
0	3	3	33	18
0	3	4	34	19
0	4	0	40	20
0	4	1	41	21
0	4	2	42	22
0	4	3	43	23
0	4	4	44	24
1	0	0	100	25
1	0	1	101	26
1	0	2	102	27
1	0	3	103	28
1	0	4	104	29
1	1	0	110	30
1	1	1	111	31
1	1	2	112	32
1	1	3	113	33

Table 2.2. Pentimal System Place Values

2.2.1   Native Addition

Using the native arithmetic, however, is easier than this, especially when the numbers get larger. About all that's necessary to remember is that five of any one unit must be carried by converting it to one of the next larger unit:

$$
\begin{array}{r}
423 \\
+\ 334 \\
\hline
\end{array}
$$

The ones (or pennies) column totals seven, which is 12, which is 2 carry 1:

$$
\begin{array}{r}
1 \\
423 \\
+\ 334 \\
\hline
2
\end{array}
$$

$1 + 2 + 3$ is six, which is 11, which is 1 carry 1:

$$
\begin{array}{r}
1 \\
423 \\
+\ 334 \\
\hline
12
\end{array}
$$

And $1 + 4 + 3$ is eight, which is 13, which is 3 carry 1:

$$
\begin{array}{r}
423 \\
+\ 334 \\
\hline
1312
\end{array}
$$

Clearly, the native arithmetic is easier once we understand it.

2.2.2 Native Subtraction

Subtraction requires borrowing, for example, converting a quarter to five nickels or a nickel to five pennies. The following subtraction of three from ten illustrates borrowing:

$$
\begin{array}{r}
20 \\
-\ 3
\end{array}
$$

Borrow a nickel from the nickels column and convert it into five pennies:

$$
\begin{array}{rl}
10 & \text{(five pennies)} \\
1 & \text{(one nickel)} \\
-\ 3 & \\
\hline
2 &
\end{array}
$$

One nickel is left:

$$
\begin{array}{rl}
10 & \text{(five pennies)} \\
1 & \text{(one nickel)} \\
-\ 3 & \\
\hline
12 &
\end{array}
$$

So we get one nickel and two pennies left.

2.3 Conversion to Pentimal

Sometimes conversions are unavoidable. For a computer to be able to store a number in binary which is input in decimal, a conversion is needed. Although conversions can be done by searching for a representation which works, there are more efficient methods. Consider the conversion of 207 into base five. To understand this conversion, it may help to look at the answer before we start:

$$1312 = 1 \cdot 5^3 + 3 \cdot 5^2 + 1 \cdot 5^1 + 2 \cdot 5^0$$

We can see that 5 can be factored out of this sum, except for the 2 at the end:

$$1312 = (1 \cdot 5^2 + 3 \cdot 5^1 + 1 \cdot 5^0) \cdot 5 + 2$$

But this just says what the quotient and remainder of 207 divided by 5 are. Notice that the remainder is our units digit. Furthermore, we can calculate this quotient and remainder using base ten, which is what we have available when we start this conversion:

$$\begin{array}{r} 41 \\ 5\overline{)207} \\ \underline{205} \\ 2 \end{array}$$ and so our ones digit is 2.

We have in base ten that:

$$207 = 41 \cdot 5 + 2$$

where again peeking at the answer shows us that:

$$41 = 1 \cdot 5^2 + 3 \cdot 5^1 + 1 \cdot 5^0$$

The quotient, 41, contains the information needed to get all the other digits. They can be obtained using more divisions:

$$\begin{array}{r} 8 \\ 5\overline{)41} \\ \underline{40} \\ 1 \end{array}$$ and adjoining this digit gives us 12.

$$\begin{array}{r} 1 \\ 5\overline{)8} \\ \underline{5} \\ 3 \end{array}$$ which gives us 312.

The last division has a zero quotient:

$$\begin{array}{r} 0 \\ 5\overline{)1} \\ \underline{0} \\ 1 \end{array}$$ or 1312

The algorithm for conversion consists of repeated division by 5, each remainder yielding a digit of the answer. It proceeds until a zero quotient is obtained.

2.4   The Binary System

Knowing the binary system is important because the native arithmetic of all existing computer processors is binary arithmetic.

Binary numbers use only two digits: 0 and 1. All binary numbers are constructed from just these two digits. Counting goes like this: 1, 10, 11, 100, 101, 110, 111, 1000, 1001, 1010, 1011, 1100, 1101, 1110, 1111, 10000, 10001, 10010, etc.

The binary system is a placeholding system. Each position except for the ones position stands for a unit which is twice the value of the next smaller unit. See Table 2.3.

2.4.1   Binary Addition

Suppose we want to add

$$
\begin{array}{r}
1101 \\
+\ 110 \\
\end{array}
$$

which is thirteen plus six. The first column does not require a carry:

$$
\begin{array}{r}
1101 \\
+\ 110 \\
\hline
1 \\
\end{array}
$$

Neither does the second:

$$
\begin{array}{r}
1101 \\
+\ 110 \\
\hline
11 \\
\end{array}
$$

The third column totals two, which is 10, which is 0 carry 1:

$$
\begin{array}{r}
1 \\
1101 \\
+\ 110 \\
\hline
011 \\
\end{array}
$$

The fourth column also totals two, which is again 0 carry 1:

$$
\begin{array}{r}
1101 \\
+\ 110 \\
\hline
10011 \\
\end{array}
$$

This is exactly how a computer adds thirteen and six. We can check that the result is nineteen.

$$
\begin{array}{rrcr}
1 \times & 16 & = & 16 \\
0 \times & 8 & = & 0 \\
0 \times & 4 & = & 0 \\
1 \times & 2 & = & 2 \\
1 \times & 1 & = & \underline{1} \\
& & & 19 \\
\end{array}
$$

32s	16s	8s	4s	2s	1s	Binary	Decimal
0	0	0	0	0	1	1	1
0	0	0	0	1	0	10	2
0	0	0	0	1	1	11	3
0	0	0	1	0	0	100	4
0	0	0	1	0	1	101	5
0	0	0	1	1	0	110	6
0	0	0	1	1	1	111	7
0	0	1	0	0	0	1000	8
0	0	1	0	0	1	1001	9
0	0	1	0	1	0	1010	10
0	0	1	0	1	1	1011	11
0	0	1	1	0	0	1100	12
0	0	1	1	0	1	1101	13
0	0	1	1	1	0	1110	14
0	0	1	1	1	1	1111	15
0	1	0	0	0	0	10000	16
0	1	0	0	0	1	10001	17
0	1	0	0	1	0	10010	18
0	1	0	0	1	1	10011	19
0	1	0	1	0	0	10100	20
0	1	0	1	0	1	10101	21
0	1	0	1	1	0	10110	22
0	1	0	1	1	1	10111	23
0	1	1	0	0	0	11000	24
0	1	1	0	0	1	11001	25
0	1	1	0	1	0	11010	26
0	1	1	0	1	1	11011	27
0	1	1	1	0	0	11100	28
0	1	1	1	0	1	11101	29
0	1	1	1	1	0	11110	30
0	1	1	1	1	1	11111	31
1	0	0	0	0	0	100000	32
1	0	0	0	0	1	100001	33

Table 2.3. Binary System Place Values

2.4.2 Binary Subtraction

Suppose we want to subtract five from twelve:

```
  1100
- 101
```

It requires borrowing:

$$10 \quad \text{(two for the ones column)}$$
$$1 \quad \text{(one for the twos column)}$$
$$1000$$
$$- 101$$

Doing the subtraction in the first column yields

$$10 \quad \text{(two for the ones column)}$$
$$1 \quad \text{(one for the twos column)}$$
$$1000$$
$$\underline{- 101}$$
$$1$$

In the two's column we subtract zero from one:

$$1 \quad \text{(one for the twos column)}$$
$$1000$$
$$\underline{- 101}$$
$$11$$

The fours column requires another borrowing:

$$10$$
$$1101$$
$$\underline{- 101}$$
$$111$$

This is how to subtract five from twelve in binary. But it is not at all how computers do this arithmetic. Computers do subtractions using negatives like this:

$$12 - 5 = 12 + (-5)$$

Since the method that we learned in school for adding a negative was to convert it to a subtraction, this might seem to be a distinction without a difference. However, computers use a different representation for negatives than just sticking a minus sign in front of the number, so there really is a difference. Representation of negative numbers is discussed in chapter 3, section 3.6.

2.4.3   Conversion to Binary

First, we observe that we can determine whether any binary number is even or odd by examining its ones digit. For example, 19 is odd and its binary representation ends in a 1.

$$10011 = 1 \cdot 16 + 0 \cdot 8 + 0 \cdot 4 + 1 \cdot 2 + 1 \cdot 1$$

Further

$$10011 = (1 \cdot 8 + 0 \cdot 4 + 0 \cdot 2 + 1 \cdot 1) \cdot 2 + 1$$

Addresses   Words

0	0 1 1 1
1	1 1 0 0
2	0 0 0 0
3	1 0 0 0
4	1 1 1 1
5	1 0 1 0

Figure 2-1. Memory with Six Four-Bit Words

So if we are working with nineteen using base ten, we have

$$19 = 9 \cdot 2 + 1$$

Suppose we convert 19 to binary. The 1 in the above equation is the units digit of 19's binary form. We got the 9 by dividing by 2.

$$\begin{array}{r} 9 \quad 1 \\ 2\overline{)19} \\ \underline{18} \\ 1 \end{array}$$

Repeating the process and writing down the remainder each time gives us the rest of the digits.

$$\begin{array}{llll} 4 \;\; 11 & 2 \;\; 011 & 1 \;\; 0011 & 0 \;\; 10011 \\ 2\overline{)9} & 2\overline{)4} & 2\overline{)2} & 2\overline{)1} \\ \underline{8} & \underline{4} & \underline{2} & \underline{0} \\ 1 & 0 & 0 & 1 \end{array}$$

The conversion is done by dividing by 2 repeatedly. Each remainder furnishes one binary digit.

2.5   Memory as a Rectangle of Bits

On all electronic computers, main memory is organized as a rectangle of bits. Figure 2-1 shows a tiny six bit by four bit memory. As shown in the figure, memory is divided widthwise into rows. Each row is called a *word*. Transfers of data to and from computer memory are done a word at a time, or in multiples of words.

The number of bits in a word is called the *word size*. The word size of the memory in Figure 2-1 is four bits. A computer with such a memory would be said to have *four-bit words*. Each word in this memory holds a number representable in four binary digits, i.e. a number from 0 through 15. So for example, a processor requesting the word located at the address 3 would be given the number 8. When designing a chess playing computer, for example, it might be a good idea to use 64-bit words, one bit for each location on the chess board.

Words in computer memory are numbered consecutively, starting from zero. These numbers are called *addresses*. In Figure 2-1, the addresses are the integers from 0 through 5. A computer with n words will have addresses from 0 through $n-1$. When requesting data transfers into or out from memory, computer processors use addresses to specify which data words are to be transferred.

The total capacity of a computer memory is the number of words in the memory times the word size, length times width. The little memory in Figure 2-1 has a capacity of 24 bits. Memory capacity is often measured in *bytes* instead of bits. One byte of memory is the same as eight bits.

Computers based on Intel processors use eight-bit words. A warning note is in order here. Because documentation from Intel and Microsoft use the term *word* to refer to a 16-bit object, this usage has become fairly standard. This is unfortunate. It is better to leave the term with its machine-dependent meaning. In any case, the number of bytes in the memory of an Intel-based machine is the same as the number of addresses.

Because the number of words in a computer memory is typically a large power of two or a small multiple thereof, several names for these large powers of two have been adapted from the metric system. For example, 2^{10} is 1024 and 1024 is approximately 1000. In the metric system the letter K, from *kilo*, is used to stand for 1000. In reference to computer memory, kilo means 1024. Other metric prefixes which have been adapted are shown in the following table.

	Exact Value	Symbol	Prefix	Approximate Value
2^{10}	1,024	K	kilo	thousand
2^{20}	1,048,576	M	mega	million
2^{30}	1,073,741,824	G	giga	billion
2^{40}	1,099,511,627,776	T	tera	trillion

Large Powers of Two

The use of the approximate equalities in this table makes possible simplified computations involving large powers of two. For example, the maximum memory capacity of an IBM AT computer is 2^{24} bytes of memory. To express this amount in more familiar terms, we may break down 2^{24} as follows:

$$\begin{aligned} 2^{24} &= 2^4 \times 2^{10} \times 2^{10} \\ &= 16 \times 1K \times 1K. \end{aligned}$$

This is approximately 16 million bytes. Since $2^{20} = 1K \times 1K = 1$ Meg, the exact amount of memory is 16 Megabytes or 16,777,216 bytes.

16s	1s	Hexadecimal	Decimal
0	1	1	1
0	2	2	2
0	3	3	3
0	4	4	4
0	5	5	5
0	6	6	6
0	7	7	7
0	8	8	8
0	9	9	9
0	A	A	10
0	B	B	11
0	C	C	12
0	D	D	13
0	E	E	14
0	F	F	15
1	0	10	16
1	1	11	17
1	2	12	18
1	3	13	19
1	4	14	20
1	5	15	21
1	6	16	22
1	7	17	23
1	8	18	24
1	9	19	25
1	A	1A	26
1	B	1B	27
1	C	1C	28
1	D	1D	29
1	E	1E	30
1	F	1F	31
2	0	20	32
2	1	21	33

Table 2.4. Hexadecimal System Place Values

2.6   The Hexadecimal System

Base sixteen is important because it is easier to read and write than binary, but is nonetheless readily convertible to and from binary.

Base sixteen is also the first base we have considered which is greater than ten. Instead of putting some numerals out of work, base sixteen requires the employment of additional numerals. Since numerals are needed for all numbers less than sixteen this means positions are open for the numbers ten, eleven, twelve, thirteen, fourteen, and fifteen. It is the custom to fill these positions with the letters A, B, C, D, E, and F.

So in base sixteen, counting goes like this: 1, 2, 3, 4, 5, 6, 7, 8, 9, A, B, C, D, E, F, 10, 11, 12, 13, 14, 15, 16, 17, 18, 19, 1A, 1B, 1C, 1D, 1E, 1F, 20, and so on. See Table 2.4.

There is value in being able to add and subtract in hex. Debuggers generally display registers in hex, and it is handy to be able to check the arithmetic being displayed without having to convert back to base ten.

Addition and subtraction are easy to do in hex if we remember that carrying and borrowing are done with 16.

2.6.1   Addition in Hex

To add

```
   47BC
 + A78
```

we start with twelve plus eight, which is twenty, which is 14H, which is 4 carry 1:

```
      1
   47BC
 + A78
      4
```

1 plus eleven plus seven is nineteen, which is 13H, which is 3 carry 1:

```
     11
   47BC
 + A78
     34
```

$1 + 7 + A =$ eighteen, which is 12H, which is 2 carry 1:

```
    111
   47BC
 + A78
    234
```

Finally, $1 + 4 = 5$:

```
    111
   47BC
 + A78
   5234
```

2.6.2   Subtraction in Hex

To subtract

$$
\begin{array}{r}
4\,7BC \\
-\ A\,4E \\
\end{array}
$$

we start by borrowing:

$$
\begin{array}{r}
1C \\
47A \\
-\ A\,4E \\
\end{array}
$$

$1C - E$ is twenty-eight minus fourteen, which is fourteen:

$$
\begin{array}{r}
1C \\
47A \\
-\ A\,4E \\
\hline
E \\
\end{array}
$$

$A - 4$ is ten minus four is 6:

$$
\begin{array}{r}
1C \\
47A \\
-\ A\,4E \\
\hline
6E \\
\end{array}
$$

Again borrowing

$$
\begin{array}{r}
171C \\
37A \\
-\ A\,4E \\
\hline
6E \\
\end{array}
$$

$17 - A$ is twenty-three minus ten, which is thirteen or D:

$$
\begin{array}{r}
171C \\
37A \\
-\ A\,4E \\
\hline
D6E \\
\end{array}
$$

Finally $3 - 0 = 3$:

$$
\begin{array}{r}
171C \\
37A \\
-\ A\,4E \\
\hline
3D6E \\
\end{array}
$$

2.6.3 Conversion to Hex

To convert a number into base sixteen, we can divide by 16 as many times as necessary. Suppose we convert 1000 into hexadecimal:

$$
\begin{array}{lll}
62\ \ 8 & 3\ \ \text{E8} & 0\ \ 3\text{E8} \\
16\overline{)1000} & 16\overline{)62} & 16\overline{)3} \\
\underline{96} & \underline{48} & \underline{0} \\
40 & 14 & 3 \\
\underline{32} \\
8
\end{array}
$$

To demonstrate the easy convertibility of base two into base sixteen, we again consider the number 1000, only this time we convert it into base two:

$$
\begin{array}{llll}
500\ \ 0 & 250\ \ 00 & 125\ \ 000 & 62\ \ 1000 \\
2\overline{)1000} & 2\overline{)500} & 2\overline{)250} & 2\overline{)125} \\
\underline{1000} & \underline{500} & \underline{250} & \underline{124} \\
0 & 0 & 0 & 1
\end{array}
$$

$$
\begin{array}{lll}
31\ \ 01000 & 15\ \ 101000 & 7\ \ 1101000 \\
2\overline{)62} & 2\overline{)31} & 2\overline{)15} \\
\underline{62} & \underline{30} & \underline{14} \\
0 & 1 & 1
\end{array}
$$

$$
\begin{array}{lll}
3\ \ 11101000 & 1\ \ 111101000 & 0\ \ 1111101000 \\
2\overline{)7} & 2\overline{)3} & 2\overline{)1} \\
\underline{6} & \underline{2} & \underline{0} \\
1 & 1 & 1
\end{array}
$$

The fact that dividing by 2 four times is essentially the same thing as dividing by 16 suggests that four stages of this conversion must correspond to one stage of hexadecimal conversion. If we group the binary digits into fours, we do in fact observe this relationship.

$$
\begin{array}{ccc}
11 & 1110 & 1000 \\
3 & \text{E} & 8
\end{array}
$$

These lumps of four digits, when treated as individual numbers, 11, 1110, and 1000, give us the hexadecimal digits 3, E, and 8. This is the base sixteen representation of one thousand. It is clear how to convert in the other direction as well. The conversion between the two is easy enough that it can be done without thinking. See Table 2.5. This makes it possible to use hexadecimal as a human readable form of binary, a kind of highlevel machine language(!). Consider the following two representations of the same number:

$$
\begin{array}{ccccccccc}
1011 & 0010 & 1001 & 0101 & 0000 & 0111 & 1010 & 1000 & 1000 \\
\text{B} & 2 & 9 & 5 & 0 & 7 & \text{A} & 8 & 8
\end{array}
$$

Binary	Hexadecimal	Decimal
0000	0	0
0001	1	1
0010	2	2
0011	3	3
0100	4	4
0101	5	5
0110	6	6
0111	7	7
1000	8	8
1001	9	9
1010	A	10
1011	B	11
1100	C	12
1101	D	13
1110	E	14
1111	F	15

Table 2.5. Hex-Binary Conversion

Suppose you had to read one of these to a hardware support person over the phone, or copy it onto a postcard. Is there any doubt that using hex would be easier and less liable to error?

Computer programs originally consisted of line after line of binary code. There is a bittersweet irony here. Filling out coding sheets with zeros and ones was a job typically done by women. As a result, many women got in on the very beginning of the computer programming field.

2.6.4   Why not Octal?

Octal numbers can be converted back and forth from binary in the same way as hex numbers, merely grouping by threes instead of fours. Octal also has the advantage over hex in that no alphabetic numerals are needed. However, the increasingly widespread use of the byte as the fundamental unit of memory has led to a decrease in the importance of octal.

2.7   Base Distinguishing Notations

Since all the digits in decimal are valid in hexadecimal, it is not possible to determine without additional information whether numeration, such as "50," is intended as decimal or hex. A common convention for indicating hexadecimal is the use of an appended H. When this convention is used, '50' just means fifty; but '50H' means fifty in hex, i.e., eighty. Occasionally, particularly with assemblers, B and D are appended to indicate binary and decimal. Appending O for octal would obviously not be a good idea. In the C language, octal is indicated by prepending a 0 and hexadecimal is indicated by prepending a 0x. This book places primary reliance on decimal, hexadecimal, and binary numeration. To distinguish these bases, the following conventions will be used:

- Hexadecimal, except in C programs, will always be indicated by an appended H. (In addition, because of a problem discussed in section 3.11, hex numeration used in the assembly language will also have a prepended 0.)

- Binary will be indicated by grouping digits into clumps of four, separated by spaces.

- Base ten numeration is the default. It is assumed for all numeration whose base is not otherwise indicated.

2.8* Fractions in Other Bases

Much computation involving fractions is done using scientific notation. Because scientific notation involves both decimal fractions and explicit powers of ten, it allows for freedom in the location of the decimal point. For example:

$$2345.6789 \times 10^2 = 23.456789 \times 10^4$$

Consequently scientific notation is sometimes referred to as *floating point* notation. The floating point property of the representation is a result of the fact that all parts of the representation, including the fractional part, use powers of ten. In order to take advantage of the floating point property in computer computations which use the binary system, all fractions and explicit powers must be binary instead of decimal.

Nondecimal placeholding fractions were used by the Babylonians and persist today in our time and angle unit systems, where we see minutes and seconds as base 60 fractions.

Decimal fractions of course are our everyday standard. For example:

$$.125 = 1 \cdot (\tfrac{1}{10})^1 + 2 \cdot (\tfrac{1}{10})^2 + 5 \cdot (\tfrac{1}{10})^3 = \tfrac{125}{1000} = \tfrac{1}{8}$$

We find this base ten fraction using long division,

```
        .125
    8)1.000
      8
      20
      16
      40
      40
       0
```

Suppose we want to find one-eighth as a pentimal fraction. We can use long division in base five using the pentimal multiplication table where necessary. (The pentimal representation of eight is 13).

$$\begin{array}{r} .0303 \ldots \\ 13\overline{)1.0000} \\ \underline{44} \\ 10 \\ \underline{0} \\ 100 \\ \underline{44} \\ 1 \end{array} \quad (3 \times 3 = 14, \text{ which is 4 with 1 to carry})$$

This is a repeating fraction similar to .33333... $= \frac{1}{3}$ in the decimal system. So one eighth in the pentimal system is

$$\tfrac{1}{13} = .030303030303...$$

an infinitely repeating fraction. Its meaning represented using ordinary decimal notation is that

$$\tfrac{1}{8} = 0 \cdot \left(\tfrac{1}{5}\right)^1 + 3 \cdot \left(\tfrac{1}{5}\right)^2 + 0 \cdot \left(\tfrac{1}{5}\right)^3 + 3 \cdot \left(\tfrac{1}{5}\right)^4 + \ldots$$

If we use long division to get the hexadecimal fraction we get a finite representation.

$$\begin{array}{r} .2 \\ 8\overline{)1.0} \\ \underline{10} \\ 0 \end{array} \quad (2 \cdot 8 = 10 = \text{sixteen})$$

This is certainly correct since $2 \cdot \frac{1}{16} = \frac{1}{8}$. In base two the same division looks like this:

$$\begin{array}{r} .001 \\ 1000\overline{)1.000} \\ \underline{1000} \\ 0 \end{array}$$

This is correct since

$$\tfrac{1}{8} = 0 \cdot \left(\tfrac{1}{2}\right)^1 + 0 \cdot \left(\tfrac{1}{2}\right)^2 + 1 \cdot \left(\tfrac{1}{2}\right)^3$$

In early Intel systems, computations based on floating point numbers were done on separate processors such as the 80387. Since the 486, these floating point units were incorporated into the main processor. In C, a programmer may send computations to the floating point unit by using a floating point data type such as `double`.

2.9* Converting Fractions

In the previous section we used long division to find a placeholding fraction, given the numerator and denominator as integers. For example, to find a base two placeholding fraction, we could do long division in base two. If we are given instead a placeholding fraction in some other base, we can use a multiplicative process to do the conversion. For example, suppose we are given the decimal fraction .33333333..., and we wish to convert that into a binary fraction. Let $b_1, b_2, b_3,...$ be the unknown digits in our binary fraction:

$.b_1 b_2 b_3...$

If we use the equality

$$.3333333... = b_1 \cdot \left(\tfrac{1}{2}\right)^1 + b_2 \cdot \left(\tfrac{1}{2}\right)^2 + b_3 \cdot \left(\tfrac{1}{2}\right)^3 + ...$$

we can determine their values as follows. Suppose we double both sides of this equation.

$$.6666666... = b_1 + b_2 \cdot \left(\tfrac{1}{2}\right)^1 + b_3 \cdot \left(\tfrac{1}{2}\right)^2 + ...$$

The integer parts of both sides must agree. The integer part of the left side is zero, so $b_1 = 0$. Hence we have our first digit and we also have the equation

$$.6666666... = b_2 \cdot \left(\tfrac{1}{2}\right)^1 + b_3 \cdot \left(\tfrac{1}{2}\right)^2 + b_4 \cdot \left(\tfrac{1}{2}\right)^3 + ...$$

If we double this equation, we get

$$1.333333... = b_2 + b_3 \cdot \left(\tfrac{1}{2}\right)^1 + b_4 \cdot \left(\tfrac{1}{2}\right)^2 + ...$$

Again the integer parts of both sides must agree, so $b_2 = 1$. Subtracting $1 = b_2$ from this equation yields the equation

$$.333333... = b_3 \cdot \left(\tfrac{1}{2}\right)^1 + b_4 \cdot \left(\tfrac{1}{2}\right)^2 + b_5 \cdot \left(\tfrac{1}{2}\right)^3 + ...$$

Continuing in this way we get $b_3 = 1, b_4 = 0, b_5 = 1, b_6 = 0$, etc. Hence the binary form of .333333 is

$.01010101...$

We have just found a binary fraction from a decimal fraction by multiplying by 2 repeatedly. To find a pentimal fraction from a decimal fraction, we begin with a similar equation and multiply by 5 repeatedly.

By definition, the base five coefficients make this equation true:

$$.3333333... = b_1 \cdot \left(\tfrac{1}{5}\right)^1 + b_2 \cdot \left(\tfrac{1}{5}\right)^2 + b_3 \cdot \left(\tfrac{1}{5}\right)^3 + ...$$

Multiplying this equation by 5 yields

$$1.666666... = b_1 + b_2 \cdot \left(\tfrac{1}{5}\right)^1 + b_3 \cdot \left(\tfrac{1}{5}\right)^2 + ...$$

The integer part of both sides must agree. Hence $b_1 = 1$. Subtracting $1 = b_1$ yields:

$$.6666666... = b_2 \cdot \left(\tfrac{1}{5}\right)^1 + b_3 \cdot \left(\tfrac{1}{5}\right)^2 + b_4 \cdot \left(\tfrac{1}{5}\right)^3 + ...$$

Multiplying this equation by 5 yields

$$3.333333... = b_2 + b_3 \cdot \left(\tfrac{1}{5}\right)^1 + b_4 \cdot \left(\tfrac{1}{5}\right)^2 + ...$$

From this we get $b_2 = 3$ and

$$.3333333... = b_3 \cdot \left(\tfrac{1}{5}\right)^1 + b_4 \cdot \left(\tfrac{1}{5}\right)^2 + b_5 \cdot \left(\tfrac{1}{5}\right)^3 + ...$$

Continuing in this way, we get $b_3 = 1, b_4 = 3, b_5 = 1$, $b_6 = 3$, etc. So the pentimal equivalent is .13131313... .

Further Reading

Number Words and Number Symbols: A Cultural History of Numbers, Karl Menninger, Dover Books: 1992.

3

LOGIC CIRCUITS AND COMPUTATION

Electronic computers are made of logic circuits. The aim of this chapter is to explain how the basic computer functions of arithmetic and storage can be done using these circuits. It culminates in a brief discussion of the ADD and MOV commands.

The most basic logic circuits are called *gates*. Gates are controller circuits. The simplest logic gate is the NOT gate. In the next section, it is shown how a NOT gate can control a flashlight.

3.1 The NOT Gate

The simple flashlight circuit shown, in Figure 3-1, is controlled by the switch at the top, which is shown in the open position. The negative end of the battery is connected directly to the bulb, but the positive end is only connected to the bulb by way of the switch. So when the switch is open, current will not flow and the bulb is off. When the switch is closed, current can flow and the bulb comes on. The control is mechanical.

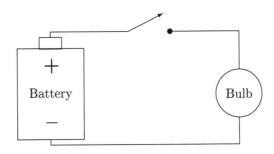

Figure 3-1. A Simple Flashlight

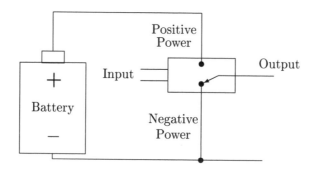

Figure 3-2. A Generic Logic Gate

3.1.1 Logic Gate Terminals

A logic gate is a circuit which works like a switch. Figure 3-2 shows a generic logic gate hooked up to a battery. As shown in the figure, a logic gate has four or more terminals.

1. *Output Terminal.* This terminal is switched so that it is connected either to the positive or the negative power terminal. The switching is done by solid-state electronics imbedded in silicon and involves no moving parts.

2. *Positive Power Terminal.* This terminal is always connected to the positive battery or power supply terminal.

3. *Negative Power Terminal.* This terminal is always connected to the negative battery or power supply terminal.

4. *Input Terminal.* A logic gate has one or more input terminals. These terminals carry the input signals which determine whether the output terminal is switched to the positive or the negative power terminal. Different types of logic gates make this determination in different ways.

Logic Value Conventions

Because the two power terminals on the logic gate are always connected to the corresponding terminals on the battery or power supply, the output terminal always supplies a connection to either the positive or the negative battery or power supply terminal. For circuits in this book

- A gate terminal connected directly or indirectly to the positive battery or power supply terminal is described as being "at logic 1."

- A gate terminal connected directly or indirectly to the negative battery or power supply terminal is described as being "at logic 0."

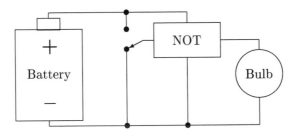

Figure 3-3. A NOT Gate-Controlled Flashlight

Because the input terminals are generally connected directly or indirectly to the battery or power supply terminals just like output terminals, they can also be described as being at logic 1 or at logic 0. The fact that the input terminals are designed to be at logic 1 or logic 0 has as a further consequence that the output of one logic gate can be connected to the input of another with predictable results.

3.1.2 Behavior of the NOT Gate

The NOT gate is a logic gate which has one input terminal. To describe the behavior of the NOT gate, all that is needed is to describe how its input determines its output. The rules are:

- If the input is at logic 1, the output is at logic 0.

- If the input is at logic 0, the output is at logic 1.

We can now put a flashlight together by hooking the output of the NOT gate to a bulb and the input to a mechanical switch. Figure 3-3 illustrates this hookup. When wires in a diagram are shown crossing at a black dot, it means that the wires are connected. When wires cross and there is no black dot, it means that they are not in contact with each other. The flashlight in this figure is ultimately controlled by a mechanical switch, just like the flashlight in Figure 3-1. When the switch is in the down position as shown in the figure, the flashlight is on. The down position connects the input terminal of the NOT gate to the negative battery terminal, which puts it at logic 0. Therefore, because of the way a NOT gate works, the output is at logic 1. This means that the output terminal is connected internally by the NOT gate to the positive power terminal and therefore to the positive end of the battery. Hence the bulb gets current and the flashlight is on.

3.1.3 Truth Table for the NOT Gate

Logic values make it easy to summarize the behavior of a NOT gate with a small table. Such a table is called a *truth table*. Table 3.1 shows the truth table for the NOT gate.

Input	Output
1	0
0	1

Table 3.1. Truth Table for NOT Gate

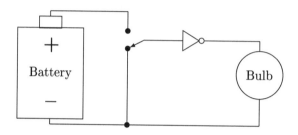

Figure 3-4. This Flashlight is On!

3.1.4   Gate Level Diagrams

A logic circuit diagram which shows the individual logic gates but not their internal make-up is called a *gate level diagram*. In a gate level diagram, the power terminals on the logic gates are usually not shown. The symbol for the NOT gate used in gate level diagrams shows only two terminals, the input and the output:

The wire shown on the left represents the input; the wire on the right is the output.

Figure 3-4 shows the diagram of the NOT gate-controlled flashlight using the schematic symbol. This diagram can be confusing because the main power connections to the NOT gate are not shown. In this figure, the only battery connection is at the signaling input to the NOT gate. Although the power connections are not shown, they must be there or the circuit will not work. Figure 3-4 represents exactly the same hookup as Figure 3-3.

3.2   Boolean Operators

The NOT gate discussed in the last section is an example of a logic gate. Logic gates are circuits whose behavior is modeled on Boolean operators.

The most basic Boolean operators are AND, OR, XOR, and NOT. In the C language, we have the symbols && for AND, || for OR, and ! for NOT. The workings of these operators can be illustrated with two examples from C. In these examples,

p	q	(p OR q)
1	1	1
1	0	1
0	1	1
0	0	0

Table 3.2. Truth Table for OR

the C language statements are evaluated using a step-by-step simplification process.

3.2.1 The OR Operator

The first example is an `if` statement involving the Boolean OR operator. In what follows, we suppose that x has already been given the value 7.

```
if ((x > 0) || (x < 5)) y = 10;
```

- First the truth values of the operands may be determined. In this case, because (x > 0) is true, it has the value 1; because (x < 5) is false, it has the value 0. These evaluations result in the following simplification of the C language statement.

```
if (1 || 0) y = 10;
```

- The Boolean OR operator may be applied next. The only thing OR sees is the truth values resulting from the operand evaluations. OR is given a 1 and a 0, from which it produces a 1.

```
if( 1 ) y = 10;
```

- The `if` can go to work next. All it sees in the parentheses is a 1. Hence it produces the simple assignment statement

```
y = 10;
```

The end result of the process is that y is set to the value 10. Notice that the OR operator never saw the value of x. It needs only 0s and 1s to do its job. Consequently, the workings of the OR operator can be described in a truth table just like the truth table for the NOT gate. Table 3.2 shows the truth table for the OR operator. In truth tables for Boolean operators, the letters p and q are often used as variables for the truth values 0 and 1. Variables which have only these two possible values are sometimes called *Boolean variables*. Notice that the decision made in the C example could have been inferred from the second line of Table 3.2.

p	q	(p AND q)
1	1	1
1	0	0
0	1	0
0	0	0

Table 3.3. Truth Table for AND

3.2.2 The AND Operator

The AND operator can also be described with a truth table. See Table 3.3. The next example shows the use of this table in evaluating a C language statement containing an AND operator.

- Again suppose that x = 7.

    ```
    if((x > 0) && (x < 5)) z = 20;
    ```

- Again the operands have the values 1 and 0.

    ```
    if(1 && 0) z = 20;
    ```

- The operation of the AND operator can be referred to the second line of Table 3.3, from which we see that a 0 results.

    ```
    if( 0 ) z = 20;
    ```

- The 0 in the parentheses results in a null statement. Nothing happens.

    ```
    ;
    ```

From these examples, it is clear that the job of the Boolean operators is to operate on truth values and produce a truth value.

3.2.3 Boolean Expressions

Just as operators in C may be nested as in the statement

```
if(((x > 0) && (x < 5)) || (x = 7)) w = 30;
```

so Boolean operators by themselves may be nested

```
((p AND q) OR r)
```

The resulting expressions are called *Boolean expressions*. Just as Boolean operators have truth tables, so do Boolean expressions. The truth table for the expression just shown is given in Table 3.4.

p	q	r	((p AND q) OR r)
1	1	1	1
1	1	0	1
1	0	1	1
1	0	0	0
0	1	1	1
0	1	0	0
0	0	1	1
0	0	0	0

Table 3.4. Truth Table for a Boolean Expression

p	(NOT p)
1	0
0	1

Table 3.5. Truth Table for NOT

3.3   Logic Gates

Table 3.5 shows the truth table for the Boolean NOT operator. It is very similar to the truth table for the NOT gate shown in Table 3.1. If we think of p as the input and (NOT p) as the output, there is in fact no difference. One should even think of the NOT gate as a silicon implementation of the NOT operator. The Boolean operators AND, OR, and XOR are also implemented in silicon.

3.3.1   The OR Gate

The OR gate is a circuit with two input terminals. It is represented in gate level diagrams with the symbol

p	q	(p XOR q)
1	1	0
1	0	1
0	1	1
0	0	0

Table 3.6. Truth Table for XOR

The inputs are shown on the left. The output is on the right. From Table 3.2, we may infer that

- If both input terminals are at logic 0, then the output terminal will be at logic 0.

- If either input terminal is at logic 1, then the output terminal will be at logic 1.

In the following circuit, for example, unless the logic values applied to all of the Filter inputs are equal to 0, the output will be at logic 1. If a logic 0 is applied to each of the Filter inputs, then the output logic value will be the same as the input logic value. In this case, one can think of the input signal as having passed through the gates. Note that the gate analogy makes sense in terms of the propogation of a signal, not the propagation of a voltage. A logic 1 applied to any of the Filter inputs guarantees that the output will be at logic 1, but this should be thought of as the *closing* of the gate. A change in the input will not make it through to the output. The circuit does *not* allow signals to pass. Hence it makes sense to think of these OR gates as *closed* when a regulatory input is at logic 1.

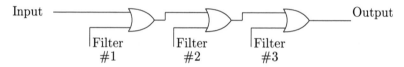

3.3.2   The AND Gate

The AND gate is also a two-input gate. Its symbol is

From Table 3.3 we may infer that

- If both input terminals are at logic 1, then the output terminal will be at logic 1.

- If either input terminal is at logic 0, then the output terminal will be at logic 0.

In the following circuit, the logic values applied to all the Filter inputs must equal 1; otherwise the output will be at logic 0. If a logic 1 is applied to each of the Filter inputs, then the input logic value passes through the gates and becomes the output value.

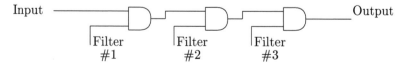

3.3.3   Boolean Circuits

AND, OR, and NOT logic gates can be used to build   up a great variety of logic circuits. For any Boolean expression, there is a corresponding circuit. For example, corresponding to the Boolean expression

((p AND q) OR r)

one can construct the circuit

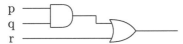

The truth table for this circuit is the same as the truth table of the Boolean expression it comes from. It is given in Table 3.4.

The truth table for the Boolean operator XOR is shown in Table 3.6. One can find a Boolean expression for XOR by using the lines of its truth table that have a logic 1 output. Using the table, we find two such lines, one where p = 1 and q = 0 and one where p = 0 and q = 1. These are the lines for which the expressions (p AND (NOT q)) and ((NOT p) AND q) are true. Hence the expression

((p AND (NOT q)) OR ((NOT p) AND q))

has the same truth table as XOR and may be used to construct a circuit for XOR

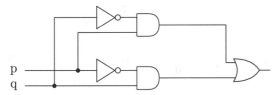

The Boolean expression ((p OR q) AND (NOT (p AND q))) also has the same truth table. Therefore the logic circuit which corresponds to this expression also works as an XOR circuit. That circuit looks like this:

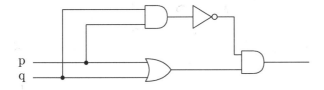

The standard symbol for XOR is

XOR may be implemented using any circuit which has the correct truth table, including the two just shown.

3.3.4 Propagation Delay

Some essential features of logic circuit behavior are left out of any description based only on Boolean expressions and truth tables. One such feature is the propagation delay, the time required for a change in an input signal to cause a change in the output. The propagation delay of a gate used in a 100 MHz processor, for example, must be less than 10 nanoseconds. This is because 100 MHz means 100 million cycles per second (cps). So the length of each processing cycle is $\frac{1}{100,000,000}$ second, which is the same as $\frac{10}{1,000,000,000}$ second or 10 nanoseconds.

Frequency		Cycle Length	
1 Hz	1 cps	1 s	1 sec
1 kHz	1,000 cps	1 ms	$\frac{1}{1,000}$ sec
1 MHz	1,000,000 cps	1 μs	$\frac{1}{1,000,000}$ sec
1 GHz	1,000,000,000 cps	1 ns	$\frac{1}{1,000,000,000}$ sec

Considering that the execution of one processing cycle might require a signal to pass through, say, five such gates in succession, the limit could drop to 2 nanoseconds or less. Reducing this time delay is one of the main goals in current fabrication technology. The less the propagation delay, the faster the clock speed at which a circuit can be run.

Also important is the amount of power dissipated. When many circuits are packed together on a chip, the temperature may increase to unacceptable levels unless the power dissipated by each circuit is reduced to a very low level. Reducing power dissipation is another primary goal of processor design.

The architecture point of view leaves these problems out of the picture. From that standpoint, all we need to know about a Boolean circuit is contained in its truth table. The architecture point of view is more often suitable in computer science than in electrical engineering.

3.4 Addition Circuits

This section shows how addition is done using logic circuits.

Consider the addition of 13 and 6 again and observe that in each column, we have two digits to add along with a carry digit from the preceding column.

```
  1 0 0
  1 1 0 1    13
+ 1 1 0      6
  0 1 1      3
```

An addition circuit which can do the work involved in one column of such an addition is called a *full adder*. It produces the sum of the two digits in that column and a carry digit from the previous column. It also produces an output carry digit. The

Input Digit #1	Input Digit #2	Input Carry	Output Sum	Output Carry
0	0	0	0	0
0	1	0	1	0
1	0	0	1	0
1	1	0	0	1
0	0	1	1	0
0	1	1	0	1
1	0	1	0	1
1	1	1	1	1

Table 3.7. Truth Table for a Full Adder

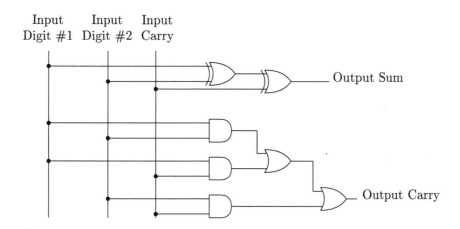

Figure 3-5. Full Adder Circuit

addition of 13 and 6 as shown requires the use of four full adder circuits. Because the binary system is being used, the Boolean truth values 0 and 1 may be used as binary digits. Table 3.7 shows the truth table for a full adder circuit. It is not hard to construct a full adder. The Output Sum circuit can be built from two XOR circuits. The Output Carry circuit can be built from three ANDs and two ORs. See Figure 3-5. A full adder has three inputs and two outputs, which together function as one column of an adding machine.

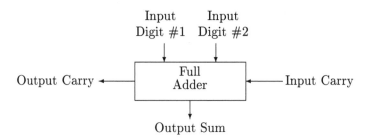

A circuit which adds four-digit binary numbers requires four full adders ganged together.

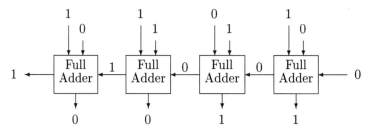

This is what the adding circuits in a four-bit processor look like. Shown here is the same calculation of thirteen plus six illustrated at the beginning of this section. In binary, that is 1101 plus 0110. The resulting total is 0011. There is also an output carry value of 1. The input carry is not used here. Surprisingly enough, there is a need for it however. We will see what that is in section 3.7.

It is one of the characteristics of a four-bit processor that it adds binary numbers four bits at a time.

A computer with a four-bit processor would not be limited to small number arithmetic, but its software would need to break large numbers down into numbers no bigger than 16.

3.5   Sequential Circuits

In all the circuits shown so far, the output is determined by the inputs. By using the truth tables of the component gates, one can construct a truth table for the whole circuit. It might seem that this should be the case with all logic circuits. However, if an output is fed back around to an input, then a vicious circle is introduced into the process of determining the truth table. Circuits with feedback loops are called *sequential circuits*.

Circuits without feedback loops are not capable of storing logic values. The output of a Boolean circuit is a function of its inputs, its *present* inputs. That means, for example, if you tried to use a Boolean circuit as a memory, then no matter what you decided upon as the memory fetch command, this input would

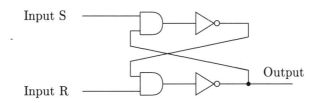

Figure 3-6. Flip-flop

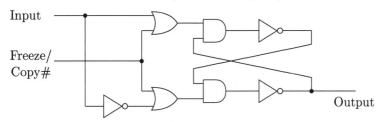

Figure 3-7. Latch

always produce the same output, namely the output specified by the truth table, so it would not be a true memory fetch. The output from a true memory fetch would depend upon what was stored at some time in the *past*.

Sequential circuits are important because they can store logic values.

3.5.1   A Flip-flop

Figure 3-6 shows an example of a circuit called a *flip-flop*. The S in the figure stands for *set* and the R stands for *reset*. The output of this circuit may be set if S = 1 and R = 0. In this case, the AND gate fed by the R input is forced to output a 0. Hence both inputs on the other AND gate are 1. Hence its output is 1 and the final output is 1.

If S = 0 and R = 1, the situation is just reversed and the final output is 0.

However, if S = 1 and R = 1, the output is not determined by the truth tables. The feedback loops make that impossible.   It turns out, however, that if the S = R = 1 state was entered from either the set or the reset state, then the final output is left alone. It does not change.

3.5.2   A Latch

Figure 3-7 shows an example of a circuit called a *latch*.   This circuit stores one bit. It is called a latch because it "latches onto" a value.

The Freeze/Copy# label in this figure uses the Intel # convention that when a signal is labeled with a meaningful word, then the meaning truthfully applies when the line is at logic 1, unless the label has a # appended, and then the opposite is the case. So the Freeze/Copy# label tells us that logic 1 means Freeze and logic 0 means Copy.

- When the Freeze/Copy# line is zero, the OR gates are opened and the circuit is turned into a flip-flop, where the input is either set or reset. The NOT gate makes the S and R inputs opposite to each other.

  The input value is copied to the output.

- When the Freeze/Copy# line becomes 1, both OR gates are forced to 1 and this freezes the output. When the output is frozen, subsequent changes in the input have no effect on the circuit. The output value remains just what it was the last time the Freeze/Copy# line turned from 1 to 0, i.e. the last time it froze.

  That output value is in storage.

3.5.3 Registers

Four latches used together in parallel can store four bits. This is an example of a *register*. A four-bit register is a collection of circuits that can store four bits. Different registers in a processor do not have to store the same number of bits, but it is easier to make things work when they do. The number of bits in a "typical" register is one of the attributes of a processor which determines whether it is called a four-bit processor, an eight-bit processor, or whatever.

The contents of a four-bit register are very naturally specified using a four-digit binary number. The four-digit binary numbers are the integers from 0 through 15. An eight-bit register holds an integer from 0 through 127.

We see that the most natural way of specifying the contents of a register leaves no room for negative numbers. The representation of negative numbers will be discussed in the next section.

3.5.4 Bit Significance

Because binary numbers are used to describe the contents of registers and memory locations, the numerical concept of a *significant digit* is useful in singling out individual bits of a specific storage location. For example, if a four-bit register holds the binary number 1100, then the four digits in order of significance are 1, 1, 0, and 0. So the most significant digit is 1, and the least significant digit is 0. The three most significant digits are 110. The three least significant digits are 100. Sometimes in this text, the most significant bits will be referred to as the *top* or *upper* bits and the least significant as the *bottom* or *lower* bits.

3.6   Negative Number Representation

The customary way to represent a negative number is to prepend a minus sign. Putting a − in front of a 3 makes a −3. This method of representing negatives is called *signed magnitude* representation. It can be implemented on the computer by allocating one bit of storage for a sign bit. To change the sign of a number that is stored using signed magnitude representation, one can simply flip the sign bit. Signed magnitude representation is not generally used for integers on the computer. The reason is that in order to do addition with signed magnitude representation, you need to do it the way it is taught to youngsters.

3.6.1   Signed Magnitude Addition

To add x and y:

Case I. If x and y are both positive, just add and make your answer positive.

Case II. If x and y are both negative, remove the negative signs, add the numbers, and tack a minus sign onto the result.

Case III. If x and y have different signs, subtract the smaller magnitude from the larger magnitude, and if the larger magnitude had a minus sign, then tack this onto the result.

Implementing signed magnitude addition with logic circuits on a chip would be a terrible waste of transistors.

3.6.2   Easy Addition

The method which is actually used with logic circuits to add x and y works like this:

Pay no attention to whether x and y are positive or negative; just add them!

Such a method would seem to be no method at all. But it works. It works because a special system for representing negatives is used, and because a register has a finite size, like an odometer.

3.6.3   Odometer Arithmetic

An odometer is an adding machine. It adds up the miles that you drive. Mileage is always considered to have a positive value. (Would a negative value imply driving backwards, or what?) However, consider the following equation, which we would ordinarily think of as making sense only for negative numbers.

$$x + 10 = 5$$

$$
\begin{array}{rl}
-1 & 99{,}999 \\
-2 & 99{,}998 \\
-3 & 99{,}997 \\
-4 & 99{,}996 \\
-5 & 99{,}995 \\
-6 & 99{,}994 \\
-7 & 99{,}993 \\
-8 & 99{,}992 \\
-9 & 99{,}991 \\
-10 & 99{,}990 \\
-11 & 99{,}989 \\
-12 & 99{,}988 \\
\cdot & \cdot \\
\text{etc.} & \cdot
\end{array}
$$

Table 3.8. Odometer Negatives

The obvious solution is x = −5. However, there is an odometer interpretation of this equation as well. Suppose you drive 10 miles in your car and the odometer reads 5 when you finish, then what did it read when you began? It must have read 99,995. Similarly if you have a car whose odometer reads 10 miles and you drive it 99,995 miles(!) then the odometer should read 5 miles when you finish. The point here is that 99,995 acts just like −5 when added on the odometer. Table 3.8 shows what odometer negatives look like. Notice that to get the number that works as the negative of a number x, you subtract x from 100,000.

Arithmetic on the odometer works this way because the odometer turns over at 100,000 miles. Computer registers turn over also—but not at 100,000.

3.6.4   Register Arithmetic

A four-bit register turns over at binary 1 0000 = 2^4 = 16. The table of negatives for a four-bit register can easily be listed completely. See Table 3.9. The only difference between this table and the odometer table is that 16 is a lot smaller than 100,000. As with the odometer, you can use subtraction instead of the table to find the number which works as the negative of some number x. In the case of a four-bit register, you subtract x from 16 instead of from 100,000. Otherwise it is the same.

But in one respect, Table 3.9 is a little alarming. For example, it gives us the fact that 11 works the same as −5. This means we now have a serious ambiguity. If a four-bit register contains 1011, we cannot tell whether this actually means 11 or −5. Some convention is needed. The convention that is used is to take the first bit as a kind of sign bit. When the first bit is 0, the number is positive (or zero). When the first bit is 1, the number is negative. The resulting system is called the *two's complement system*. When the two's complement system is used, the ambiguity is

Decimal		Binary
−1	15	1111
−2	14	1110
−3	13	1101
−4	12	1100
−5	11	1011
−6	10	1010
−7	9	1001
−8	8	1000
−9	7	0111
−10	6	0110
−11	5	0101
−12	4	0100
−13	3	0011
−14	2	0010
−15	1	0001

Table 3.9. Four-Bit Register Negatives (Ambiguous!)

Decimal		Binary
−1		1111
−2		1110
−3		1101
−4		1100
−5		1011
−6		1010
−7		1001
−8		1000
	7	0111
	6	0110
	5	0101
	4	0100
	3	0011
	2	0010
	1	0001

Table 3.10. Four-Bit Two's Complement Representation

cleared up. Table 3.10 illustrates the four-bit case. We see from Table 3.10 that in the four-bit two's complement system, there is no 11, just a −5. The ambiguity is gone if we accept this system.

Notice that although the first bit in a two's complement system is a sign bit, it is not just a sign bit. For example, if we change the sign bit on 1011, we get 0011. This changes −5 to 3, not 5.

3.6.5   Signed vs. Unsigned Numbers

If all arithmetic done on computers were done using two's complement representation, there would never be any problem interpreting the contents of a numerical register. But unfortunately this is not the case. Sometimes arithmetic is done and it is assumed that the numbers are represented using the plain binary system. So when a four-bit register has a 1011 in it, does this mean −5 or 11? If we are using two's complement, then we know it is −5. But we could be using just plain binary! Then we have 11. Computing practice is not consistent about this. Both systems are used. It could be either one. It is up to the software to make the distinction. The terminology *signed* vs. *unsigned* is often used. Signed integers are two's complement integers. Unsigned integers are plain binary integers.

Although when we are adding numbers, it doesn't matter if the numbers are signed or unsigned — the adding hardware works either way — many other operations require different implementations depending on whether the operand is intended as a signed or an unsigned number. Consider inequality testing. Suppose four-bit hardware is asked to determine whether 1011 < 0010 is true or not. While 0010 represents 2 in both the signed and the unsigned systems, 1011 is −5 as a signed number and 11 as an unsigned number. The signed interpretation, −5 < 2, yields a true, whereas the unsigned interpretation, 11 < 2, yields a false. The hardware must make a different response in the two cases. This means that a single "less than" command cannot work. Two are needed, one for signed numbers and one for unsigned numbers. This issue comes up over and over again in assembly language.

In the C language, integers may be declared as `unsigned int` or as `signed int`. The unspecified `int` declaration means the same as `signed int`.

3.7   Subtraction Using Negation

This section explains how subtraction may be done using the circuits described so far.

3.7.1   Two's Complementation

Since we have an adder that works with negatives, we should be able to use it to do subtractions, such as $5 - 3$, since

$$5 - 3 = 5 + (-3)$$

But there is a problem. Converting 3 to −3 is not as easy as just sticking on a minus sign or flipping a bit. If it were, tables such as Table 3.8 and Table 3.9 would not be necessary. Although we do have a formula which explains these tables, it is unfortunately based on subtraction. For example, according to the formula for the four-bit table, to get the negative of 3, you subtract 3 from 16. But since our goal is to find a way to do subtraction, we appear to be trapped in a vicious circle. The situation is not as bad as it seems, however. Subtracting 3 from 16 in binary can be done even if we don't know how to subtract and even though the binary representation of 16 requires one more bit than our four-bit registers can hold. We are saved by two facts.

i) $16 - x = (15 - x) + 1$.

ii) Subtracting from 15 can be done by just flipping the bits. Notice what happens when we subtract 3 from 15 in binary.

$$\begin{array}{r} 1111 \\ - \ 0011 \\ \hline 1100 \end{array}$$

The bits in 0011 are flipped and we get 1100. We have hardware that can flip bits. We can feed each bit into a NOT gate. Adding 1 then gives the result.

$$\begin{array}{r} 1100 \\ + \quad 1 \\ \hline 1101 \end{array}$$

The unused input carry on the addition circuit comes into its own here. (See section 3.4.) It's just what's needed to add 1 to a total. The process of flipping the bits and adding one is called *two's complementation*. It subtracts a number from the turnover value. The turnover value for an n-bit two's complement number is 2^n. If $n = 4$, this value is 16.

So we may do $5 - 3$ as an addition

$$\begin{array}{r} 0101 \\ + \ 1101 \\ \hline 0010 \end{array}$$

or to really see how the computer does it,

$$\begin{array}{r} 1 \\ 0101 \\ + \ 1100 \\ \hline 0010 \end{array}$$

The final carry bit is ignored. That is how a computer subtracts 3 from 5.

The use of the word *complement* is justified by the fact that

$$16 - (16 - x) = x$$

Note that this faithfully reflects the fact that

$$-(-x) = x$$

3.7.2   Two's Complementation in Hex

The two's complement process is done by flipping the bits and adding one. If we think of flipping the bits of a hex digit, we see that this can be done by subtracting from 15. To do the two's complement of a number in hex then, we can subtract each of its digits from fifteen and then add one. For example, given an eight-bit number 23H,

$$
\begin{array}{c}
\text{FF} \\
-\ 2\,3 \\
\hline
\text{DC}
\end{array}
\quad \text{and then} \quad
\begin{array}{c}
\text{DC} \\
+\ \ 1 \\
\hline
\text{DD}
\end{array}
$$

Hence the two's complement of 23H is DDH. On the other hand if we use the fact that finding the two's complement is really subtraction from the turnover value, we can just do the subtraction.

$$
\begin{array}{c}
1\,0\,0 \\
-\ 2\,3 \\
\hline
\text{DD}
\end{array}
$$

3.7.3   Conversions

When debuggers display register contents for us, negatives will be shown to us in hex. Consequently, it is worthwhile to become handy with two's complement values in hex. Suppose we are shown the 16-bit value FF42H, and we would like to know what value it represents. First we observe that if we take this to be a signed number, then it is negative since its first bit is 1 — if the first hex digit is any of the hex digits 8, 9, A, B, C, D, E, or F, then the first binary digit is 1. To find the corresponding positive number, we can perform the two's complement in hex.

$$
\begin{array}{c}
1\,0\,0\,0\,0 \\
-\ \text{FF}\,4\,2 \\
\hline
\text{BE}
\end{array}
$$

And BEH is $11 \times 16 + 14 = 190$. Consequently, the represented value is -190.

You could also convert everything to binary, take the two's complement, and then convert to decimal. Of course you could also convert FF42H to decimal and subtract the result from 65,536! Probably working in hex as much as you can is the easiest.

3.8*   Placeholding Two's Complement

Two's complement can be thought of as a placeholding system. If the place value of the most significant bit is thought of as standing for the negative of its ordinary binary value, then this yields a place value interpretation for two's complement numbering. Table 3.11 shows the place values in the four-bit two's complement system. Using the table, we see that -5 can be expressed as $(-8) + 2 + 1$.

−8s	4s	2s	1s	Binary	Decimal
1	1	1	1	1111	-1
1	1	1	0	1110	-2
1	1	0	1	1101	-3
1	1	0	0	1100	-4
1	0	1	1	1011	-5
1	0	1	0	1010	-6
1	0	0	1	1001	-7
1	0	0	0	1000	-8
0	1	1	1	0111	7
0	1	1	0	0110	6
0	1	0	1	0101	5
0	1	0	0	0100	4
0	0	1	1	0011	3
0	0	1	0	0010	2
0	0	0	1	0001	1

Table 3.11. Four-Bit Two's Complement Place Values

3.9 Memory Circuits

The latch circuit shown in Figure 3-7 has the property that if a logic 0 is applied to the Freeze/Copy# line, then the value on the Input propagates through to the Output. On the other hand, if a logic 1 is applied to the Freeze/Copy# line, then the Output signal is held to whatever value it had at the time of the "freeze." This value is in storage and the input is ignored.

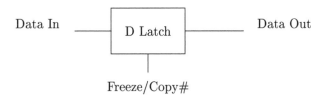

To see how this circuit might serve as one bit of a memory circuit, imagine many of these circuits arranged in a rectangle, each row forming a word of memory. Each row would respond to a selection signal picking that row out from all the other rows in memory. The memory would be required to remain dormant whenever the selection signal was not present. To use this circuit as one bit of a memory, let us suppose we have a W/R# control signal and a selection signal, Sel. W stands for write, which means that the processor wants to write to the memory circuit. R stands for read and means that the processor wants to read from the memory circuit. All the circuits in the entire memory will be connected to the same W/R# signal, but only the circuits in the same word are connected to a single Sel signal.

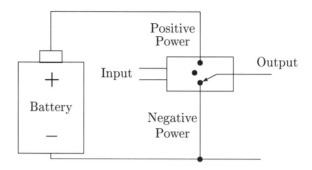

Figure 3-8. A Tri-State Logic Gate

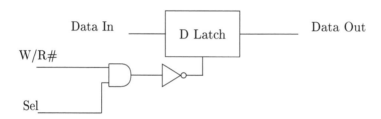

When Sel is 0, the NOT gate outputs a 1, which freezes the circuit. When Sel is 1 and the W/R# input is 0, meaning the processor wants to read, then again the circuit remains frozen. When Sel is 1 and the W/R# is 1, then the NOT gate outputs a 0, which causes the Data In to be stored.

This circuit would work alright except for the fact that the number of Data wires for the entire memory is the same as the number of bits in one word. For example, this means that the least significant bit of the word must share its Data Out wire with the corresponding Data Out wire from every other word in memory as well as with the corresponding Data In wire. The same goes for each of the other bits. A memory with four-bit words has only four data wires, regardless of how many words it has. To avoid causing massive conflicts, circuits which have what is called a *tri-state output* are used.

3.9.1 Tri-State Outputs

Figure 3-2 shows a generic logic gate. The output of this gate can be switched either to the positive or the negative power terminal. Because its output has two possible values, it is called a *two-state gate*. Figure 3-8 shows a generic tri-state logic gate. Its output has three possible values. The output of this gate can be a logic 1 or a logic 0, but the output can also be switched to a disconnected state so that the output is not hooked up to anything. This is sometimes referred to as

Control	Input	Output
0	0	X
0	1	X
1	0	0
1	1	1

Table 3.12. Truth Table for Tri-State Buffer

a *don't care* state and is sometimes denoted by the letter X. When a logic gate switches to this state, it releases control over its output. If there is conflict on the horizon, switching to this state is a good way to avoid it. A simple tri-state circuit is the tri-state buffer whose truth table is given in Table 3.12. The symbol for this circuit is

When a tri-state buffer is added to the latch, as shown in Figure 3-9, the data wire can be shared by the input and the output. The processor, of course, needs a tri-state buffer on its end too. This circuit has only three external connections. Suppose we represent it as follows as shown in Figure 3-10. Four of these circuits used in parallel could store four bits, all under the control of the same two signals, W/R# and Sel.

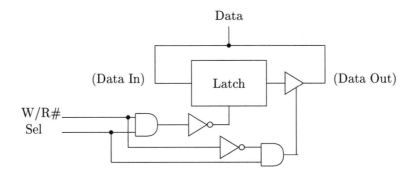

Figure 3-9. A One-Bit Memory Circuit

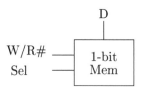

Figure 3-10. One-Bit Memory

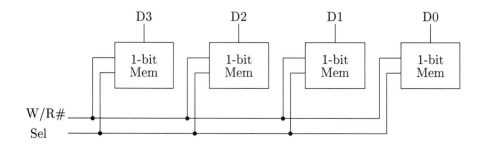

Suppose we represent a four-bit memory like this:

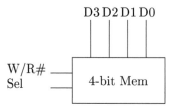

Figure 3-11 shows a memory consisting of four of these circuits. Two address wires suffice to address this memory. This memory circuit has four words. Each word holds four bits. The data wires D0, D1, D2, and D3 are all shared. The address wires A0 and A1 control the four different Sel inputs. The address wires select which of the four Sel wires is selected. The other three will have the value 0. It is not possible to turn on two at a time.

If we imagine this as the memory of a tiny little computer, then this computer would have a four-bit data bus, a two-bit address bus, and a one-bit control bus. To fetch an item from memory the processor for this little computer would put its W/R# pin at logic 0 and a two-bit address on the address bus. This would activate the Sel signal for exactly one word of memory. If we imagine a fetch-execute cycle in progress, the processor would need a two-bit register to keep track of the address of the instruction it was executing. All processors performing the fetch-execute cycle need such a register. It is often called the *Program Counter*. In Intel machines, it is called the *Instruction Pointer*.

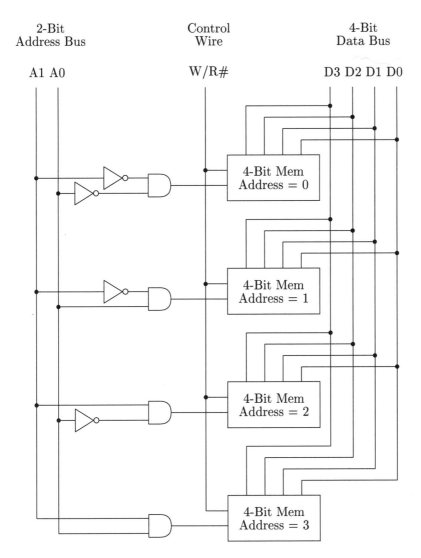

Figure 3-11. Four-Word Memory. Each Word Holds Four Bits

Definition of Memory Capacity

Any *physical memory* is an object or device which is stable in more than one state. Its capacity is the number of its stable states. Since a computer memory is laid out as a rectangle of objects with two stable states each, the number of stable states in the memory is $2^{l \times w}$, where l and w are the length and width of the rectangle. l is also called the number of words, and w is the width of each word in bits. For convenience, the capacity is often given (in bits) as just $l \times w$, i.e. the base two logarithm of the number of stable states. The capacity in bytes, of course, is one eighth of the capacity in bits.

SRAM vs. DRAM

When memory circuits are built out of logic circuits, it is called *static memory* or *SRAM*. Memory circuits can also be made out of capacitors. A charged capacitor represents a stored 1; a discharged capacitor represents a stored 0. Since fewer transistors are required, these circuits can be packed with greater density on a chip. Small, closely packed capacitors have the disadvantage that they discharge rapidly. They require constant rechecking. Every capacitor which is not completely discharged must be pumped back up again. Because the memory is being constantly "refreshed," it is called *dynamic memory*, or *DRAM*. Dynamic memory is like a bookshelf without the shelf, except that in the case of a book falling four feet, say, to the floor, you would have .5 seconds to catch it before it hit the floor. These little capacitors discharge in .0001 seconds. The memory refresh must be done approximately every 100 μs. Unlike many developments which have numerous contributors, dynamic memory was invented by a single person, Ted Hoff, around 1970. Dynamic memory is cheaper and slower than static memory. Static memory is usually used for cache memory, while dynamic memory is used for RAM.

One drawback of DRAM is that it makes hardware debugging much more difficult. The simplest way to do hardware debugging would be to slow the computer's clock way down. Aberrant behavior could then be observed as it happened. But because of DRAM's rapid refresh requirements, there is no easy way to do this.

3.10   x86 General Registers and their Ancestry

One of the reasons behind the market success of the Intel x86 line of processors has been that each new processor in the line was designed subject to the requirement that it be compatible with previous processors. Intel never wiped the slate clean and started from scratch as Motorola and IBM did with the PowerPC chip and DEC   did with the Alpha processor. This minimized the amount of hardware and software retooling necessitated by an upgrade. Consequently, a description of the x86, and in particular its registers lends itself to a historical approach. We begin with the 8080 processor.

3.10.1   8080 Registers

The 8080 was the first really mass-produced microprocessor. It was used as the CPU in several early microcomputers, including the Atari. This processor has registers A, B, C, D, H, and L, which are all eight-bit registers. The very first personal computer also utilized the 8080 processor. It was the Altair, which appeared on the cover of *Popular Science* magazine of January 1975. The fact that its registers, memory addresses, and data transfers were all eight bits in size makes this computer

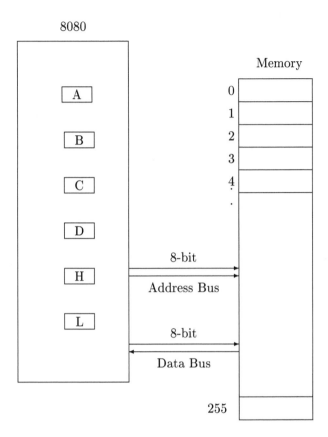

Figure 3-12. Altair Computer

a very good example of an eight-bit computer. All the registers shown are eight-bit registers. The address bus and the data bus each have eight wires.

The L register is used to store addresses. The Altair memory has bytes numbered 0 to 255. This memory is shockingly small, but on the other hand it was filled one byte at a time by flipping eight bit switches!

There are extant versions of the 8080 on the market, the   8085 and the Z80. Radio Shack's TRS-80 was based on the Z80.

When IBM introduced the PC, they chose the Intel 8088 as its   processor because in its dealings with memory and the system board, it acts like an eight-bit processor. In particular, it acts a lot like the 8080 processor.

3.10.2   8086 Registers

Although the Altair was a nearly pure example of an   eight-bit computer, the 8080 processor did have some 16-bit features. In particular, it was designed so that it could be used with a 16-bit memory addressing system. It did this by allowing two of the eight-bit registers, the H and the L, to pair up and form a 16-bit register, which could then be used for addresses. When this high byte-low byte pair was referenced by a command, an X was used in the command. For example the 16-bit increment command was INX. The eight-bit command was INR. The X stood for *extended*, and was used whenever 16-bit register pairs were being   referenced. When the 16-bit 8086 processor, shown in Figure 3-13, was designed this X was recruited for use in the 16-bit register designations AX, BX, CX, and DX. The 16-bit registers AX, BX, CX, and DX are pairs of high and low byte registers AH and AL, BH and BL, CH and CL, DH and DL. The other 16-bit registers, SP, BP, SI, and DI, have no X in their names and are not byte pairs. The data bus has 16 wires. Also shown are the 65,536 ($= 2^{16}$) memory locations in one 8086 memory segment. In spite of the above picture, the 8086 is not really a good example of a 16-bit computer. The address bus has 20 wires, and there is a clumsy mechanism for using a handful of segments at a time. So the memory is not actually limited to 64K, but there is no convenient way to use all 2^{20} bytes at once.

3.10.3   80386 Registers

Many of the wrinkles visible in the design of the 8086 are smoothed out in the 80386, shown in Figure 3-14. The eight registers whose names begin with E are all extensions of the corresponding registers on the 8086. The bottom half of each 32-bit register is a 16-bit register inherited from the 8086. The address bus and the data bus each have 32 wires. Also shown are the 4,294,967,296 ($= 2^{32}$) memory locations which an 80386 is capable of addressing. An 80386 computer is a very good example of a   32-bit computer. The 80486 and the Pentium are also 32-bit processors. In fact, in terms of registers sizes, memory addressing, and so on, there are no changes at all. Up until the Pentium II and Pentium Pro were released, the main   developments consisted in increasing the speed without changing the basic architecture. Figure 3-14 could just as well be labeled "Pentium Computer" as "80386 Computer," except that the Pentium has a 64-bit data bus.

3.11   The MOV Command

This section introduces the MOV command. It is a very important instruction. MOV is a storage command. It copies a value into a location. It has many different valid forms. The **reg,imm** and **reg,reg** forms are especially important.

3.11.1   MOV **reg,imm**

- **reg** stands for *register*. It may be any of the registers listed in Table 3.13.

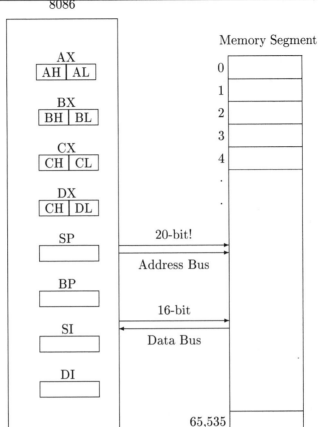

Figure 3-13. 8086 Computer (Partial Model)

- **imm** stands for *immediate*. The term *immediate* is used to refer to a numerical value given directly by a decimal or hexadecimal representation as opposed to a register or memory location containing that value.

For example, in

    MOV AX, 54

the number 54 occurs as an immediate value. This command stores the number, 54, into the 16-bit register AX. This register is the same as the bottom 16 bits of the register EAX. The top 16 bits are unmodified. Since 54 = 36H, the command is the same as the command

    MOV AX, 36H

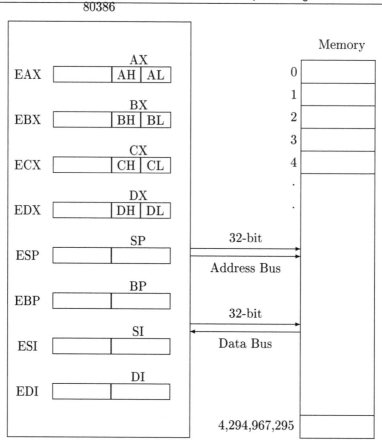

Figure 3-14. 80386 Computer (Partial Model)

The value assigned to the location must fit. The command

    MOV AL, 999

is not valid because 999 will not fit into an eight-bit register.
    NASM and Edlinas allow signed integers. Hence

    MOV AL, −128

is valid and does the same thing as

    MOV AL, 128

But

8-bit	16-bit	32-bit
AH	AX	EAX
AL	BX	EBX
BH	CX	ECX
BL	DX	EDX
CH	BP	EBP
CL	SP	ESP
DH	SI	ESI
DL	DI	EDI

Table 3.13. x86 General Registers

MOV AL, −129

is not valid in Edlinas because −129 is not in the eight-bit signed range. NASM doesn't balk until it gets to −257. NASM allows characters to represent ASCII codes. For example,

MOV AL, 'A'

stores the ASCII code for the letter A, which is 65, in AL.

Code using 32-bit registers will not run on x86 processors prior to the 80386. Although it is a characteristic of so-called "32-bit code" to use 32-bit registers, some "16-bit code" does also. The actual difference between 32- and 16-bit code is discussed in chapter 5, section 5.5.

3.11.2   MOV reg,reg

MOV reg,reg copies from the second register into the first. The two-operand commands described in this book use the syntax   COMMAND destination, source. Hence the command

MOV EAX, EBX

does not change the EBX register. It means

let EAX = EBX

not move EAX to EBX.

There are assemblers which use the opposite syntax, such as the AT&T-style assembler used by gcc. In its syntax, the exact same command is written

```
movl %ebx,%eax
```

The two registers used in a MOV command must be the same size. The following command, for example, is not valid.

MOV EBX, DX

3.11.3   Ambiguity Problem

According to the append H hex convention discussed in chapter 2, section 2.7, the register names AH, BH, CH, and DH are also valid hexadecimal names for the numbers ten, eleven, twelve, and thirteen. This would make commands such as

    MOV BL, AH

ambiguous. This command would be a valid example of both the **reg,reg** form and the **reg,imm** form of the MOV command. The customary resolution of this ambiguity is to require all hexadecimal numbers used in assembly language commands to begin with one of the digits 0, 1, ... 9. This modification of the append H convention will be observed in this text and is required by both NASM and Edlinas. Hence MOV BL, AH is actually not a valid example the **reg,imm** form. It is an example of the **reg,reg** form. To store the immediate value ten into BL we must use either

    MOV BL, 0AH

or

    MOV BL, 10

3.12   Addition and Subtraction Commands

This section describes the **reg,imm** and **reg,reg** forms of the ADD and SUB commands. These are very fundamental arithmetic instructions.

3.12.1   ADD **reg,imm**

    ADD reg,imm

means to add the immediate value to the register. For example

    ADD BL, 10

can be thought of as

    let BL = BL + 10

3.12.2   ADD **reg,reg**

The command

    ADD reg,reg

means to add the contents of the second register to the first. So the command

    ADD BL, AL

means

    let BL = BL + AL

The register AL is not changed by this command.

3.12.3 SUB reg,imm

The command

SUB BL, 10

for example, means

let BL = BL −10

3.12.4 SUB reg,reg

SUB BL, AL

for example, means

let BL = BL − AL

3.13* Multiplication and Division Commands

If the multiplication command were to function similarly to the ADD and SUB command, we would expect to see commands such as

MUL EAX, EBX

which would mean to multiply the contents of the register EAX by the value in EBX. However, the multiply command does not work like this. One reason is that because multiplying numbers together typically doubles them in size, it does not make sense to use the same size registers for the answer as for the multiplied numbers.

3.13.1 The MUL Command

The syntax for the multiply command is

MUL reg

reg may be any of the 24 general registers listed in Table 3.13. If the register used is an eight-bit register, for example

MUL BH

then the command means:

let AX = AL · BH

When an eight-bit register is used, it always multiplies by AL and stores the result in AX. When a 16-bit register is used, for example,

MUL BX

then the command means

let DX:AX = AX · BX

where the 32-bit answer is stored in two 16-bit registers. The top 16 bits are stored in DX, the bottom 16 bits in AX. When a 32-bit register is used, for example,

MUL EBX

then the command means

let EDX:EAX = EAX · EBX

A single register is all that you specify when you use the MUL command. The other registers are always implied. The situation is similar to that with the ADD command on the 8080 processor, where addition results are always stored in the A register. The command ADD B in 8080 assembly language means

let A = A + B

Unlike the ADD and SUB commands, the MUL command has no immediate form. The command

MUL 7

is *not* valid.

3.13.2   The DIV Command

The DIV command closely resembles the MUL command in syntax and is essentially its inverse. It forms both a quotient and a remainder

	dividend	remainder	quotient
32-bit form	EDX:EAX	EDX	EAX
16-bit form	DX:AX	DX	AX
8-bit form	AX	AH	AL

For example, if AX held the value 17 and BH held the value 3, then

DIV BH

would store 2 in AH and 5 in AL. The command would be recognized as an eight-bit command because BH is an eight-bit register.

Division by zero produces an error called an *exception*. Exceptions are dealt with in chapter 9.

It is important to note that because of the sizes of the registers involved in division, zero is not the only divisor which can cause an exception. For example, when AX is divided by a number stored in an eight-bit register, the quotient is supposed to be stored in AL, an eight-bit register. But dividing a 16-bit number by an eight-bit number does not always produce a number which can be stored in eight bits. For example, $1024 \div 2 = 512$, or in hex, $400H \div 2 = 200H$. But 200H requires at least ten bits of storage. This means that the following code will cause an exception:

```
MOV AX, 400H
MOV BH, 2
DIV BH
```

This error is called a *division overflow*.

3.13.3 Negative Numbers and Congruences

Two's complement representation is used for negative numbers, in part because it allows addition and subtraction hardware to be used irrespective of whether the bits being operated on are intended as signed integers or as unsigned integers. The mathematical explanation for why two's complement representation works like this is based on a concept due to C. F. Gauss, a remarkable nineteenth century mathematician.

Gauss defined $a \equiv b(\bmod\ m)$ to mean that a and b differ only by some exact multiple of m. In two's complement representation, a negative number and the positive number used to represent it differ by the turnover value of the registers being used. If four-bit registers are being used, then each negative and its positive representation differ by 2^4, or 16, as shown in Table 3.9. In Gauss' notation, for example, $-5 \equiv 11 \pmod{16}$. So when the computer does $(-2) + (-3)$ as $14 + 13$, it depends on the fact that $14 + 13 = 27 \equiv -5 \pmod{16}$. The four-bit addition hardware produces 11 because a carry of 16 is lost. But that is okay. Eleven is the correct representative for -5.

Congruence Addition Theorem

This reasoning is summarized in the following theorem due to Gauss:

If $a \equiv b \pmod{m}$ and $c \equiv d \pmod{m}$
then $a + c \equiv b + d \pmod{m}$

This theorem says that congruences can be added just like equations. Gauss devised the congruence notation in order to make the point that a congruence is similar to an equation.

Congruence Multiplication Theorem

The following theorem states that congruences can also be multiplied just like equations.

If $a \equiv b \pmod{m}$ and $c \equiv d \pmod{m}$
then $a \cdot c \equiv b \cdot d(\bmod\ m)$

Because of this nice theorem, we should be able to use both signed and unsigned numbers with MUL just like ADD and have no problems! Except for one thing.

We want to double the register size as we go. So the theorem we really need is this one:

If $a \equiv b \pmod{m}$ and $c \equiv d \pmod{m}$
then $a \cdot c \equiv b \cdot d \pmod{m^2}$

Unfortunately, this isn't a theorem. It's a falsehood. For example, in the eight-bit case where m $= 256$ and $m^2 = 65,536$, if $a = -16$, $b = 240$, and $c = d = 2$, we get $a \cdot c = -32$ and $b \cdot d = 480$. So the theorem says

$-32 \equiv 480 \pmod{256}$, which is correct.

Removing the eight-bit turnover value of 256 from 480 leaves 224. Hence if we considered the answer to be 224 unsigned or -32 signed, then everything would be okay. Two hundred twenty-four is the two's complement positive that is equivalent to -32 in the eight-bit system. But we're not content with eight bits. We want 16. And

$-32 \equiv 480 \pmod{65,536}$ is wrong.

In the 16-bit system, -32 is represented by 65504, not 480. Consequently, we can't use MUL (or DIV) for both signed and unsigned numbers. MUL and DIV work for unsigned numbers. There are different commands which work for signed numbers: IMUL and IDIV. This is an example of the issue raised in section 3.6.5.

Further Reading

The Microprocessor, A Biography, Michael S. Malone, Springer: 1995.

The Anatomy of a High-Performance Microprocessor, Shriver and Smith, IEEE: 1998.

4

ASSEMBLY LANGUAGE

A computer program is something which can be stored in a computer's memory. If the memory has one-byte words, we can then say that the computer program consists of bytes. These bytes are also called *machine language*. Writing a program by listing these bytes explicitly is called *machine language programming*. It is the original form of programming. It is definitely the most tedious. Assembly language was devised as a way of specifying machine code without actually having to write it down. Assembly language may be mere shorthand or it may involve complex *macros*, some of which may even resemble `if` or `while` statements in C. But whether it is primitive or fancy, its defining characteristic is that it gives the programmer control over the machine language.

Three good reasons for learning assembly language are

1. In truly time-critical sections of code, it is sometimes possible to improve performance by coding in assembly language.

2. It is a good way to learn how a particular CPU works.

3. In writing a new operating system or in porting an existing system to a new machine, there are sections of code which must be written in assembly language.

Assembly languages are written to fit hand-in-glove with a specific processor. Given the considerable variety of processors and instruction sets, one might expect there to be a considerable variety in the instruction formats for the various assembly languages as well. But this is not the case. Assembly languages generally follow one universal format which might be called the *four field format*.

4.1   The Four Field Format

According to this format every assembly language program consists of lines. Every line consists of four fields. The four fields are the label field, the mnemonic field, the operand field, and the comment field.

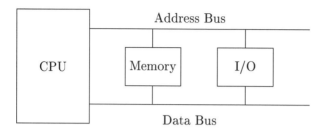

Figure 4-1. All Computers are Divided into Three Parts

1. The label field is used for a label which specifies the target of a jump instruction. A jump is the same as a *go to* instruction. Examples of jump instructions are given in section 4.4.

2. The mnemonic field contains an instruction specifier. Examples of mnemonics are MOV, ADD, SUB, etc. The word *mnemonic* suggests that it makes the machine code easy to remember, although it doesn't; it makes the machine code unnecessary to remember.

3. The operand field contains the object or objects on which the instruction is operating. If there is more than one operand, they are separated by commas. As we noticed above, ADD takes two operands. JMP on the other hand takes one. Some mnemonics take none at all.

4. The comment field contains documentation. It begins with a semicolon. In any computer language, documentation is important. In assembly language, documentation is especially important because an assembly language program is especially hard to read without it. A line may consist of nothing but a comment.

Program 4.1 is an example of an x86 assembly language program. The reader should note the consistent four field layout even though some of the fields on some of the lines are empty. Many of the instructions in Program 4.1 are making their first appearance here in this book. These new instructions are all discussed in this chapter.

4.2   Computers from the CPU Standpoint

Computers are often described as consisting of three parts: the CPU, the memory, and the input/output, or I/O system. A diagram drawn according to this picture looks like Figure 4-1. Included in the I/O system are the monitor, the keyboard, the hard drive, the printer, the modem, the sound card, and the CDROM. These

```
      ;
      ; Greatest common divisor program
      ;
            MOV EDX, 0        ; 0 is the only Edlinas input port
            IN EAX,[DX]       ; Get the user's first input
            MOV ECX, EAX      ; Get the input out of harm's way
            IN EAX,[DX]       ; Get the user's second input
            MOV EDX, EAX      ; Use EDX for the larger of the two inputs
ORD:        SUB EAX, ECX      ; Use EAX as a working copy of EDX
            JZ GCD            ; When equality is obtained we are done.
            JNS NXT           ; We want EDX to be larger. No swap needed
            MOV EAX, ECX      ; Swap EDX and ECX (Takes three MOV's)
            MOV ECX, EDX
NXT:        MOV EDX, EAX      ; If there was no swap then EDX = EDX-ECX
            JMP ORD           ; End of the loop
GCD:        MOV EAX, EDX      ; The GCD is in EDX
            MOV EDX, 1        ; We need EDX for the output port number
            OUT [DX],EAX      ; Display the answer to the user
            RET
```

Program 4.1

are all just I/O devices. This is a processor-centric view. Just as members of a group sometimes categorize people in terms of how they relate to the group, this picture of a computer defines parts of a computer according to how they relate to the CPU. Since assembly language is all about working with the CPU, however, it is a useful point of view for us to adopt.

If we imagine the CPU in the picture to be a 386, then we can think of the data bus as a set of 32 wires connected to 32 pins on the CPU, and the address bus as another set of 32 wires also connected to the CPU. Notice that the memory and I/O systems are connected to the processor in essentially the same way. If we imagine viewing the bits flowing on the buses, a data transfer between the CPU and the memory looks almost exactly like a data transfer between the CPU and the I/O system. The difference actually boils down to a single pin on the CPU. This pin is called the M/IO# pin. When this pin is at logic 1, it signals a memory transfer. When it is at logic 0, it signals an I/O transfer. The above diagram does not really make sense without an M/IO# wire. It also needs a W/R# wire to signal whether data is to flow into or out of the processor. These wires are called *control wires* and are part of the *control bus*.

The reader is urged to compare Figure 4-1 with Figure 3-11, which shows in greater detail how the wires from the three different buses hook up to a memory circuit.

4.2.1   Memory vs. I/O

In Table 4.1 we see two **imm** forms of the MOV command compared with the corresponding I/O commands. These commands carry out transfers between the AL register and the memory or I/O device located at address 12. The processor

	Memory	I/O
Read	MOV AL,[12]	IN AL,[12]
Write	MOV [12],AL	OUT [12],AL

Table 4.1. Examples of Memory and I/O Transfer Commands

signals read vs. write using the W/R# pin and memory vs. I/O using the M/IO# pin. Otherwise the transaction is very similar.

One significant difference between memory and I/O addressing on the x86 is that memory addresses undergo processing before they leave the processor. This processing has two stages: segmentation and paging. Segmentation is described in chapter 12 and paging is described in chapter 8.

Another difference between the I/O system and the memory is that they do not have the same range of valid addresses. As discussed in chapter 3, the range of valid memory addresses varies from one x86 processor to another. (It depends on the number of address pins the processor has.) The range of valid I/O addresses on the other hand is the same on all x86 processors. It is the 16-bit range from 0 to 65,535. Incidentally, this means that the I/O system does not need to be connected to all 32 address wires, only to the bottom 16. The addresses in this range are called *ports* or *port numbers*.

Many existing I/O devices, such as disk drives, printers, and serial ports, use a handful of ports each. Table 4.2, for example, lists the eight addresses used by the standard serial ports. (Clearly the port numbers 1 through 4 in the table are *not* port numbers in the specific sense we are considering here. But the following hex addresses are *perfect* examples of these port numbers.) A relatively complete

Com Port	I/O Addresses
1	3F8H–3FFH
2	2F8H–2FFH
3	3E8H–3EFH
4	2F8H–2FFH

Table 4.2. Standard Serial Port I/O Addresses

list of the port numbers used on a standard PC may be found in Appendix A of Shanley's *ISA System Architecture*. The I/O ports in use on a Linux machine may be accessed via the `/proc` directory using the command

> `linuxbox$ cat /proc/ioports`

The close similarity of memory and I/O transfers is not fully reflected in x86 assembly language, which has many commands involving memory access but only a few, IN and OUT for example, controlling I/O access. The use of MOV and many other commands to access memory is discussed in chapter 6, section 6.2. The IN and OUT commands are discussed next.

4.2.2 The IN Command

The input command transfers data from an I/O port into the processor. There are six valid forms of this command

> IN EAX, [DX]
> IN AX, [DX]
> IN AL, [DX]
> IN EAX,[imm]
> IN AX,[imm]
> IN AL,[imm]

where **imm** is any one-byte number. Notice that the general

> COMMAND destination, source

format is adhered to in this instruction. The valid destination registers are EAX, AX, and AL. The I/O device whose port number is stored in DX or given by **imm** is the source.

Notice that DX is a 16-bit register. This makes sense because a port number is a 16-bit number. Most Intel assemblers, including NASM, do not use brackets around the port number. If you do, however, you can think of the command IN AL, [DX], for example, as

> let AL = [DX]

where the [DX] refers to data located at the address DX. This is done in Edlinas for the sake of consistency. Memory commands use brackets in the same way. Brackets become a dereferencing operator like * in the C language. In both Edlinas and NASM, all references to data in memory by means of an address use brackets around the address. NASM does not use brackets for I/O references. Hence, in using NASM, the brackets in the IN and OUT instructions are omitted.

Because the **imm** forms of the IN command accept only one-byte ports, only the bottom 256 of the 65,536 ports are accessible using the **imm** forms. Notice that the IN command was not given as IN reg, [reg]. This is because forms such as IN EBX, [DX] and IN EAX, [CX] are *not* valid.

4.2.3   The OUT Command

The output command transfers data from the processor to an I/O device. The six valid forms of this command are

```
OUT [DX], EAX
OUT [DX], AX
OUT [DX], AL
OUT [imm], EAX
OUT [imm], AX
OUT [imm], AL
```

where again **imm** is any one-byte number. The order of the operands is opposite to what it is in the IN command because the data is flowing in the opposite direction. The source is either the EAX, the AX, or the AL register, and the destination is an I/O device. Again, NASM doesn't use brackets with OUT.

4.2.4   Memory Mapped I/O

When addresses in the memory address space are connected, in fact, to I/O devices, this is referred to as *memory mapped I/O*. The video buffer on the standard PC is an example. Characters stored at the 4000 bytes starting at the memory address B8000H are output to the monitor.

Using a separate address space for I/O devices is not the only conceivable approach to I/O addressing. Many architectures use a single set of addresses and simply reserve some of them for I/O.

Reserved addresses are also used on PCs for ROM, or *read-only memory*. If memory writes are done to read only memory, the processor will send the appropriate write signals out onto the buses, but no change will be made in the "stored" data.

4.3   Simple Assembly Language Programs

Simple high-level language programs often have a three-part format: input data, do calculations, and then output the results. Using Edlinas, simple programs of the same style can be written in x86 assembly language.

4.3.1   Edlinas Ports

The imaginary machine simulated by Edlinas uses only two port numbers.

- 0 is the port for the keyboard input.

- 1 is the port for the screen output.

Keyboard input is echoed at the lower left of the screen and output is displayed at the lower right. When IN EAX, [DX] is used with Edlinas, the value stored in DX should be 0. When port 0 is addressed, the user is prompted for an input value. When OUT [DX],EAX is used, the value stored in DX should be 1. When port 1 is used, the output value is displayed in base ten at the bottom right of the screen. The use of these two ports allows very simple programs to be written in genuine x86 assembly language and run on the Edlinas simulator.

Programs using Edlinas ports will not run under DOS or Unix. In chapter 8, section 8.4.7 it is shown how these I/O commands to the simulated machine may be replaced by calls to the C library functions `scanf()` and `printf()`. In this way, simple Edlinas programs using real I/O can be run under Linux.

4.3.2   The RET Command

Programs are set in motion by the operating system. When the program is finished, it must return control to the operating system. RET does this. Subprograms also use RET to return control to a calling program. RET works using the stack and is discussed in chapter 7, section 7.2.

4.3.3   Program to Add Two Numbers

We now have all the commands we need to write some simple but complete programs. Here is an Edlinas program to add two numbers:

```
MOV EDX, 0       ; Making all 32 bits zero makes DX zero.
IN EAX, [DX]     ; User enters the first number via port zero.
MOV EBX, EAX     ; Get the first number out of the way.
IN EAX, [DX]     ; User enters the second number.
ADD EAX, EBX     ; Add the first number to the second.
MOV EDX, 1       ; The Edlinas output port is one.
OUT [DX], EAX    ; The result is output to the user.
RET              ; End the simulation.
```

Program 4.2

4.4   Assembler Programs with Jumps

High-level languages need loops in order to be able to do their work. These loops must be turned into assembly code by a compiler. For example, as illustrated in Figure 4-2, to do a C language `while` loop in the most straightforward way requires both a conditional jump forward and an unconditional jump backward.

4.4.1   The JMP Command

The fetch-execute cycle works by calculating the address in memory of the next instruction. This address is normally determined by just going to the first address

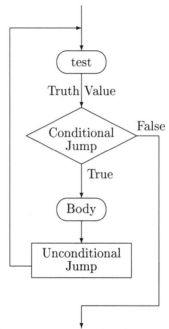

Figure 4-2. while(test) Body;

beyond the current instruction. In order to support if-then statements or loops in high-level languages, however, jumps are needed. The JMP command transfers execution to the address specified by a label.

The JMP command has the form

   JMP label

The label is created by the programmer. It is wise to devise labels which help in understanding the program. For this purpose, long labels are useful. On the other hand, the screen space used by Edlinas is very limited and so labels beyond three characters are truncated when they are displayed unless they are on a line by themselves. The label in the label field specifies the target of the jump and often has a colon appended to make it clear that it is a label and not an arcane mnemonic. Many jump commands may point to the same target, but no two lines may carry the same label in their label field. In the following program, the last line transfers control to the preceding line. This program continues adding 2 to the EAX register forever. It is an infinite loop. Infinite loops are usually written only by mistake.

4.4.2   Conditional Jumps and Flags

A *conditional jump* is a jump carried out on the basis of a truth value. The information on which such decisions are based is contained in one-bit registers called

```
          MOV EAX, 0
          MOV EBX, 2
XYZ:      ADD EAX, EBX
          JMP XYZ
```

Program 4.3

flags. When a flag contains 1, it is referred to as being *set*. When it contains 0, it is referred to as being *cleared*. Two very important flags are the zero flag and the sign flag.

The Zero and Sign Flags

The ADD and SUB commands affect not only their destination registers but also many of the flags. Suppose the command

```
    ADD EAX, EBX
```

is executed. The result of this command will be in the EAX register. If this result is 0, then the zero flag is set. If it is not 0, then the zero flag is cleared.

The value given to the sign flag after an ADD instruction is the value of the most significant bit of the result. This bit is 1 if the result is negative when viewed as a signed number. Thus if executing the ADD EAX, EBX command gives EAX a value which is negative, as a four-byte signed number, then the sign flag is set; otherwise the sign flag is cleared.

4.4.3   The JZ, JS, JNZ, and JNS Commands

The following conditional jump commands all have the same format as the JMP command.

```
    JZ    label
    JS    label
    JNZ   label
    JNS   label
```

They each take a label in the operand field. The meanings of these commands are as follows:

```
    JZ    Jump if the zero flag is set.
    JS    Jump if the sign flag is set.
    JNZ   Jump if the zero flag is not set.
    JNS   Jump if the sign flag is not set.
```

The following assembly language program illustrates the use of the JS instruction in a program to determine which of two user inputs is larger. Program 4.4 seems air tight. In fact it has a bug.

```
          ; If the first input is larger output 1
          ; If the second input is larger output 2
          ; The program uses subtraction:
          ; B < A is true if and only if B − A is negative.
          ; A subtraction followed by a JS does the job
          ;
          MOV EDX, 0
          IN EAX, [DX]
          MOV EBX, EAX    ; The first input is now in EBX
          IN EAX, [DX]     ; The second input is now in EAX.
          SUB EBX, EAX    ; This is (first − second).
          JS SIB           ; Second is Bigger
          MOV EAX, 1       ; Otherwise First is Bigger
          JMP END          ; Don't drift into the other case!
SIB:      MOV EAX, 2       ;
END:      MOV EDX, 1       ; Either way now EAX is ready.
          OUT [DX], EAX
          RET
```

Program 4.4

4.5   Assembler Programs with Loops

Conditional jumps are used to implement loops and if-then statements. Suppose we consider the following program, which does multiplication using repeated addition. For example to do 7×5 we can do $5 + 5 + 5 + 5 + 5 + 5 + 5$. In Program 4.5

```
          ;
          MOV EDX, 0
          IN EAX,[DX]      ; First input is the multiplier
          MOV EBX, EAX    ; Put Multiplier in EBX
          IN EAX,[DX]      ; Second input is the multiplied number
          MOV ECX, 0       ; Initialize the running total.
RPT:      ADD ECX, EAX    ; Do one addition.
          SUB EBX, 1       ; One less yet to be done.
          JNZ RPT          ; If that's not zero, do another.
          MOV EAX, ECX    ; Put the total in EAX
          ADD EDX, 1       ;
          OUT [DX], EAX    ; Output the answer.
          RET
```

Program 4.5

the number 1 is added in one line and subtracted in another. There are special commands for this which take less memory space.

The INC and DEC Commands

The following increment and decrement commands add and subtract 1:

> INC reg

and

> DEC reg

reg may be any of the 24 general registers. These commands are often used to increment or decrement a loop counter. In Program 4.5, SUB EBX, 1 can be replaced by DEC EBX and ADD EDX, 1 can be replaced by INC EDX.

4.6   Signed Comparisons

4.6.1   Comparison-Based Jumps

High-level languages often use comparisons in if-then statements. Using the sign flag to test the result of a subtraction, as was done in section 4.4, seems to be a reasonable way to implement this testing since it is a mathematical fact that

> B < A if and only if B − A is negative.

Since the sign flag indicates the sign of the result of a subtraction we would seem to be on solid ground. But in fact this is not true.

4.6.2   The Overflow Flag

Suppose we are using one-byte signed numbers and we wish to test whether

> $100 < -50$

In one-byte registers:

> $100 - (-50) = -106$

An overflow has occurred. The result is negative. The sign flag is set and the comparison will be judged as true! Using the sign flag to determine a jump gives the wrong answer. But since an overflow always changes the sign of a result to the opposite of what it should be, the jump condition can be fixed.

1. If no overflow has occurred, jump if the sign flag is set.

2. If an overflow has occurred, jump if the sign flag is not set.

The x86 processor has an overflow flag. It is used in order to implement this fixed-up jump condition. If we use SF for the binary value of the sign flag and OF for that of the overflow flag, we can restate the fixed jump condition as just

Jump if (SF XOR OF)

This jump condition will produce a jump following a subtraction such as

SUB AL, BL

if and only if AL < BL. There is an x86 command for this jump. The mnemonic for it is JL, which stands for *jump if less than*.

4.6.3 The CMP Command

When a subtraction is performed only for the sake of a comparison, it may be done with the CMP instruction. This command sets the flags in the exact same way as SUB but has the advantage of not wasting register space by storing an unneeded result. Using the JL and CMP instructions we can rewrite the Program 4.4 as follows:

```
        ; If the first input is larger output 1
        ; If the second input is larger output 2
        ; The program uses subtraction:
        ; B < A is true if and only if B − A is negative.
        ;
        MOV EDX, 0
        IN EAX, [DX]
        MOV EBX, EAX    ;The first input is now in EBX
        IN EAX, [DX]    ;The second input is now in EAX.
        CMP EBX, EAX    ; This is first − second.
        JL SIB          ; Second is Bigger
        MOV EAX, 1      ; Otherwise First is Bigger
        JMP END         ; Don't drift into the other case!
SIB:    MOV EAX, 2      ;
END:    MOV EDX, 1      ; Either way now EAX is ready.
        OUT [DX], EAX
        RET
```

Program 4.6

Program 4.6 works correctly for all numbers in the unsigned four-byte range.

4.6.4 More Jump Commands

Following a CMP EAX, EBX command, the JL command executes a jump if the condition EAX < EBX is true. The commands

```
CMP EAX, EBX
JL ABC
```

mean

> Compare EAX to EBX and
> Jump if EAX is less than EBX .

What is going on here is subtraction and flag checking, but the well-designed syntax allows us to overlook that. The *less than* condition is not the only condition conveniently accessed following a CMP command. A list of several other conditional jump commands is given here.

JL	less than	$EAX < EBX$
JLE	less than or equal	$EAX \le EBX$
JG	greater than	$EAX > EBX$
JGE	greater than or equal	$EAX \ge EBX$
JE	equal	$EAX = EBX$
JNL	not less than	$EAX \not< EBX$
JNLE	not less than or equal	$EAX \not\le EBX$
JNG	not greater than	$EAX \not> EBX$
JNGE	not greater than or equal	$EAX \not\ge EBX$
JNE	not equal	$EAX \ne EBX$

Because these various jump commands are so easily interpreted, they turn the compare command into a kind of syntactical windfall.

4.7 Unsigned Comparisons

In section 4.6 it was shown how flags could be used to determine the truth values of inequalities so that these inequalities could be used in conditional jumps. The conditions obtained work for unsigned numbers.

But suppose we consider the same example

$$100 < -50$$

that we considered in the last section and note that when this same inequality is stated in terms of unsigned numbers it becomes

$$100 < 206$$

This inequality has the opposite truth value. So a "jump if less than" command for unsigned numbers must execute a jump in this case. The JL command will not do so. The signed jump commands of the previous section do not work for unsigned numbers. If AL = 64H = 100 and BL = CEH = 206, then a JL will not execute a jump because it is acting on $100 < -50$. An unsigned "jump if less than" is needed.

4.7.1   The Carry Flag

In the case of unsigned numbers, the inequality $A < B$ turns out to be easier to test than its signed counterpart. Since a subtraction of unsigned numbers $A - B$ cannot go out of range on the high side, it is out of range if and only if it is negative. Out of range errors for unsigned numbers are called *carry errors*. Hence $A < B$ is true if and only if the subtraction $A - B$ produces a carry error. So a flag which signals carry errors will signal negative results of a subtraction. The x86 processors have a carry flag to indicate these errors. Using CF to denote the value of this carry flag, we can easily state the condition used to implement the unsigned "jump if less than" command as "jump if CF."

Like the sign flag, the zero flag, and the overflow flag, the carry flag responds to conditions occurring whenever ADD or SUB are used. Unlike these other three flags, it is   unaffected by the INC and DEC commands.

4.7.2   Out of Range Flag Summary

Arithmetic commands such as ADD and SUB are performed on binary bits without any information specifying whether the bits are being used to represent signed or unsigned numbers. It is the responsibility of the software to keep track of this.

When the software uses the processor to do arithmetic on signed numbers, then it should consult the overflow flag to determine whether or not an out of range error has occurred. When the software uses the processor to work on unsigned numbers, then the software should consult the carry flag to check for an out of range error.

The hardware has no way of knowing whether the numbers are signed or unsigned. And it doesn't matter.

For example, on one-byte registers the command to add FFH to FFH may be coming from software that is working with signed numbers. In this case the sum FEH is not a problem. The software sees the arithmetic that has just happened as

$$-1 + -1 = -2.$$

This is okay.

On the other hand the command may be coming from software that is using unsigned numbers. In this case the software sees the arithmetic that has just happened as

$$255 + 255 = 254.$$

This is not okay. The true answer, 510, has gone out of the one-byte unsigned range, 0-255. Hence the addition of FFH to FFH clears the overflow flag because the signed arithmetic answer is okay and sets the carry flag to notify software that there is an unsigned, out of range error.

As another example, suppose that one-byte registers receive a command to add 40H to 40H. The sum is 80H. If the command has come from software working with unsigned numbers then the arithmetic just done will appear as

$64 + 64 = 128$.

This is okay.

Suppose that the command has come from software working with signed numbers. Then the arithmetic looks like this:

$64 + 64 = -128$.

This is not okay. The true answer, $+128$, is outside the one-byte signed range, -128 to $+127$. The hardware sets the overflow flag because this is an out of range error in the signed number system, and clears the carry flag because there is no out of range error in the unsigned system. The hardware does not know which system the software is using, so it has to take care of both flags.

Both the carry and the overflow flags are out of range indicator flags. The carry flag is set if the arithmetic interpreted in the unsigned system has produced an out of range error. The overflow flag is set if the arithmetic interpreted in the signed system has produced an out of range error.

4.7.3   Still More Jump Commands

Given that we need a different command for "jump if less than" for use with unsigned numbers, we also need a different mnemonic. Moreover, considering all the other jump conditions, "greater than," "greater than or equal to," etc., we need a whole new set of commands and mnemonics. To systematize this new set, the words *above* and *below* are used in place of the phrases *greater than* and *less than*. Hence the "jump if less than" command which works for unsigned numbers uses the mnemonic JB, for "jump if below." The full set of these commands is as follows:

JB	below	$EAX < EBX$
JBE	below or equal	$EAX \le EBX$
JA	above	$EAX > EBX$
JAE	above or equal	$EAX \le EBX$
JNB	not below	$EAX \not< EBX$
JNBE	not below or equal	$EAX \not\le EBX$
JNA	not above	$EAX \not> EBX$
JNAE	not above or equal	$EAX \not\ge EBX$

4.8   Linux .s files

One of the intermediate steps that gcc uses in the translation of a C source program into an a.out file is an assembly language file. This file is the output of the compiler proper and the input to the assembler, gas. To see these assembler files, one can direct gcc to output the assembler file once this stage is reached using the -S switch. This output has a .s file extension. Consider for example the following C program, mult.c:

```
main()
{
    int x, y;
    register int a, b, c;
    printf("Enter a number:  ");
    scanf("%d", &x);
    printf("Multiply it by what number?  ");
    scanf("%d", &y);

    a = x;
    b = y;
    c = 0;

    while (b != 0)
    {
        c = c + a;
        b = b - 1;
    }

    printf("The result is %d.\n.",c);
}
```

Program 4.7

Suppose that the numbers x = 5 and y = −7 are entered. This program actually outputs the correct answer, −35, and to calculate it, the loop executes $2^{32} - 7 =$ 4,294,967,289 times. Note that

$$(2^{32} - 7) \times 5 = 2^{32} \times 5 - 7 \times 5$$

Each time the running total, b, exceeds the turnover value of 2^{32}, 2^{32} is dropped from the total. This happens four times. The resulting value of b is $2^{32} - 35$, which is the two's complement representation of −35.

One of the main practical uses of assembly language programming is in the coding of loops that execute so many times that an improvement in the time required for each execution actually makes a noticeable difference in the total run time. In a test on a 120 MHz Pentium, the 5×-7 calculation required 110.90 seconds. To obtain the assembly code for this program, one can use the command

```
linuxbox$ gcc -S mult.c
```

The resulting file, mult.s, is the assembly code which was used by gcc to produce the executable file. The syntax of this assembly code differs from that of the widely used Intel assembly language used in this book, but it can still be deciphered. Comments for this purpose are added. The first line uses TEST. It is an instruction

```
.L2:
        testl %esi,%esi  ; Is ESI = 0
        jne .L4          ; If not go to L4
        jmp .L3          ; otherwise go to L3
.L4:
        addl %ebx,%edi   ; Let EDI = EDI + EBX
        decl %esi        ; Let ESI = ESI - 1
        jmp .L2          ; Go to L2
.L3:
```

Program 4.8

similar to CMP, which will be discussed in the next chapter. %esi refers to the ESI register. Like CMP, the TEST command sets the zero flag if ESI = 0. The l at the end of many of these commands is used to specify the length of the operand, "long" in this case, and that means four bytes. Notice that the add uses a "COMMAND source destination" operand order, the opposite of that used in this book.

The loop consists of the six instructions shown. If we note that we can take some jumps out of the loop by testing whether ESI is zero at the end of the loop, we can reduce the loop from six instructions to three. The only change made was

```
.L2:
        testl %esi,%esi
        jne .L4
        jmp .L3
.L4:
        addl %ebx,%edi
        decl %esi
        jne .L4          ; If ESI isn't 0 go to L4
.L3:
```

Program 4.9

to the jump at the end of the loop. The modified file was compiled using using gcc.

```
linuxbox$ gcc mult.s
```

The resulting program was run and the computation of 5×-7 took 76.14 seconds on the same machine.

4.8.1 The Pentium's Dual Pipeline

If we look at the time for each instruction to execute, in the first case we get

$$\frac{110.0}{4,294,967,289\times6} = 4.303 \text{ ns}$$

This arithmetic assumes that the program spent all of its time in the loop. Comparing this with the length of one clock cycle,

$$\frac{1}{120,000,000} = 8.333 \text{ ns}$$

we find the amazing result that the time for two instructions to execute, 8.606 nanoseconds, is just a little over one clock cycle. Since one instruction per clock cycle is ideal under ordinary circumstances, what we have here is something special. It is an illustration of the Pentium's dual pipeline. When possible, the Pentium pairs instructions off and executes two at once. This is how rates of more than one instruction per clock cycle can be achieved. (There is actually another pipeline for floating point numbers.) The instruction pairing also explains why the 2:1 improvement we might have expected when we reduced the number of instructions in the loop from six to three did not materialize. What happened apparently was that the number of instruction pairs went from three to two, one of the two "pairs" being half-empty. The time 76.14 nanoseconds is .687 of 110.9 nanoseconds. This is approximately two-thirds, suggesting the use of two instruction pairs instead of three for each pass through the loop.

5

MACHINE LANGUAGE

Machine language is the language seen by the processor. The bytes fetched in the fetch-execute cycle are bytes of machine code. Assembly language can be defined as language which gives the programmer control over the machine code. Assembly language specifies machine code. This characteristic feature of assembly language will not be apparent without some familiarity with machine language. In this chapter the main features of x86 machine code are presented.

The process of converting assembly code into machine code is called *assembling*. A program which takes assembly language as input and produces machine language as output is called an *assembler*. It is similar to a compiler but it operates at a lower level.

Conversely, the process of turning machine code into assembly language is called *unassembling*. A program which does this is called an *unassembler*.

5.1   Assembling Simple Programs

To tell the whole story of the machine code for the x86 processors involves a lot of tricky detail. However, it is quite easy to specify machine code for the subset of the x86 assembly language used in all the numbered programs used in sections 4.3 through 4.5. Coding for this portion of x86 assembly language is given in Table 5.1. Most of the machine code is given in hex, but some of the bytes have to be given in binary. The number of bytes varies from one to six. The first line of the table, for example, shows that the code for MOV reg,reg is a two-byte code, the first of which is given in hex and the second in binary. The bytes given in binary are those which incorporate register codes. S S S in the binary coding represents the three-bit code for the *source* register. D D D represents the three-bit code for the *destination* register. The register codes are given at the bottom. Each "imm" occurring in a command specifies four additional bytes, which must be supplied by the programmer. Examples follow. Using Table 5.1, Program 5.1 can be machine assembled as follows:

		First Byte		Second Byte		4 More
MOV	reg, reg	89		1 1 S S S D D D		
MOV	reg, imm	1 0 1 1 1 D D D				___
ADD	reg, reg	01		1 1 S S S D D D		
ADD	reg, imm	81		1 1 0 0 0 D D D*		___
SUB	reg, reg	29		1 1 S S S D D D		
SUB	reg, imm	81		1 1 1 0 1 D D D*		___
INC	reg	0 1 0 0 0 D D D				
DEC	reg	0 1 0 0 1 D D D				
IN	EAX, [DX]	ED				
OUT	[DX], EAX	EF				
RET		C3				
JMP	imm	E9				___
JZ	imm	0F		84		___
JNZ	imm	0F		85		___
JS	imm	0F		88		___
JNS	imm	0F		89		___

3-Bit Register Codes			
EAX	000	ESP	100
ECX	001	EBP	101
EDX	010	ESI	110
EBX	011	EDI	111

Table 5.1. Some 32-Bit Machine Coding

* If reg is EAX, there is a shorter machine code.

5.1.1   Register Codes

The first byte of the first command, BA, is encoded using the 1011 1DDD code given for MOV reg,imm. The DDD bits are filled in with the register code 010 for EDX, which results in a binary code of 1011 1010 or a hex code of BA.

The second MOV command, MOV ECX,EAX is encoded as 89 C1 using the first line of the chart which specifies the second byte as 11 SSS DDD. EAX is the source register and its code is 000. ECX is the destination register and its code is 001. The resulting second byte is 11 000 001, which is C1.

Label	Source Code	Address	Machine Code
	MOV EDX, 0	0	BA 00
		2	00 00
		4	00
	IN EAX, [DX]	5	ED
	MOV ECX, EAX	6	89 C1
	IN EAX, [DX]	8	ED
	MOV EDX, EAX	9	89 C2
ORD	SUB EAX, ECX	B	29 C8
	JZ GCD	D	0F 84
		F	11 00
		11	00 00
	JNS NXT	13	0F 89
		15	04 00
		17	00 00
	MOV EAX, ECX	19	89 C8
	MOV ECX, EDX	1B	89 D1
NXT	MOV EDX, EAX	1D	89 C2
	JMP ORD	1F	E9 E7
		21	FF FF
		23	FF
GCD	MOV EAX, EDX	24	89 D0
	MOV EDX, 1	26	BA 01
		28	00 00
		2A	00
	OUT [DX], EAX	2B	EF
	RET	2C	C3

Program 5.1

5.1.2 Little Endian Immediate Codes

The first and last MOV commands in this program both contain immediate values. Both of these store four-byte values in four-byte registers. Notice in the last MOV command, the four-byte immediate value 00000001H is stored as 01 00 00 00.

5.1.3 Relative Jumps

The jump encoding used by x86 processors uses relative rather than absolute addresses when this is feasible. All the jump instructions in this program encode jumps as relative jumps. An absolute jump would specify an actual address as the target of a jump, whereas relative encoding specifies the number of bytes to jump starting from the beginning of the next instruction. This value may be interpreted as a signed number, a negative value for a backwards jump. The encoded value is added by the processor to the address of the next instruction to obtain the address of the instruction being jumped to. For example, the JMP NXT instruction has a little endian encoded 4; counting four bytes from the 89 byte that begins the MOV EAX, ECX, brings you to the 89 byte that begins MOV EDX, EAX. This command is the target of JMP NXT. The JMP ORD instruction contains the relative jump value FFFFFFE7H = −25. Counting backwards 25 bytes from the 89 byte that begins the MOV EAX, EDX, brings you to the 29 byte that is the first byte of the code for SUB EAX, ECX.

5.1.4   Short Jumps

The relative jump values in the program are each encoded in four bytes, in spite of the fact that the values 17, 4, and −25 fit easily in the one-byte signed range. There are alternate encodings which can be used to save space on one-byte jumps. These jumps are called *short jumps*. The short jump encoding for the JNS NXT instruction, for example, is 79 04. The machine codes for the conditional short jumps can be obtained from their 32-bit counterparts by dropping the 0F byte and subtracting 10H from the second byte. The short code for the JMP command is EB. In Edlinas, a long jump can be converted to a short jump using the s key. In NASM, the unadorned JMP instruction always means a short jump. A JMP instruction which can't be encoded in one-byte gets an error message. To specify a jump which uses the longer encoding, JMP NEAR is used. In the present context, jumping "far" would seem to make more sense than jumping "near," but a *far jump* actually refers to a jump which uses absolute encoding as will be seen in chapter 12.

Since most jumps are no more than 128 bytes, it makes sense to have a special encoding for them. The instruction set for the 8086 actually had only the short versions of the conditional jumps. The 0F long jump codes did not appear until the 80386.

5.2   Opcode Space

The machine codes given in the last section can be used to assemble a great variety of simple programs. On the other hand, taken together they represent only a small portion of the complete x86 instruction set. In this section an overview of the entire set of x86 machine codes is given. Table 5.2 shows what information is conveyed by the first byte of machine code.

Most of the entries in the table contain both mnemonic and operand information. In a few cases, this information specifies both completely. The entry in the table for the byte EE, for example, is

```
OUT
[DX],AL
```

In other cases, the mnemonic is given but a class of allowable operands are described using letter *keys*.

- r stands for *register.*

- m stands for *memory.*

- i stands for *immediate.*

- b stands for *byte*

- 2 stands for *2 bytes.*

- v means 32 bits or 16 bits.

- e means E in 32 bits and disappears in 16 bits.

These keys were used by Stephen Morse in the excellent book *80386/387 Architecture.*

Consider the entry in the table for the byte 03.

> **ADD**
> rv,rmv

Since the first operand position contains rv, this indicates that the first operand must be a 16- or a 32-bit register. Since the second position contains rmv, the second operand must be a 16- or 32-bit register or memory operand. Since EDI and EAX are 32-bit registers, we see that **ADD EDI,EAX** is an example of an instruction which can be encoded with code whose first byte is 03. Another example is **ADD EDI,[1234H]**. The type of information conveyed by the first byte of code can be broken down into cases.

1. In a few cases, this one-byte suffices to completely specify an instruction. F4, for example, specifies the halt instruction, **HLT**.

2. In many other cases, although the first byte determines which operation is to be performed, it does not specify the operands. In these cases, a second byte is often sufficient to carry the operand information. This second byte is called the ModRM byte. For example, if the first byte is 89, then the table entry is **MOV** rmv,rv. In addition to specifying the operation **MOV**, the rmv,rv operand keys convey information on how the ModRM byte is to be interpreted.

3. There are also cases where the first byte does not fully specify an operation, but merely a general type of operation, and the ModRM byte is used to complete the specification of the operation as well as carry operand information. For example, if the first byte is C2, then the table entry is Shift rmv,ib. In these cases the full interpretation of the ModRM byte requires moving to Table 5.3. *Shift* is not a mnemonic. It is only a pointer into Table 5.3. This is indicated in the table by the fact that not all of its letters are upper case.

4. If the first byte is 0F, then a whole raft of possibilities is opened up. The information conveyed by 0F is merely "go to Table 5.4."

	0	1	2	3	4	5	6	7	8	9	A	B	C	D	E	F
0	ADD rmb,rb	ADD rmv,rv	ADD rb,rmb	ADD rv,rmv	ADD AL,ib	ADD eAX,iv	PUSH ES	POP ES	OR rmb,rb	OR rmv,rv	OR rb,rmb	OR rv,rmv	OR AL,ib	OR eAX,iv	PUSH CS	386 space
1	ADC rmb,rb	ADC rmv,rv	ADC rb,rmb	ADC rv,rmv	ADC AL,ib	ADC eAX,iv	PUSH SS	POP SS	SBB rmb,rb	SBB rmv,rv	SBB rb,rmb	SBB rv,rmv	SBB AL,ib	SBB eAX,iv	PUSH DS	POP DS
2	AND rmb,rb	AND rmv,rv	AND rb,rmb	AND rv,rmv	AND AL,ib	AND eAX,iv	ES:	DAA	SUB rmb,rb	SUB rmv,rv	SUB rb,rmb	SUB rv,rmv	SUB AL,ib	SUB eAX,iv	CS:	DAS
3	XOR rmb,rb	XOR rmv,rv	XOR rb,rmb	XOR rv,rmv	XOR AL,ib	XOR eAX,iv	SS:	AAA	CMP rmb,rb	CMP rmv,rv	CMP rb,rmb	CMP rv,rmv	CMP AL,ib	CMP eAX,iv	DS:	AAS
4	INC eAX	INC eCX	INC eDX	INC eBX	INC eSP	INC eBP	INC eSI	INC eDI	DEC eAX	DEC eCX	DEC eDX	DEC eBX	DEC eSP	DEC eBP	DEC eSI	DEC eDI
5	PUSH eAX	PUSH eCX	PUSH eDX	PUSH eBX	PUSH eSP	PUSH eBP	PUSH eSI	PUSH eDI	POP eAX	POP eCX	POP eDX	POP eBX	POP eSP	POP eBP	POP eSI	POP eDI
6	PUSHA PUSHAD	POPA POPAD	BOUND rv,m2v	ARPL rm2,r2	FS:	GS:	OpLen	AdLen	PUSH iv	IMUL rv,rmv,iv	PUSH ib	IMUL rv,rmv,ib	INSB	INSD	OUTSB	OUTSD
7	JO ib	JNO ib	JB ib	JAE ib	JE ib	JNE ib	JBE ib	JA ib	JS ib	JNS ib	JP ib	JNP ib	JL ib	JGE ib	JLE ib	JG ib
8	Immed rmb,ib	Immed rmv,iv		Immed rmv,ib	TEST rmb,rb	TEST rmv,rv	XCHG rmb,rb	XCHG rmv,rv	MOV rmb,rb	MOV rmv,rv	MOV rb,rmb	MOV rv,rmv	MOV rm,segr	LEA rv, m	MOV segr,rm	POP rmv
9	NOP	XCHG eAX,eCX	XCHG eAX,eDX	XCHG eAX,eBX	XCHG eAX,eSP	XCHG eAX,eBP	XCHG eAX,eSI	XCHG eAX,eDI	CWDE CBW	CWQ CDQ	CALL FAR s:m	FWAIT	PUSHF	POPF	SAHF	LAHF
A	MOV AL,[iv]	MOV eAX,[iv]	MOV [iv],AL	MOV [iv],eAX	MOVSB	MOVSD	CMPSB	CMPSD	TEST AL,rb	TEST eAX,iv	STOSB	STOSD	LODSB	LODSD	SCASB	SCASD
B	MOV AL,ib	MOV CL,ib	MOV DL,ib	MOV BL,ib	MOV AH,ib	MOV CH,ib	MOV DH,ib	MOV BH,ib	MOV eAX,iv	MOV eCX,iv	MOV eDX,iv	MOV eBX,iv	MOV eSP,iv	MOV eBP,iv	MOV eSI,iv	MOV eDI,iv
C	Shift rmb,ib	Shift rmv,ib	RET i2	RET	LES rm,rmp	LDS rm,rmp	MOV rmb, ib	MOV rmv, iv	ENTER i2, ib	LEAVE	RETF i2	RETF	INT 3	INT ib	INTO	IRET
D	Shift rmb, 1	Shift rmv, 1	Shift rmb,CL	Shift rmv,CL	AAM	AAD		XLATB	87 space	87 space	87 space	87 space	87 space	87 space	87 space	87 space
E	LOOPNE short	LOOPE short	LOOP short	JeCXZ short	IN AL,[ib]	IN eAX,[ib]	OUT [ib],AL	OUT [ib],eAX	CALL iv	JMP iv	JMP FAR s:m	JMP ib	IN AL,[DX]	IN eAX,[DX]	OUT [DX],AL	OUT [DX],eAX
F	LOCK		REPNE	REP REPE	HLT	CMC	Unary rmb	Unary rmv	CLC	STC	CLI	STI	CLD	STD	IncDec rmb	Indir rmv

Table 5.2. First Byte of Opcode Space

5. If the first byte is in the range D8-DF, then the command is a floating point command. These commands are not dealt with in this text.

6. There are also prefix bytes which modify the subsequent commands. In Table 5.2, the prefix bytes such as the **LOCK** prefix F0 are shown as *bottom-sitters*.

These various cases are dealt with one by one in the following sections.

5.3   The ModRM Byte

The ModRM byte is used to carry operand information when the first byte cannot do so. The ModRM byte consists of three parts.

Mod		R			M		
7	6	5	4	3	2	1	0

1. Bits 7 and 6 are the Mod bits. When the Mod bits are 11, the M bits designate a register. Otherwise the M bits are used for memory coding.

2. Bits 5, 4, and 3 are the R, or register, bits and are often designated using a slash notation, /r.

3. Bits 2, 1, and 0 are the M, or memory, bits, and are used to specify or help specify a memory location except when the Mod bits are 11.

5.3.1   rv,rmv Coding

The entry in Table 5.2 for the byte 03 is

    ADD
    rv,rmv

We can use this entry to assemble the **ADD EDI,EAX** command. The **ADD EDI,EAX** command requires a ModRM byte. The m in the second operand position specifies not only that the second operand may be a memory operand, but also that it must be encoded in the M bits of the ModRM byte. Since the second operand is the register EAX, the bit code for EAX, 000, occupies the M bits in the ModRM byte. Since we are using a register for the M bits, the two Mod bits must be 11. The first operand, which as the r indicates must be a register, is therefore encoded in the R bits of the ModRM byte. EDI is the first operand and its code is 111. Consequently the ModRM byte is:

Mod		R			M		
7	6	5	4	3	2	1	0
1	1	1	1	1	0	0	0

1111 1000 = F8H

Combining the 03 with the ModRM byte yields the code 03 F8 for ADD EDI,EAX.

If in this code we change the two Mod bits from 11 to 00, we get the code for ADD EDI,[EAX]. Here the M bits are used for an actual memory operand. The codes 01 and 10 are used to code for immediate displacements such as ADD EDI,[EAX + 5], where the displacement is either of type **ib** or **iv**. Hence the code for ADD EDI,[EAX + 5] is 03 78 05. The code for ADD EDI,[EAX + 87654321H] is 03 B8 21 43 65 87. If this coding were done uniformly, however, it would leave no room in the coding space for the complicated formats seen in chapter 6, section 6.2.3. To make space for coding these formats, the code for the ESP register is removed to provide an escape into another byte of the coding space called the *SIB byte*.

5.3.2   rmv,rv Coding

When the **rmv** and **rv** keys are reversed, this turns the three-bit codes around. As an example, suppose we want to code the instruction MOV EDI, EAX. The entry for 8B matches and could be coded with the same ModRM byte as the ADD EDI,EAX code. But the entry 89 also matches:

> MOV
> rmv,rv

Using this entry, we note that the first operand may be a register and is coded in the M bits. Hence the code for EDI goes into the least significant bits. The second operand, EAX, is coded in the R bits.

Mod		R			M		
7	6	5	4	3	2	1	0
1	1	0	0	0	1	1	1

1100 0111 = C7H

Hence, using the 89 entry in Table 5.2, we obtain the encoding 89 C7 for MOV EDI,EAX.

5.3.3   Nonregister R Bits

In some cases, the first byte is insufficient to specify an operation, but the R bits of a ModRM byte are used to complete the specification. These cases are listed in Table 5.3. SUB ECX, 32 is an example. The entry in Table 5.2 for 83 is

> Immed
> rmv,ib

Since the row of Table 5.3 labeled "Immed" has a SUB under /r = /5, we learn that instructions matching

> SUB
> rmv,ib

can be coded using 83 as the first byte and 101 for the R bits of the ModRM byte. Since the first operand, ECX, is not memory, the Mod bits must be 11, and the M bits will be filled with 001, the code for ECX. So the required ModRM byte is

/r	/0 000	/1 001	/2 010	/3 011	/4 100	/5 101	/6 110	/7 111
Immed	ADD	OR	ADC	SBB	AND	SUB	XOR	CMP
Shift	ROL	ROR	RCL	RCR	SHL	SHR	SAR	
Unary	TEST i		NOT	NEG	MUL	IMUL	DIV	IDIV
IncDec	INC	DEC						
Indir	INC	DEC	CALL m	CALL FAR m	JMP	JMP FAR	PUSH	

Table 5.3. Instructions Specified by R Bits

Mod	R				M		
7	6	5	4	3	2	1	0
1	1	1	0	1	0	0	1

1110 1001 = E9H

The ib stands for an immediate byte. So the code for **SUB ECX,32** is 83 E9 20.

5.4   386 Space (0F + ...)

On an 8086, the byte 0F codes for the   instruction **POP CS**. On subsequent processors this instruction was removed to make the 0F code available for a significant expansion in the instruction set. Table 5.4 reveals the space which was opened up. Like Table 5.2, it shows the information conveyed by a single byte, in this case the byte following an initial 0F byte. A few of the instructions in Table 5.4 appeared first on the 80286, the 80486,   or the Pentium, but most of them appeared first on the 80386. The bulk of the instructions new to the 80286 are in Table 5.2.

1. As with Table 5.2, sometimes one entry specifies exactly one instruction. For example, 0F CA is the code for the instruction **BSWAP EDX**, (Byte SWAP the EDX register).

2. Sometimes a ModRM byte is needed to convey operand information.   The **XADD** instruction whose first two bytes are 0F C1 is an example of this.

3. Sometimes a ModRM byte is used to specify an operation. For example, if the first two bytes of the instruction are 0F 01, then we must check R bits of the ModRM byte to determine the operation. From Table 5.5 we see that if the register bits in the ModRM byte were 011 then the instruction would be an **LIDT** instruction (Load the Interrupt Descriptor Table).

	0	1	2	3	4	5	6	7	8	9	A	B	C	D	E	F
0	LocalT	GlobalT	LAR rv,rmv	LSL rv,rmv		LOADALL	CLTS		INVD	WBINVD						
1																
2	MOV r2,CRr	MOV r2,DRr	MOV CRr,r2	MOV DRr,r2	MOV r2,TRr		MOV TRr,r2									
3	WRMSR	RDTSC	RDMSR													
4																
5																
6	MMX space	MMX space	MMX space	MMX space	MMX space	MMX space	MMX space	MMX space	MMX space	MMX space	MMX space	MMX space			MMX space	MMX space
7		MMX space	MMX space	MMX space	MMX space	MMX space	MMX space	MMX space							MMX space	MMX space
8	JO iv	JNO iv	JB iv	JAE iv	JE iv	JNE iv	JBE iv	JA iv	JS iv	JNS iv	JP iv	JNP iv	JL iv	JGE iv	JLE iv	JG iv
9	SETO rmb	SETNO rmb	SETB rmb	SETAE rmb	SETE rmb	SETNE rmb	SETBE rmb	SETA rmb	SETS rmb	SETNS rmb	SETP rmb	SETNP rmb	SETL rmb	SETGE rmb	SETLE rmb	SETG rmb
A	PUSH FS	POP FS	CPUID	BT rm,r	SHLD rmv,rv,ib	SHLD rmv,rv,CL		IMUL rv,rmv	PUSH GS	POP GS	RSM	BTS rmv,rv	SHRD rmv,rv,ib	SHRD rmv,rv,CL		IMUL rv,rmv
B	CMPXCHG rmb,rb	CMPXCHG rmv,rv	LSS rv,rmp	BTR rm,r	LFS rv,rmp	LGS rv,rmp	MOVZX rv,rmb	MOVZX rv,rm2			Bits	BTC rm,r	BSF r,rm	BSR r,rm	MOVSX rv,rmb	MOVSX rv,rm2
C	XADD rmb,rb	XADD rmv,rv						CMPXCHG8 m8	BSWAP EAX	BSWAP ECX	BSWAP EDX	BSWAP EBX	BSWAP ESP	BSWAP EBP	BSWAP ESI	BSWAP EDI
D	MMX space	MMX space	MMX space	MMX space		MMX space			MMX space	MMX space	MMX space	MMX space	MMX space	MMX space		MMX space
E		MMX space	MMX space		MMX space	MMX space			MMX space	MMX space		MMX space	MMX space	MMX space	MMX space	MMX space
F	MMX space	MMX space	MMX space	MMX space	MMX space	MMX space			MMX space	MMX space	MMX space		MMX space	MMX space		

Table 5.4. 386 Space

/r	/0 000	/1 001	/2 010	/3 011	/4 100	/5 101	/6 110	/7 111
LocalT	SLDT rm2	STR rm2	LLDT rm2	LTR rm2	VERR rm2	VERW rm2		
GlobalT	SGDT m6	SIDT m6	LGDT m6	LIDT m6	SMWS rm2		LMSW rm2	
Bits					BT rmv,ib	BTS rmv,ib	BTR rmv,ib	BTC rmv,ib

Table 5.5. 0F Instructions Specified by R Bits

4. Some of the codes refer to MMX instructions. These instructions are discussed in the Intel book, *The Complete Guide to MMX Technology*.

We learn that instructions matching Table 5.5 contain 80486, Pentium, and MMX instructions as well as 80386 instructions.   For example, the XADD and BSWAP instructions first appeared on the 80486 and the CPUID and RDTSC first appeared on the Pentium.

5.5   32-Bit vs. 16-Bit Code

To this point we have discussed machine codes for commands involving 32-bit general registers only. We are now ready to consider the coding of the 16-bit general registers.

The MOV ECX,EAX command, as noted in section 5.1, can be encoded as 89 C1. The corresponding 16-bit command is MOV CX,AX. Surprisingly, the code for this command is also 89 C1! The 80386 was designed to use the same encodings for the 16-bit registers as for the 32-bit registers. Clearly there is a problem with this. When the processor fetches the bytes 89 C1, which instruction should be executed, MOV ECX,EAX or MOV CX,AX? It so happens that the decision is based on a single bit in the processor. This bit determines whether code is interpreted as 32-bit code, in which case 89 C1 means   MOV ECX,EAX, or 16-bit code, in which case 89 C1 means MOV CX,AX.

When the bit is set it does not mean that the instruction   MOV CX,AX is unavailable. To encode the fact that the 32-bit coding presumption is wrong a one-byte prefix 66 is used. So in 32-bit code 66 89 C1 is the code for MOV CX,AX Similarly the MOV ECX,EAX instruction is available in 16-bit code. The code for it is 66 89 C1 This prefix is called the *operand size prefix*. It means that the operand size is not the default size.

Typically the bit is set while running Linux for example, and   cleared while running DOS. Except where specifically stated otherwise, code given in this book assumes the processor's bit is set for the 32-bit default.   Hence, 89 C1 means MOV ECX,EAX and 66 89 C1 means MOV CX,AX. Now that we see how the code 89 C1 can have either one of two possible meanings, it is easy to explain the v in

	32-Bit Code	16-Bit Code
MOV ECX, EAX	89 C1	66 89 C1
MOV CX, AX	66 89 C1	89 C1

Table 5.6. 32- vs. 16-Bit Coding Example

Codes for 8-Bit Registers			
AL	000	AH	100
CL	001	CH	101
DL	010	DH	110
BL	011	BH	111

Table 5.7. Codes for 8-Bit Registers

the entry in the first chart for the code 89:

    MOV
    rmv,rv

The v in each operand marker stands for variable where variable refers to the fact that the size may be either 16 or 32 bits. Similarly the e in register designations such as eAX refers to the fact that in 32-bit coding EAX is intended and in 16-bit coding AX is intended.

5.6   The 8-Bit Registers

Although the 32-bit and 16-bit register commands are forced to share opcodes, the eight-bit registers generally have dedicated opcodes. For example, the opcode 8A designates an eight-bit **MOV** instruction. The entry in Table 5.2 for 8A is

    MOV
    rb,rmb

rb stands for *register byte* and is coded for in the register bits of the ModRM byte. **rmb** stands for *register* or *memory byte* and is coded for in the memory bits of the ModRM byte. 8A C1 is the code for **MOV AL,CL**. Table 5.7 lists the eight-bit register codes. The code for CL goes into the M bits and the code for AL goes into the R bits.

Mod		R			M		
7	6	5	4	3	2	1	0
1	1	0	0	0	0	0	1

Combining the two bytes yields 8A C1.

5.7   Linux .o Files

Programs in C which include calls to functions such as `printf()` or `scanf()` require
linking to the compiled code for these functions. This code is stored in libraries
such as `libc.so`. Once this linking is done, the program becomes much longer. In
order to examine the machine code of a program, it is easier to look at the code
before this linking is done because there is so much less of it. This code is stored in
object modules with a `.o` file extension. The analogous files in DOS are the .OBJ
files. To instruct the gnu C compiler to produce a `.o` file, the -c switch can be used.
The command

```
linuxbox$ gcc -c mult.c
```

produces a `mult.o` file. This file contains the machine code of the program, in
addition to tables which allow the linker to do its job.

To examine an object code file, one may use either the ob program (object
dump) which comes with this book or the   od program (octal dump) which is a
standard Unix utility. To get od to display in hex, use the switches -tx and -Ax.

```
linuxbox$ od -tx -Ax mult.o
```

ob has no switches:

```
linuxbox$ ob mult.o
```

6

MEMORY

In chapter 4, section 4.2 we noted that the MOV command can be used to transfer data to and from memory just as IN and OUT can be used to transfer data to and from I/O devices. For the programmer, using MOV to access memory is simple: just enclose an address in brackets. In neither DOS nor Linux, however, are the addresses enclosed by brackets actual memory addresses. In DOS an address processing mechanism called *segmentation* is used, and in Linux another one called *paging* is used. But these mechanisms can be circumvented. In this chapter we make the simplifying assumption that this is done so that addresses enclosed in brackets are actual hardware addresses. Programs written on this basis run under Edlinas. Segmentation and paging will be dealt with later. Segmentation is discussed in chapter 12, and paging is discussed in chapter 8.

6.1 4-Byte Data Width

Data transfer between a processor and its memory is easy when word size and register size agree. For example, the 8080 processor fetches eight-bit words into its eight-bit registers. Eight-bit registers are, of course, mainly a thing of the past. But eight-bit words we still have. Intel has implemented many measures so that its new processors would run old software. One of these has been the maintainence of eight-bit words, despite the fact that both processor registers and data transfers long ago outgrew the eight-bit size. The 386 processor, for example, has 32-bit registers and 32-bit data transfers.

When register and word sizes don't match, simple transfer commands no longer make sense. For example, without some further protocols in place the command

    MOV [19H], EAX

does not make sense. The memory location referred to, like all Intel memory locations, is an eight-bit location. But EAX on the other hand is a 32-bit register.

6.1.1 Storage Protocols

Two further protocols are used.

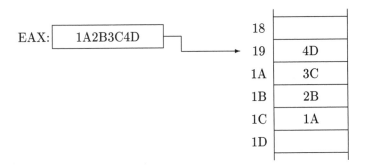

Figure 6-1. MOV [19H], EAX

- When an n byte transfer is indicated by an address a, the memory bytes referred to are those at the addresses a, $a + 1$, ..., $a + n - 1$. All architectures do this.

- When an n byte number is stored in memory, its bytes are stored in order of significance, least significant bytes in the lowest addresses. Numerically increasing addresses correspond to increasing byte significance. Not all architectures do this.

These two protocols make it possible to interpret the MOV [19H], EAX command. As shown in Figure 6-1, the bytes in EAX are stored in addresses 19H, 1AH, 1BH, and 1CH. The least significant byte in EAX is stored in 19H, the next in 1AH, and so on. Program 6.1 demonstrates the use of this instruction. When Program 6.1 is

```
; Tiny Edlinas program which stores an input number into memory.
;
        IN EAX, [0]
        MOV [19H], EAX
        RET
```

Program 6.1

run under Edlinas, it is loaded starting at address 0. Since memory locations up to the address 20H are all displayed when this program is loaded, the execution of the MOV instruction is directly observable.

6.1.2 Little and Big Endian Architecture

Architectures which use the byte ordering given in the second of these protocols are called *little endian*. Architectures which do the opposite are called *big endian*.

All Intel processors are little endian. Examples of big endian processors are

Motorola's 6800 and 68000 processors. MIPS and PowerPC processors can work in either mode.

In order to encourage software developers to migrate away from competing hardware, a common strategem is to incorporate compatibility features. A compatibility feature added to the 486 processor is the **BSWAP** instruction. It reverses the byte ordering of any 32-bit general register. Its format is simply:

BSWAP reg

For example if the EAX register contained the number 12345678H, then following the execution of the **BSWAP EAX** command, it would contain the number 78563412H.

6.1.3 Alignment

The discrepancy between the four-byte data transfer size and the one-byte word size which exists in 386 and 486 systems   is not fully reflected in the hardware. In fact the one-byte word size is a kind of fiction maintained for the benefit of the software. Although memory on these systems is forced to emulate a one-byte word memory, words are actually four bytes wide. The two lowest bits of the 32-bit address bus are in fact not there. The wires on the address bus are A31 through A2. A1 and A0 are missing. From a hardware point of view, a 386 addresses 2^{30} 32-bit words. The $2^{32} \times 8$ bit memory is a fiction. But because the fiction is consistently maintained, software which believes this fiction does work. But it doesn't work as well as software which takes the true state of affairs into account. For example the command

MOV EAX, [10H]

accesses four bytes of memory whose 32-bit addresses are

    0000 0000 0000 0000 0000 0000 0001 0000
    0000 0000 0000 0000 0000 0000 0001 0001
    0000 0000 0000 0000 0000 0000 0001 0010
    0000 0000 0000 0000 0000 0000 0001 0011

Note that these addresses differ only in the "non-existent" bottom two bits. These four bytes are actually just one four-byte word. The command can be accomplished with a single memory transfer. On the other hand the command

MOV EAX, [12H]

which also accesses four bytes of memory, cannot be carried out in the same way. The 32-bit addresses of these four bytes are

    0000 0000 0000 0000 0000 0000 0001 0010
    0000 0000 0000 0000 0000 0000 0001 0011
    0000 0000 0000 0000 0000 0000 0001 0100
    0000 0000 0000 0000 0000 0000 0001 0101

To access these four bytes, two distinct memory transfers are required. In code which is accessing a large number of consecutive memory locations, four bytes at a time, performance will be cut in half if the addresses called are not those whose bottom two bits are zero, i.e. a multiple of four. Memory transfers which straddle four-byte word boundaries are said to be *out of alignment*. Starting with the 486 processor, a flag was added which detects memory transfers that are out of alignment.

6.2   Addresses in Brackets

The use of MOV to access memory just scratches the surface of available memory commands. All of the entries in Table 5.2 containing operand keys that contain an **m** describe commands that access memory. From the table, we can see that MOV, ADD, OR, ADC, SBB, AND, SUB, and XOR   all allow memory operands in either the source or the destination operand position. Memory operands may be supplied using several different formats.

6.2.1   The [imm] Format

All the memory operand examples presented so far have used the [imm] format with the MOV instruction. Illustrating the [imm] format with the ADD command we have both

>   ADD reg,[imm]

and

>   ADD [imm],reg

where **imm** can be any four-byte number.

As we all know, memory may be used for storage of many kinds of data, including text, graphics, and numbers. In the following paragraphs we look at how it is used in connection with numbers, in particular with big numbers.

64-Bit Arithmetic

Memory space is much larger than processor space. When numbers become too large for the processor to work with, the arithmetic can be done piecemeal, with pieces small enough for the processor to handle loaded in from memory as they are needed. Some features of the processor are designed with this kind of arithmetic in mind. The ADC instruction is a case in point. This instruction makes it possible to do piecemeal addition of large numbers. Suppose that we have the numbers 1111222233334444H and AAAABBBBCCCCDDDDH stored at locations 100H and 108H in memory, and that we want to add them. Using the ADD instruction on the bottom four bytes of these numbers will set the carry flag. Using the ADC instruction on the next four bytes takes account of the carry. The ADC instruction is very similar to the ADD instruction. It means let destination = destination + source + carry flag

whereas the ordinary ADD instruction means

let destination = destination + source

The addition can then be carried out in two stages, the first one using ADD and the next one using ADC.

```
ADC            1  |              ADD
   1111 2222 | 104          3333 4444 | 100
   AAAA BBBB | 10C          CCCC DDDD | 108
   BBBB DDDE |              0000 2221 |
```

In order for the carrying to work, it is important that nothing disturb the carry flag between the low order addition and the high order addition. The following code does this arithmetic using the eight bytes starting at 100H as the destination and the eight bytes starting at 108H as the source. When this program finishes, the

```
                      ; 8 byte Destination at 100H
                      ; 8 byte Source at 108H
   MOV EAX,[108H]     ; Bottom 4 Source bytes
   ADD [100H], EAX    ; Add to bottom 4 Destination bytes
   MOV EAX,[10CH]     ; Top 4 Source bytes
   ADC [104H], EAX    ; Add to top 4 Destination bytes
```

Program 6.2

eight-byte sum is located in the eight bytes starting at the address 100H. When the ADC instruction finishes, the overflow, carry, and sign flags will be correct for eight-byte arithmetic. The zero flag does not work so well for eight bytes. When set, it need *not* indicate that the eight-byte sum is 0.

Powers of 3

Expanding on this idea, we can code a little 64-bit power of 3 calculator using the following algorithm:

```
Initialize y = 3
Then repeat:
      x = y
      y = y + x
      y = y + x
```

Program 6.3 has no input or output. It can be observed by stepping through it in Edlinas. The [imm] format is useful in referring to a few fixed locations in memory. It is not useful in processing a long succession of bytes in memory.

```
; Edlinas program which finds 64-bit powers of 3.
; Store the 8 bytes of x starting at memory address 100H.
; Store the 4 least significant bytes of y in EAX.
; Store the 4 most significant bytes of y in EBX.
;
; y = 3
            MOV EAX, 3
            MOV EBX, 0
            MOV EDX, 1
; x = y
ABC:        MOV [100H], EAX
            MOV [104H], EBX
; y = y + x
            ADD EAX,[100H]
            ADC EBX,[104H]
; y = y + x
            ADD EAX,[100H]
            ADC EBX,[104H]
            INC EDX ; Keep track of the exponent.
;
            JMP ABC
```

Program 6.3

6.2.2   The [reg] Format

Long successions of bytes occur in both arrays and in very large numbers. The [reg] format is much better suited to deal with these situations than is the [imm] format. Using MOV to illustrate the [reg] format, we have both

```
       MOV reg,[reg]
```

and

```
       MOV [reg],reg
```

In the first of these, the [reg] source operand refers to the location in memory whose address is in the register whose name is in brackets. For example, the code

```
       MOV EBX, 10H
       MOV EAX, [EBX]
```

transfers four bytes into the EAX register from memory starting at address 10H.

As an example of the usefulness of the [reg] format, suppose we consider the problem of adding two 256-byte numbers.

```
ADC  |              ADC  |        ADD  |
 8 8 | 1FC           2 2 | 104     4 4 | 100
 7 7 | 2FC    . . .  A B | 204     C D | 200
 B E |                2 1 |        2 1 | 100
```

In Program 6.2 the addresses were accessed directly using the [imm] format. Each four bytes of the addition were done using two instructions, a MOV and an ADC. Using that same technique here to do add 256-byte numbers would require multiplying the number of instructions needed by 64. Consequently we would need 128 lines of code. If we use the [reg] format, on the other hand, we may use a register for the source and destination addresses and increment them in a loop. If we use EDI for the *destination index* and ESI for the *source index*, then we begin by storing 100H in EDI and 200H in ESI. We must then increase these pointers four bytes at a time as we traverse the two big numbers. This code is much shorter than the 128

```
;
; Code which adds two 256-byte numbers y and x:
; y = y + x
;
; Assume the 256 bytes of y are stored starting at memory address 100H.
; Assume the 256 bytes of x are stored starting at memory address 200H.
; Use EDX to store a decrement counter for the y = y + x loop.
;
        MOV EDI, 100H ; Initialize pointer into y.
        MOV ESI, 200H ; Initialize pointer into x.
;
; y = y + x
        MOV EDX, 40H   ; Loop needs 64 iterations.
        CLC            ; Clear the carry flag.
XYZ:    MOV EAX,[ESI]  ; 4 Source bytes into the Processor.
        ADC [EDI],EAX  ; Do the addition.
        INC ESI        ;
        INC ESI        ;
        INC ESI        ; This is ugly.
        INC ESI        ;
        INC EDI        ; But using ADD here would
        INC EDI        ; clear the carry flag.
        INC EDI        ;
        INC EDI        ;
        DEC EDX        ; Decrement the loop counter.
        JNZ XYZ        ; See if the loop is finished.
```

Program 6.4

lines which would have resulted from using the [imm] format.

At first sight it would appear that we could do better by using ADD instructions in place of multiple INC instructions. But this would actually ruin everything. Because we are using a loop to proceed four bytes at a time from the least significant to the most significant bytes, we encounter a problem with the carry flag. If in between two executions of the ADC instruction we move four bytes down the number using an ADD instruction, we have messed up the carry flag. In chapter 4 it is noted that the carry flag is unaffected by the INC and DEC instructions. The reason for this arcane little exception suddenly becomes clear. Multibyte arithmetic needs a carry flag which can survive loop counter adjustments. Because they don't affect the carry flag, the INC and DEC instructions can be used to carry out harmless loop counter adjustments. Adding 4 by using four INC instructions is not beautiful, but it works.

This code is not bad from the standpoint of taking up memory space since memory is cheap. But it is bad from the standpoint of adding execution time to a loop. If there is one place where execution time is costly it is in the middle of a nested loop, and that is exactly where those extra INC instructions are.

Another memory format is useful in dealing with this problem.

6.2.3   The [reg+scale*reg+imm] Format

The most general memory format is the [reg + scale * reg + imm] format, where *scale* is a scale factor which must be either 1, 2, 4, or 8. The register which is multiplied by the scale factor is called the *index register*. The other register is called the *base register*. Some fields may be omitted. This gives us the effect of a variety of formats, including

```
[scale*reg + imm]
[reg + scale*reg]
[reg + reg + imm]
[reg + imm]
[reg + reg]
```

in addition to the [reg] and [imm] formats already discussed. It is a little hard to believe that instructions with this degree of complexity are hardcoded into the processors. But the cost in terms of instruction length for all this complexity is actually just one more byte of code for instructions which utilize this general format. The byte is called the SIB byte, both for *scaled-index-base* byte and *sibling* of the ModRM byte.

Taking up the problem of the repeated INC instruction in Program 6.3, note that a scale factor of 4 would increase the address by 4 whenever the index register was incremented by 1. In the code shown in Program 6.5 the [scale*reg + imm] format is used to refer to both source and destination memory locations. In this code we see that a single INC instruction takes the place of eight INC instructions in Program 6.3.

```
; Edlinas program which finds 256-byte powers of 3.
; Store the 256 bytes of x starting at memory address 100H.
; Store the 256 bytes of y starting at memory address 200H.
          MOV EBX, 3 ; Initialize base.
          MOV EDX, 1 ; Initialize exponent.
; y = 3
          MOV EAX, 0 ; Do the adding in EAX.
          MOV EDI, 40H ; Loop needs 64 iterations.
ZRO:      DEC EDI
          MOV [4*EDI + 200H],EAX
          JNZ ZRO
          MOV [4*EDI + 200H],EBX
;
; x = y. Main infinite loop starts here.
;
LUP:      MOV EDI, 40H ; Loop needs 64 iterations.
          MOV ESI, EBX ; Initialize main loop counter.
BEG:      DEC EDI
          MOV EAX,[4*EDI + 200H]
          MOV [4*EDI + 100H],EAX
          JNZ BEG
; y = y + x
AGN:      MOV ECX, 40H ; Loop needs 64 iterations.
XYZ:      MOV EAX,[4*EDI + 200H]
          ADC EAX,[4*EDI + 100H]
          MOV [4*EDI + 200H], EAX
          INC EDI
          DEC ECX
          JNZ XYZ
;
          DEC ESI
          JNZ AGN
;
          INC EDX
          JMP LUP
```

Program 6.5

One variation which is not permitted is the use of memory references in both operand positions. There are no x86 processor instructions which use memory as both source and destination operands. The instruction

```
ADD [EAX],[EBX]
```

for example, does not exist. There are however instructions which involve both reading from and writing to memory; INC [EAX],for example both reads from and writes to the memory location whose address is in EAX. Architectures called *load/store* architectures do not allow mixing processor operations with memory operations. The only commands in a load/store architecture which access memory are *load* and *store*.

6.2.4   16-Bit Addresses

In section 6.2.2 the [reg] format for memory addressing was presented where **reg** could be any of the eight 32-bit general   registers. The 8086 and 80286 also use a [reg] format. Not all eight 16-bit registers are permitted, however, only BP, BX, SI, and DI. There is also a [reg + reg + imm] form. **imm** must be a 16-bit number. If two registers are used, the only allowed combinations are, BP + SI, BP + DI, BX + SI, and BX + DI. Since these restrictions are easy to forget, programmers not accustomed to 16-bit addresses may find themselves using disallowed forms of address. Most programmers will prefer to avoid 16-bit addressing whenever possible.

These 16-bit forms of memory address can be used on an 80386. When they occur in 32-bit code, a special prefix, 67H, has to be applied to the machine code to notify the processor that the memory address bits in the ModRM byte are coded using the old 16-bit coding system. This prefix is called the *address size prefix*. It is similar to the operand size prefix discussed in chapter 5, section 5.5.

6.2.5   CISC vs. RISC

An x86 computer is generally considered to be a complex instruction set computer (CISC). This is partly because of complicated addressing, as in the [EDX + 4*ESI + ABC] memory operand. Machines such as the SUN and MIPS workstations are based on the idea that by simplifying the instructions and having fewer of them, they become easier and faster to execute. This can more than make up for the fact that it takes more of these little instructions to write a program. Computing based on this philosophy is called RISC, reduced instruction set computing. The RISC vs. CISC issue is not an either–or issue like little endian vs. big endian. RISC is a set of features which may be adopted partially, in varying degrees. One reason that the 486 and Pentium processors were able to compete with the early RISC PowerPC processors is that they adopted a piecemeal RISC philosophy. Although CISC instructions are allowed on a Pentium, it works faster if programmed using a RISC-like subset of the total instruction set.

Their names notwithstanding, the Pentium II and Pentium Pro   have gone over to a totally RISC architecture. The instruction set used internally is a pure RISC instruction set. Traditional x86 instructions are converted internally to RISC instructions before they are executed. In a sense, the "end of the line" tag hung on the Pentium by Apple marketers was correct. But ironically, 386 assembly language is now stronger than ever.

6.3   Operand Size Ambiguity

In most two-operand instructions, both operands must have the same size.   So when a memory operand is used in such a context, the number of bytes it refers to can be determined if the other operand is a register operand. For example, in ADD [EBX],AX the memory operand [EBX] must refer to two bytes of memory since AX is a two-byte register. However, when a memory operand is used with an immediate operand, the result is ambiguous. For example, the following command is ambiguous:

> MOV [EBX], 5

Similarly, when a memory operand is used with a unary operation such as NEG (which takes the two's complement of a number), the operand size is indeterminate. An instruction such as

> NEG [EBX]

might well refer to one, two, or four bytes of memory. Under these circumstances, an assembler has to make a choice. NASM chooses to produce an error message. In 32-bit code Edlinas defaults to a four-byte reference when the reference is ambiguous. In 16-bit code, the default is two-byte. To indicate the one-byte case in Edlinas you may use the customary but clumsy notation

> NEG BYTE PTR [EBX]

In NASM, the code is

> NEG BYTE [EBX]

To indicate a four-byte reference in NASM, the code is

> NEG DWORD [EBX]

A two-byte reference is indicated using WORD as a qualifier. These qualifiers clearly do the job. The implied concession that a word is 16 bits is unfortunate. In light of notation such as BYTE PTR, the AT&T practice of adding a letter to the mnemonic doesn't seem so bad. In fact, the Intel assembler does use mnemonics of this sort in a few cases such as LODSB and STOSB (load string byte and store string byte).

6.4   Labels

In programming jumps, labels are used as a convenience. Using a label with a jump instruction makes it unnecessary to count the number of bytes upstream or downstream to the jump target. Counting these bytes requires assembling the intervening code and has to be done over again any time the intervening code is changed. So labels are a great convenience. But still they are only a convenience.

Labels may also be used in accessing memory storage locations. In Program 6.6 we see ABC used as the label for a location where an input byte is stored. In the

; Tiny Edlinas program which uses a label to reference a data storage location.
;

```
            IN AL, [0]          ; E4 00
            MOV [ABC], AL       ; 88 05
                                ; 09 00
                                ; 00 00
            RET                 ; C3
ABC:        NOP                 ; 90
```

Program 6.6

machine code for the MOV [ABC], AL instruction, the label ABC is replaced by a number. Based on the encoding of jump instructions discussed in chapter 5, we should expect to see ABC replaced by the number 1, since the label ABC occurs one byte past the beginning of the next instruction. Based on the MOV instructions in section 6.2, we should expect to see ABC replaced by the address of the instruction on which the label ABC occurs, in this case 9, if we assume that it is loaded starting at 0, as it would be by Edlinas.

6.4.1 Address Encoding

There are two common methods for encoding the address of some targeted memory location.

- Relative Encoding. The numerical difference between the address of the targeted location and the address of the following instruction is used in the machine code.

- Absolute Encoding. The target address itself is used in the machine code.

All the jump instructions discussed in chapter 5 use relative encoding. Absolute encoding is used for jump instructions used in 8080 code and also in so-called *far jumps* in x86 machine code. The existence of some absolute encoding is almost unavoidable. (The only alternative would be to design the processor to take over the job of memory allocation.)

All memory accessing instructions in x86 machine code, MOV, ADD, etc., use absolute encoding.

6.4.2 Program Loading

Dormant programs usually reside on the hard disk or some other secondary storage device. To execute, they need to be in memory. To get a program to execute, the user passes its file name to the operating system (by typing it on the command line for example), to execve() in the case of Linux. execve(), not the user or the programmer, decides where in memory the program will be loaded. Since programmers have no control over the location of their programs in memory, it makes using instructions that use absolute memory encoding problematic when labels are used to refer to memory. In fact it makes assembling programs using memory labels into plain unaided machine code impossible. Executable code resulting from programs using memory labels must be accompanied by tables identifying all the points in the code where an absolute address occurs. These tables are called *relocation tables*. All object code files, .o files in Linux, contain relocation tables. When a program is loaded into memory, these tables are used to fix each absolute address in the machine code so that it points to the address which is valid given where the program is actually loaded.

The Edlinas simulator loads all programs starting at the address zero. We can count the bytes in Program 6.6 from there to the line with ABC on it. If we do we, find that the NOP instruction occurs at address 9. That is why the machine code given for the MOV [ABC], AL instruction in Program 6.6 shows the label ABC encoded as 9. The instruction MOV [9], AL could therefore be used in place of MOV [ABC], AL. If this program were to be relocated so that it started at the address 100H, then the code for the ABC label in the MOV instruction would need to be 109H instead of 9.

6.4.3 Variables

In high-level programming languages, variables are often implemented as labelled memory locations. Although a compiler may use a register, a more typical implementation of a variable is as a labelled memory location. This is true particularly for global variables.

6.4.4 Arrays

As an example of how these addressing modes might be used to handle array programming, consider the following C code which counts how many zeros and ones there are in the part of an array, x[70][100], where the rows of interest are from 20 through 29 and the columns are from 50 through 54. To code this in assembler, we can use EBX for num_zeros, ECX for num_ones, and the label ABC for the beginning of the array x. To reference the array location x[i][j] we need to use the fact that the address &x[i][j] is i*100*4 + j*4 bytes past &x[0][0] = ABC. The 100 in i*100*4 comes from the declaration int x[70][100] which tells us that every row contains 100 four-byte locations. Although we might like to use EDI for i and ESI for j and reference x[i][j] using [ABC + 400*EDI + 4*ESI], this much latitude does not exist in the coding space. The multiplier 4 is allowed on one register, but neither a multiplier of 400 nor having two scaled registers is allowed. Hence it makes sense to use EDX for 400*i. [ABC + EDX + 4*ESI]

```
num_zeros = 0;
num_ones = 0;
for(i = 20; i < 30; i = i + 1)
for(j = 50; j < 55; j = j + 1)
{
    if (x[i][j] == 0)
        num_zeros = num_zeros + 1;
    if (x[i][j] == 1)
        num_ones = num_ones + 1;
}
```

Program 6.7

6.5 Immediate Storage

The job of an assembler is to produce object code files. An assembly language program is the input to an assembler. Except for comments, all the lines of all the assembly language files we have worked with so far have consisted of instructions which are translated into processor instructions as was done in chapter 5. Automatic translation by the assembler is a great convenience and is mostly what assembly language is all about. Nonetheless it is sometimes desirable to forego translation and specify object code bytes directly. Two notable occasions for this are

- Data bytes need to be inserted directly.

- Processor instructions need to be assembled by hand.

The following syntax is used to insert immediately given bytes directly into the machine code.

6.5.1 Byte Definition Assembler Directive

In NASM, the command

   db imm

stores any one-byte number into the object code file. db stands for *define byte*. Instructions such as db which do not translate into processor instructions are sometimes called *pseudo-instructions*. Since they are actually instructions to the assembler, it is better to call them *assembler directives*. Assembler directives typically lack the universality of processor instructions which usually follow the format laid down by the manufacturer. Edlinas follows the Unix tradition that all assembler directives begin with a dot, and uses .db.

Without the initial dot, the define byte syntax is very widespread. When used with labels it works in both Microsoft and Turbo assemblers. In these assemblers

```
              MOV EBX, 0        ; num_zeros
              MOV ECX, 0        ; num_ones
              MOV EDX, 8000     ; 400 * 20, Initially i = 20
;
; Outer loop begins here.
;
OTL:          MOV ESI, 50       ; Let j = 50
;
; Inner loop begins here.
;
INL:          MOV EAX, [ABC + 4*ESI + EDX]
                                ; ABC = &x[0][0].
                                ; EDX = &x[i][0] − &x[0][0]
                                ; 4 * j = &x[i][j] − &x[i][0]
                                ; ESI = j
              CMP EAX, 0        ; Check for zeros
              JNE NOZ           ;
              INC EBX           ; Count zeros
NOZ:          CMP EAX, 1        ; Check for ones
              JNE NOO
              INC ECX           ; Count ones
NOO:          INC ESI           ; j = j + 1
              CMP ESI, 55       ; Check that j < 55
              JL INL            ; Inner loop ends here.
              ADD EDX, 400      ; Increase EDX by 100 * 4
              CMP EDX, 12000    ; 8000 + 10 * 100 * 4
              JL OTL            ; Outer loop ends here.
ABC:          NOP               ; Begin array here.
```

Program 6.8

the define byte directive has the flavor of a data type declaration. This "data type" is used to resolve ambiguities of the kind noted in section 6.2. For example, if the label ABC is used in a program with the line

ABC DB 3 ; ABC is of type byte

then a command such as

NEG [ABC]

means the same thing as

NEG BYTE PTR [ABC]

In NASM (and in Edlinas) programs, there is no type significance attached to db. Common embellishments of the simple syntax also work in both.

    db imm, imm, ...

where a sequence of one-byte numbers follows the db, stores a seqence of bytes into the object code file.

In Edlinas, it is also possible to use an integer multiplier on the left. For example, the following code stores zero into one hundred bytes of memory.

    .db 100 * 0

In NASM the same effect can be achieved using the code

    TIMES 100 db 0

6.5.2 Hand Coding of Instructions

Because a new processor often uses an instruction set which is the same as an old instruction set except for one or two new instructions, it is often worthwhile to use an old assembler to program a new processor. New instructions can be utilized by hand coding them. Open source advocates may well note that if the assembler were an open source program, it could simply be reprogrammed to handle the new instruction. But that is another question.

```
; Using immediate storage to encode the CPUID instruction.
;
        MOV EAX, 0
        db 0FH,0A2H        ; Immediate storage
```

Program 6.9

6.5.3 Initializing Data

In C it is easy to get the impression that there is no difference between a declaration with an initialization such as

    char x = 2;

and a declaration followed by an assignment such as

    char x;
    x = 2;

In fact, however, there is a difference. In the second case there is an implied processor instruction which stores the immediate value 2. In the first case, however, no processor instruction is implied. The storage indicated may be performed by storing the 2 at a program internal address by the assembler before the program is ever loaded.

```
; Tiny Edlinas program which uses a label to access stored data.
;
        MOV AL,[ABC]
        OUT [1], AL
        RET
ABC:    .db 3
```

Program 6.10

7

THE STACK

The *stack* is a portion of memory which is shared with the operating system. It is used by programs for communication with subprograms, for temporary storage, and when making system calls. It is called the stack because it has a "last stored first retrieved" policy. It is in fact an example of the data structure that is called a stack. Because it is used by the operating system as well as by the programmer, it must be used responsibly. Misusing the stack is a very easy way to crash a program, or the whole system, if the operating system is unprotected.

7.1   Push and Pop Operations

The following figure shows the stack and the ESP register. This register has the job of keeping track of the stack. It does this by holding the address of the top of the stack. The SP in ESP stands for *stack pointer*. Although the ESP is called a general register because it is accessible to the programmer like the registers EAX, EBX, etc., writes to ESP should be done only with great care.

Suppose that ESP contained the address 19H as in Figure 7-1. Then storing the byte 76H on the stack would fill the location 18H and the stack pointer would be changed, as shown in Figure 7-2. This kind of operation is called a *push*. The one-byte push shown here is essentially the same as the following two operations:

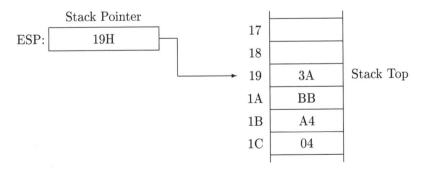

Figure 7-1. Before Push

111

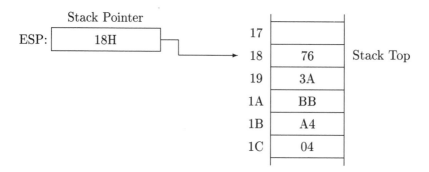

Figure 7-2. After Push

DEC ESP ; Move the pointer to the first vacancy.
MOV [ESP],76H; Store 76H at the address in ESP.

In fact, the x86 does not allow one-byte pushes. All pushes must be either two-byte or four-byte pushes. The number of bytes pushed is determined by the size of the operand on the PUSH instruction.

7.1.1   The PUSH Command

The most common form of the PUSH instruction is

PUSH reg

Allowable registers include the 16- and 32-bit general registers, but not the eight-bit registers. Memory and immediate operands can also be used with PUSH, but the register operand form is the most useful.

Figure 7-3 and Figure 7-4 show the effect of a PUSH EAX instruction.

PUSH EAX

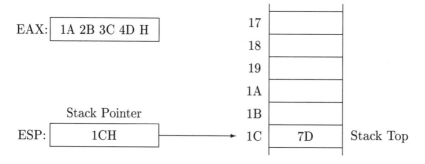

Figure 7-3. Before PUSH EAX

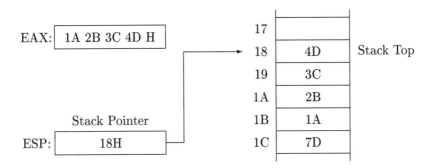

Figure 7-4. After PUSH EAX

is very similar to

    SUB ESP, 4
    MOV [ESP], EAX

Because the stack pointer points to the last occupied location rather than the first unoccupied location of the stack, a PUSH must be carried out by subtracting from the stack pointer first and then transferring the bytes to the stack rather than the other way around. Having the stack pointer point to the first available location would be a reasonable policy if all pushes and pops were the same size. But since pushes and pops may be either two or four bytes, this is not a tenable policy.

7.1.2 The POP Command

The opposite operation is called a *pop*. Like the PUSH instruction, POP takes register and memory operands, which may be either two or four bytes. Unlike PUSH, it does not take immediate operands. As with pushes, the size of the operand determines the number of bytes to be popped. Since BX is a two-byte register, POP BX pops two bytes off the stack.

    POP BX

is very similar to

    MOV BX, [ESP]
    ADD ESP, 2

One use for the stack is simply for storage when there are not enough registers available. Suppose there are values in EAX and EBX which are important and need to be saved, but that also a computation has to be done which uses the registers EAX and EBX. This is a situation which calls for using the stack. Before the computation is done, the values in the registers EAX and EBX may be saved on the stack. After the computation is finished, they may be restored again. The following code does this:

```
PUSH EAX
PUSH EBX
...
; Computation
...
POP EBX
POP EAX
```

The order of the pops is the exact reverse of the order of the pushes. This is because of the "last stored first retrieved" character of a stack. The values in EAX and EBX at the end should be the same as at the beginning. But this will only be true if the intervening computation uses the stack responsibly. This means that each push should be matched with a pop. If pushes and pops are not balanced, then the values popped into EBX and EAX at the end of computation will not be the same as their original values.

When writing a user program to be run in Unix, it is not necessary to initialize the stack by storing a value in ESP. In fact, since the stack is already set up, storing an arbitrary value in ESP would disrupt the existing stack and crash the program. When writing a program to run in Edlinas, however, it is necessary to initialize ESP.

7.2   Subprograms

High-level programming languages use subprograms in order to reduce complex tasks to simpler components. In C, subprograms are functions. A function may be called as though it were another C instruction. If the function subpr() has been defined, then it may appear in a line of a main program, as in Program 7.1.

```
main()
{
    int x, y, z;
...
    subpr(); This subprogram is defined separately.
...
}
```

Program 7.1

7.2.1   The CALL and RET Commands

Coding an assembler program which has a subprogram is done using the CALL and RET instructions. RET stands for return. These commands work like jump to and jump back commands. The format of the CALL instruction is very similar to the format of the JMP instruction.

```
subpr()
{
    int a, b, c;
...
    return c;
}
```

Program 7.2

CALL label

As with the JMP instruction, the label is created by the programmer and refers to the line whose label field it occupies.

When the subprogram is done, control needs to be transferred back to the main program; in particular the next instruction executed in the main program needs to be the instruction following the CALL instruction. To make this possible, the processor pushes the address of the next instruction onto the stack before it leaves the main program. CALL does this. The RET instruction pops this address off the stack and jumps to it.

For example, Program 7.3 is a program that accepts a user input, uses a subprogram which adds 1 to the EBX register to increment the number, and then outputs the result back to the user.

```
;
            MOV ESP, 2000H ; initialize the stack
;
; Edlinas programs must initialize the stack
; Unix programs must not.
;
            IN EAX,[0]        ; Get a user input
            MOV EBX, EAX      ; EBX is where the subroutine works.
            CALL subpr        ; Leave for the subroutine.
            MOV EAX, EBX      ; Back now from the subroutine!
            OUT [1], EAX      ; Output the incremented value
            RET               ; Go back to Edlinas.
;
subpr:
            INC EBX           ; Subprogram does its job.
            RET               ; Go back to the main program.
```

Program 7.3

For a more involved example, consider the following algorithm. This algorithm is at the heart of a well-known, unsolved mathematics problem called the Collatz Problem.

> If x is even divide it by 2
> If x is odd multiply it by 3 and add 1 to it.
>
> Repeat this process until x = 1.

Suppose we want a program which executes this algorithm and counts how many steps are required until the value of x becomes 1.

Since it requires a loop to determine whether a number is even or odd, or to divide it by 2, if we are using only add, subtract, and conditional jump commands, it makes sense to devise a subprogram to do this. Specifically, suppose we assign the subprogram the task of examining the EAX register and storing half of EAX in EBX if EAX is even, and zero in EBX otherwise. We may code this subprogram as follows:

```
HAF:   MOV ECX, EAX
       MOV EBX, 0
AGN:   INC EBX        ; Count the subtractions
       SUB ECX, 2     ; Repeatedly subtract 2
       JG AGN         ;
       JZ DUN         ; It comes out even
       MOV EBX, 0     ; It's not even.
DUN:   RET
```

Program 7.4

With this subprogram we may now write a main program which executes Program 7.4.

7.3   Parameter Passing

One of the most important functions of the stack is that it is used for parameter passing. For example, suppose the character code converting function `tolower()` is called in a C program.

The `tolower()` function in the standard C library ctype.h converts the character codes to lower case. For example, on a machine using ASCII, code it will return 97, the ASCII code for 'a', if given 65, the ASCII code for 'A', as an input parameter. The input parameter is pushed onto the stack. So the assembler code for the same function call looks like this:

```
MOV EBX, 65
PUSH EBX
```

```
            MOV EDX, 0
            IN EAX, [DX]
ABC:        CMP EAX, 1        ;
            JE FIN            ;If EAX = 1 then it's over.
            INC EDX           ;Use EDX as the counter.
            CALL HAF          ;This is the subroutine call!
            CMP EBX, 0        ;EBX = 0 means EAX is odd
            JE ODD            ;
            MOV EAX, EBX      ;If not then EBX is half of EAX
            JMP ABC           ;
ODD:        MOV EBX, EAX      ;Triple EAX and add 1
            ADD EAX, EBX      ;
            ADD EAX, EBX      ;
            INC EAX
            JMP ABC           ;
FIN:        MOV EAX, EDX      ;EDX contains the final count.
            MOV EDX, 1
            OUT [DX], EAX
            RET
```

Program 7.5

```c
#include <ctype.h>

main()
{
    int x,y;

    x = 65; /* x = 'A' */
    y = tolower(x); /* y = 'a' */
}
```

Program 7.6

```
        CALL tolower
        ADD ESP, 4
```

Although it might seem like a natural idea to use the stack for the return value, it is more common to use a register. In gnu C for the x86, returned integer values are stored in the EAX register. Languages differ as to whether the subprogram or the main program is responsible for popping the parameters off the stack. In Fortran, Basic, and Pascal the subprogram pops the stack, but in C the calling program does. This is the reason for the **ADD ESP, 4** instruction in the calling programs just shown.

Languages also differ in the order in which parameters are pushed onto the stack. C pushes parameters starting from the right. Suppose we have defined an integer power function ipow():

```
int ipow(int base, int exponent);
```

The assembler code to call this function to calculate 2^3 looks like this:

```
MOV EBX, 3
PUSH EBX
MOV EBX, 2
PUSH EBX
CALL ipow
ADD ESP, 8
```

After this call, the result ipow(2, 3) = 8 will be stored in the EAX register.

7.3.1   The Global Assembler Directive

In the .o files produced by the gnu compiler, symbols such as printf or tolower which need external linkage are coded differently in the symbol tables. Without this special coding the gnu linker will pass them by and linkage will fail. In order to receive this special encoding, the assembly language source code must specially indicate symbols which are to receive this treatment. There is an assembler directive recognized by the gnu assembler and by Edlinas which will cause the assembler to encode a symbol in the symbol table as available for linkage. It's syntax is

```
.globl symbol
```

In NASM the syntax is:

```
global symbol
```

7.3.2   Calling Assembler from C

The HAF subprogram would not work if called from C because it does not return values in the EAX register. Also, it does not push the registers it uses. In the code below, ECX is pushed because it is used and the calling program could be using it for something else. We also need to make the function name visible using the global directive.

We have just written a function in assembler which we can call from a C program. The C program will store the calling parameter on the stack. It will be buried under the return address pushed by the calling program and the contents of ECX which were just pushed. These two items occupy eight bytes on the stack, so the calling parameter is accessed at the address ESP + 8. The result is stored in EAX instead of EBX. To save the object code as a .o file while in Edlinas, use the **o** key. To produce an object code file using NASM, enter

```
          global half ; or .globl in Edlinas
half:     PUSH ECX          ; ECX is used, so push it.
          MOV ECX, [ESP + 8]
                            ; Stack top + 2 integers
          MOV EAX, 0
AGN:      INC EAX           ; Count the subtractions
          SUB ECX, 2        ; Repeatedly subtract 2
          JG AGN            ;
          JZ DUN            ; It comes out even
          MOV EAX, 0        ; It's not even.
DUN:      POP ECX
          RET
```

Program 7.7

```
linuxbox$ nasm -f elf half.asm
```

The `-f elf` switch specifies the format of the object code file which in current Linux is elf. This format is discussed further in chapter 8.

Program 7.8 is a C program which calls the function `half()` whose assembly code is shown in Program 7.7. If Program 7.8 is saved in a file `collatz.c`, then to compile it and link it with `half()`, use `gcc` on both files

```
linuxbox$ gcc collatz.c half.o
```

7.4 Recursion

In recursion, much of the work of computation is done by the parameter-passing mechanism.

A recursive definition can very often be easily turned into a computationally effective, if not efficient, program. This is typically illustrated using the Fibonacci numbers.

$$\text{fib}(k) = \begin{cases} 1 & \text{if } k < 2 \\ \text{fib}(k-1) + \text{fib}(k-2) & \text{otherwise.} \end{cases}$$

Program 7.9 shows how this recursive definition can be turned into C code. In assembly language, we can code this easily, provided we recall that used registers other than EAX must be pushed. Program 7.10 shows how we can get by using only ECX and EAX. To test this program from C, one can use a small calling program such as Program 7.11. To test a program like this using Edlinas, it is also necessary to initialize the stack, as is shown in the first line of Program 7.3.

```
main()
{
    int count,x,y;
    count = 0;

    printf("Enter a number:  ");
    scanf("%d", &x);

    while(x != 1)
    {
        count = count + 1;
        y = half(x); /* This is the subroutine call!  */
        if(y != 0)
            x = y;
        else
            x = 3*x + 1;
        printf("\n x = %d.", x);
    }
    printf("\n There were %d iterations.\n\n.",count);
}
```

Program 7.8

```
int fib(int k)
{
    int d;

    if(k < 2)
        d = 1;
    else
        d = fib(k-1) + fib(k-2);

    return d;
}
```

Program 7.9

```
        global fib
fib:    PUSH ECX          ; Gives us access to ECX
        MOV EAX, [ESP + 8]
                          ; Access parameter
        CMP EAX, 2        ; if k < 2
        JAE ELS           ;
        MOV EAX, 1        ; Put the return value in EAX
        JMP DUN
ELS:    DEC EAX           ; Get k−1
        MOV ECX, EAX      ; EAX will be overwritten!
        PUSH EAX          ; Pass k−1 as parameter
        CALL fib          ; Get back fib(k−1) in EAX
        ADD ESP, 4        ; Get rid of parameter
        DEC ECX           ; Get k−2
        PUSH ECX          ; Pass k−2 as parameter
        MOV ECX, EAX      ; Put fib(k−1) into ECX
        CALL fib          ; Get back fib(k−2) in EAX
        ADD ESP, 4        ; Get rid of parameter
        ADD EAX, ECX      ; Add the two partial results
        POP ECX           ; Restore the original value
        RET
```

Program 7.10

```
main()
{
    int x, y;
    ;
    printf("Enter a number:  ");
    scanf("%d", &x);
    ;
    y = fib(x);
    ;
    printf("%d\n", y);
}
```

Program 7.11

8

LINUX USER PROGRAMS

At the beginning of chapter 6 it was noted that memory addresses used in Linux user programs are not true memory addresses. The main reason for this is that Linux needs to prevent the user from having direct access to memory. See Figure 8-1.

Linux is a multitasking system. A multitasking system has many user jobs and an operating system, which are all running at once. On a machine where any job can overwrite the memory belonging to another job, a multitasking system is impossible. Multitasking requires memory protection. Linux uses paging to implement a memory protection system.

Paging was originally designed as a system for economizing on memory. Linux uses it for this purpose as well as for memory protection. Paging works by intercepting each memory access encountered in the user's machine code. In other words, every memory reference in a user program is turned into a request for memory access which is required to go across the desk of the paging system for approval. This means that paging gets control over memory access. In order for this to happen, the processor has to have paging wired into it.

Neither the 8086 nor the 80286 processors support   paging. The first Intel processor with paging support is the 80386.

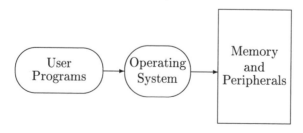

Figure 8-1. Protected Operating System such as Linux

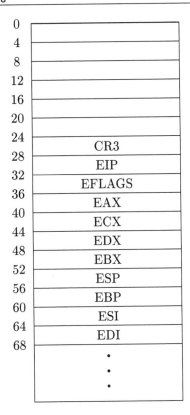

0	
4	
8	
12	
16	
20	
24	CR3
28	EIP
32	EFLAGS
36	EAX
40	ECX
44	EDX
48	EBX
52	ESP
56	EBP
60	ESI
64	EDI
68	

Figure 8-2. Task State Segment

8.1 Multitasking

Before multitasking operating systems existed, computer programs were executed in sequence, i.e., one after the other. No program was able to begin executing until the program ahead of it was finished. Operating systems which ran programs in series like this were called *batch* operating systems. A multitasking system allows programs to take turns using processors. An operating system program called the *scheduler* acts as a referee and forces user programs to yield to one another even when they are not finished. At any given moment, there may be many user programs taking turns and waiting for processor time. Each of these programs is called a *task* or a *process*. A distinction has to be made between a program and a process since one program can be called several times by several users all at once. Each separate instance of a program is a process. In Linux we can list the processes by using the

```
linuxbox$ ps aux
```

command. Or to conduct a more detailed examination, we can explore the /proc directory.

A multitasking system such as Linux is continually juggling its processor resources, passing them from process to process. Each time a process gets bumped from a processor, it has to save its current state. Part of the work of saving is done by a hardwired routine which is executed when the x86 does a *task switch*. It saves all current registers to a region in memory called the *task state segment*. The task state segment holds the frozen state of a task which is not currently running. Every task has its own task state segment. These task state segments make it possible to switch from one task to another. Figure 8-2 shows the basic layout of a task state segment, including the space for all the general registers, and a register called the *CR3 register*. Some space that is unmarked in this figure is discussed in chapter 13.

8.2 Paging

As discussed in chapter 4, section 4.2, x86 I/O addresses do not undergo processing. If the DX register contains a number such as FC30H, then the execution of the IN AL,[DX] command causes the 16 bits of DX to be applied directly to the address bus.

FC30H = 1111 1100 0011 0000

So on the address bus we get

A15	A14	A13	A12	A11	A10	A9	A8	A7	A6	A5	A4	A3	A2	A1	A0
1	1	1	1	1	1	0	0	0	0	1	1	0	0	0	0

The top 16 bits are just 0.

Memory addresses on the other hand are not handled in such a straightforward fashion. A MOV AL,[0FC30H] will not result in these same bits being pumped out onto the address bus. Memory addresses undergo a two-step process.

1. Segmentation

2. Paging

Only at the end of this process, and then only if everything goes well, is there a physical address which can be pumped out onto the address bus. Since Linux does not use segmentation, discussion of it is deferred to chapter 12.

8.2.1 Virtual Memory

All addresses lie in the 0 to 4 Gig range. Although it would make sense that different tasks be required to use different parts of the 4 Gig space, Linux does not work this way. Linux may allocate the same addresses to different tasks at the same time. These addresses are not real. They are called virtual addresses. Just as a fraudulent accountant keeps two sets of books, one for the auditors and one for the true state of affairs, Linux must keep a set of virtual addresses for *each* task, plus one set of real addresses for the actual physical locations on disk and in RAM.

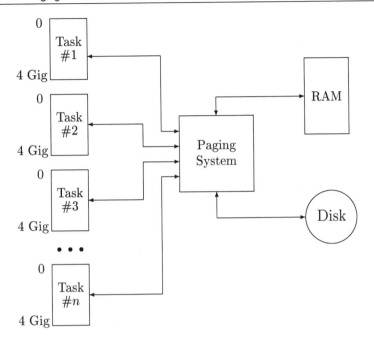

Figure 8-3. x86 Virtual Memory System

The translation between the virtual addresses and the real ones is done using extensive sets of tables called *page tables*. Each process has its own set of tables.

Figure 8-5 shows the situation which results. The reader will note that memory has been seriously overbooked. There are typically many processes running. Each process uses potentially 4 Gig of virtual address space. But the typical computer has much less RAM than would be needed to supply all processes with 4 Gig! At first sight, paging seems to be a very bad idea. But in fact it economizes greatly on memory usage and is one of the reasons computers are able to run big programs as fast as they do. Airlines overbook in order to keep their planes occupied. The cost of free airline tickets now and then to bumped passengers is more than paid for by keeping the seats full. Likewise, the occasional *page fault* is more than made up for by keeping memory busy.

Paging works by copying temporarily idle portions of memory onto disk. As suggested by its name, it works in units called *pages*.

4K Pages

On an x86 machine, a page is 4,096 bytes. In order to set up a paging system, four areas need to be divided up into pages:

1. The available physical memory is broken up into pages. Since $4{,}096 = 2^{12} = 4K = 1000H$, every page starts at an address ending in three hex zeros. Pages in physical memory are sometimes called *page frames*.

2. Each task's 4 Gig virtual address spaces is also divided into pages. 4 Gig corresponds to 1 Meg of pages.

$$4 \text{ Gig} \div 4K = (4 \times 2^{30}) \div (4 \times 2^{10}) = 2^{32} \div 2^{12} = 2^{20} = 1 \text{ Meg.}$$

Again, every page starts at an address ending in three hex zeros.

3. The portion of the hard disk used for paging is also divided into pages. This portion is often called the *swap space*. Since most disks are formatted into 512-byte sectors, this means the number of sectors allocated to the swap space must be a multiple of eight. $4{,}096 = 8 \times 512$.

4. The page tables used to translate virtual addresses are themselves set up in units of pages. These tables are described in section 8.3.1.

Note that pages of virtual memory, physical memory, and disk all have the same size. This facilitates data transfers in page size quantities.

8.2.2   Paging vs. Swapping

The term *swap space* is unfortunate since "swapping" traditionally refers to copying entire processes to and from the disk. When demand for memory on a multitasking system exceeds the available RAM, a very simple solution to this problem is to just copy some process out to the disk. That is what swapping does. Swapping does not increase memory efficiency. It just prevents memory from overloading. It can be done by the operating system on its own. It does not require any special hardware support. Swapping was common in Unix systems before paging was invented. Linux does not use swapping and never has.

Although swapping solves the problem of memory unavailability, it does not do very well in terms of making memory usage efficient. Copying whole processes into and out of memory tends to fragment memory just as copying files onto and off of a disk tends to fragment a disk. Furthermore, by treating processes as wholes, it misses out on the possibility that by keeping just the most important parts of each process in memory, it may be possible to run all the processes without much ongoing disk access. Failing this, it may at least be possible to greatly reduce the fraction of the processor's time which is wasted in servicing memory faults.

Page Faults

Using paging, all the processes are run as though they were all in memory simultaneously. When a machine instruction is encountered which refers to a memory location actually on disk, this is called a *page fault*. When a page fault occurs, some page frame in RAM has to be chosen so that the needed page may be loaded into it

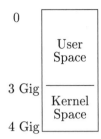

Figure 8-4. Single Process View of Memory

from the disk. If no page frame is free, then some page of memory has to be chosen for transfer to the disk so as to free up a page frame. This memory page is copied to the disk and the page containing the missed address is copied into RAM. There are many different algorithms in use which choose pages to be expelled from memory. Such algorithms are referred to as *paging algorithms*. Many paging algorithms choose pages for expulsion on the basis of usage. Unused pages get expelled.

8.2.3 Kernel Addresses

Although Linux may and often does allocate the same virtual addresses to different tasks, it uses a special set of virtual addresses for kernel memory and these are never duplicated.

- Kernel addresses lie in the range from C0000000H to FFFFFFFFH, i.e., 3 to 4 Gig.

- User addresses in the range from 0 to BFFFFFFFH, i.e., 0 to 3 Gig.

Figure 8-4 illustrates this memory policy from the standpoint of a single process. Figure 8-5 shows it from the standpoint of the entire system. User virtual addresses are allotted individually. Kernel addresses are system-wide.

Before version 2.1.39 of Linux, the separation of kernel and user memory was accomplished using the segmentation process. Linux currently makes no use of segmentation. Now the separation is accomplished simply as an allocation policy. This incidentally makes x86 Linux more like Alpha Linux. The Alpha architecture has no segmentation. Segmentation is discussed in chapters 12 and 13.

8.2.4 Kernel Pages

The Linux paging algorithm never pages kernel memory out to disk. The Linux kernel is therefore always in RAM.

This is one reason that compiling Linux specially for each machine is worthwhile. If the kernel is compiled with code which isn't needed, such as device drivers for

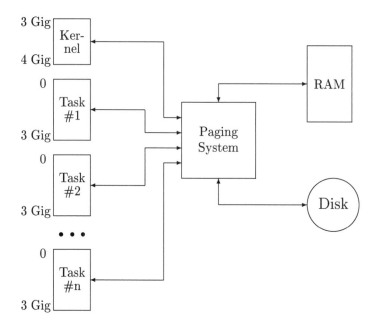

Figure 8-5. Linux Virtual Memory System

devices the machine doesn't have, RAM will be permanently occupied by code which is never used.

It is also the reason that machines require approximately 4 Meg of RAM, depending on the Linux version, to run Linux at all.

8.2.5 Kernel Modules

Although kernel memory is never touched by the paging system, it has been possible since Linux version 2.0 to add or delete chunks of kernel memory, provided they have been compiled separately as modules. The commands

```
linuxbox$ insmod module
```

for "install module" and

```
linuxbox$ rmmod module
```

for "remove module" do change the amount of RAM occupied by the kernel. To inspect memory to find out the amount of memory available, the Linux command

```
linuxbox$ free
```

is useful.

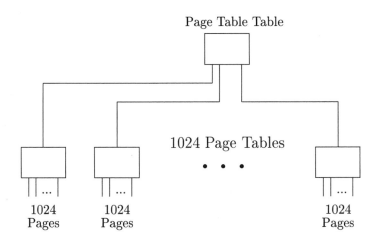

Figure 8-6. x86 Page Table Structure

8.3   Address Translation

Linux user memory addresses are virtual addresses, not actual physical addresses. Linux uses paging to translate virtual addresses to RAM addresses. x86 paging obtains its translations from page tables set up by the operating system. Since the translation process is hardwired into the processor, x86 page tables must have the two-tiered structure shown in Figure 8-6.

8.3.1   Two-Tiered x86 Page Tables

Each table in this structure has 1024 four-byte entries. The size of each table therefore is 4K. Note that each table is also a page.

A page table table lists the locations of 1024 page tables. Each page table lists the locations of 1024 pages. Each page contains 4096 bytes. The total memory referenced by a page table table is therefore $1024 \times 1024 \times 4096 = 2^{10} \times 2^{10} \times 2^{12} = 2^{32} = 4$ Gigabytes. This is the size of one virtual address space.

8.3.2   Address Parsing

All virtual addresses are 32-bit quantities. These 32 bits are broken up as follows:

32 bits = 10 bits + 10 bits + 12 bits.

These bits are allocated as shown in Figure 8-7. The two ten-bit numbers are indices

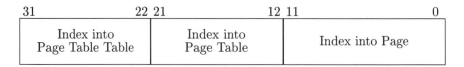

Figure 8-7. Virtual Address Translation

into tables with $1024 = 2^{10}$ entries. A ten-bit number is a number from 0 to 1023. The 12-bit number is an index into a page. A page has 2^{12} bytes. A 12-bit number is a number from 0 to 4095. It picks out one byte from a page.

8.3.3   Translation Example

Suppose we have a virtual address of 1A2B3C4DH. This 32-bit address is broken into its three parts:

```
   1   A   2   B   3   C   4   D
0001 1010 0010 1011 0011 1100 0100 1101   Virtual Address
0001 1010 00                              Index into Page Table Table
            10 1011 0011                  Index into Page Table
                      1100 0100 1101      Index into Page
```

Translation begins at the page table table. The first ten bits pick out an entry from this table. In our example, these bits are: 0001 1010 00 = 0110 1000 = 68H = 104. Indices start at zero. The first item fetched is the 105th four-byte entry in the page table table. If all goes well, this entry contains an address. In section 8.3.4 it is shown how to extract this address. The address is the address of a page table. The next ten bits, 10 1011 0011, equal 2B3H, or 691, which is the number of an entry in the page table. Again if all goes well, we may extract an address from this entry. This address is the RAM address of the page on which the information being sought is located. Suppose that this address happens to be 1234000H. The last 12 bits of the virtual address, 1100 0100 1101 = 0C4DH, are the offset within the page. The translated address is then 1234C4DH.

8.3.4   Page Table Entries

Suppose a memory address is encountered by the processor for the first time in a read command such as

    MOV AL,[12345678H]

As just explained in section 8.3.3, a table entry for this address is obtained. This entry is four bytes in size. Its least significant bit is called the *present bit*. In the diagram shown here, it is marked "P P" for page present.

Figure 8-8. Page (Table) Table Entry

When the present bit is set, it means that the sought after page is located in RAM. In this case the calling program is lucky and the page table entry just read provides the physical address of the page containing the required byte. Since all page frames in physical memory are stored at addresses whose bottom 12 bits are zero, the address can be given using its upper 20 bits. That is what the top 20 bits of the page table entry provide. Once the address of the page is determined, the memory read is completed as shown in section 8.3.3.

8.3.5 Memory Protection

When the present bit is not set, there are two possibilities:

1. It may mean that the page containing the sought after byte is located on disk. In this case, a Page Fault results.

2. It may also mean that the address is not valid at all! In this case, a Segmentation Fault results.

The first possibility is no surprise. The idea of paging is to put some memory pages out onto the disk. When a program tries to access them, this is of course a problem. Problems like this are dealt with in chapter 9, section 9.4.

The second possibility is somewhat foreign to the idea of paging as a memory economizing feature. But it brings out exactly what we mean when we say that Linux uses paging to "protect" memory. Because the page tables are under the control of the operating system, it gives the operating system an opportunity to intercept every single memory request. This is how Linux keeps potentially overwhelming demands for memory under control. Only addresses on pages which it has allocated to processes will have the present bit in the page tables set. Any reference to an unallocated page results in the dreaded "Segmentation Fault" error message.

8.3.6 The CR3 Register

Translation begins at the page table table. Each task has its own page table table. The physical address of the page table table is stored in a register called CR3. CR stands for *control register*. The control registers were added to the x86 processors starting with the 386. For more discussion of these registers see chapter 13, section 13.1.

CR3 is reloaded automatically every time the x86 processor changes from one task to another. This is what makes it possible for each task to have its own set of virtual addresses. The kernel memory in the last one-fourth of the address space (see section 8.2.3) is there because Linux puts it there. This address space is shared because the page tables which translate these addresses are shared. The last one-quarter of every page table table on the system is identical.

8.3.7   Kernel Memory Access

The fact that kernel addresses are stored in all the page tables on the system might lead us to believe that kernel memory can be used by all processes on the system. In a way this is true. In chapter 9, section 9.7 we will see how user code may invoke system calls to get access to kernel memory. However, user code by itself does not have this kind of access. It is blocked by the U_S user-supervisor bit of the table entries for kernel memory. (See Figure 8-8.)

This bit, if it is 1, does not block access. If it is 0, it is checked against a two-bit privilege, value stored in a special register called the CPL register. This register and the privilege levels stored in it are discussed in chapter 9, section 9.6. Access is blocked if the value in the CPL register is 3. When user programs are running, the CPL register holds 3. This is the basic protection that kernel memory has against access by user programs.

8.3.8   Paging Page Tables

Entries in the page table table look just like entries in the page table. The present bit in each means the same thing. If it is cleared it means that the sought after item is not present. Just as a page of some process's memory can be paged out to disk, so can a page table. Just as 4K of address space in a page can be marked as unallocated, so can the 4 Meg of address space under a page table be marked as unallocated.

A missing page table causes a page fault or a segmentation fault, just like a missing page of user memory.

8.4   Program Segments

Consider Program 8.1. When this program is run, the line labelled ABC wipes itself out. This program is an example of *self-modifying code* Once upon a time in the bad old days, self-modifying code was sometimes used to save a few bytes of memory space. Today self-modifying code is not considered good programming. Tom Shanley put it more bluntly when he wrote that programmers who create self-modifying code should be "cast into the pits." Ordinarily, the only reason that a running program is modified is that something has gone wrong. Running programs should not get modified.

```
; Program which self-destructs.
;
        IN AL, [0]
ABC:    MOV [ABC], AL
        RET
```

Program 8.1

8.4.1 Non-Writeable Memory

Unix requires that running programs be protected from accidental modification by being stored in memory which is "not writeable." Linux uses bit 1 of the page table entry to implement this requirement. This is the bit marked "W_R" for Write Read in the diagram. If this bit is cleared, the indexed page is not writeable. When the processor encounters a write command such as

```
MOV [87654321H],AL
```

this bit is checked. First the page table entry for the address 87654321H is fetched. Assuming the present bit in the entry for this page is set, then because this instruction is a write command, bit 1, the write or read bit, is checked. If this bit is not set, the processor will not execute the instruction and Linux issues a "Segmentation Fault" error message. Faults are described in greater detail in chapter 9, section 9.4.

Unix protects code by marking it as nonwriteable.

8.4.2 Writeable Memory

Data space used for computation needs to be in memory which is writeable. Consider Program 8.2. The label XYZ just marks stored data. The code is perfectly

```
; Tiny NASM program which crashes trying to increment a byte of stored data.
;
        global main
main:   MOV AL,[XYZ]
        INC AL
        MOV [XYZ], AL
        RET
XYZ:    db 3
```

Program 8.2

reasonable. But because the entire program is stored in nonwriteable memory, a segmentation fault occurs when the processor attempts to execute the MOV [XYZ], AL instruction. This is a problem.

- On the one hand Linux protects the code in Program 8.2 by storing it on pages which are not writeable.

- On the other hand the label XYZ in Program 8.2 marks writeable space. It therefore cannot be stored on the same page as the executable lines of the program.

Because write protection for code is implemented using page table entries, then at least two different pages are needed for Program 8.2, one with write protection and one without it. No page can be shared by write-protected code and writeable data space.

8.4.3   Text and Data Segments

Programs have to be broken up. The different pieces of an executable file are called *segments*.

The machine code could be broken up when it was loaded, but this would place unreasonable demands on the loading program. In order that the segments do not have to be created at load time, the executable file is divided into segments. Eventually we will describe five different kinds of segments. So far we have made a case for two:

- Text segments. Executable code needs a segment which is stored in pages whose Write Read bit is cleared. It is called the text segment.

- Data segments. Some programs need space in the executable file where data can be written. It is stored in pages whose Write Read bit is set. It is called the *data* segment.

8.4.4   Text and Data Sections

Just as an executable file has segments, an object code file has *sections*. One of the linker's jobs is to put together a text segment from the text sections of all the object code files being linked, a data segment from all the data sections, etc. Linkers have a lot of work to do.

Who creates the sections in the object code files? Object code files are created by assemblers.

8.4.5   Section Definition Directives

Assemblers do not separate code into text and data sections acting on their own. At least, most assemblers are not that smart. The programmer needs to help out by using directives that specify which code goes into which section. The following NASM directive can be used to initiate sections.

```
    section .text
```

specifies a text section. Similarly,

```
    section .data
```

initiates a data section.

With these directives we can direct NASM to produce a `.o` file with both text and data sections. Adding these directives to Program 8.2 gives us Program 8.3, which will compile and run without crashing.

```
; Tiny program which increments a byte of stored data.
;
        global main
        section .text
main:   MOV AL,[XYZ]
        INC AL
        MOV [XYZ], AL
        RET
        section .data
XYZ:    db 3
```

Program 8.3

8.4.6 Segments in C Code

Program 8.4 can be used to determine the addresses of pages allocated to itself.

8.4.7 Calling C from Assembler

Calling functions involves using the stack. When functions are called using assembler, it is possible to see exactly how the stack is used in a function call. Once you know how to use the stack to call a function, you can call C library functions to get actual input and output for assembler programs which run under Linux.

In order to call `printf()` and `scanf()` using assembler, it is necessary to push strings onto the stack. This is because the first argument of each of these functions is always a string. The `db` assembler directive introduced in chapter 6, section 6.5.1 can be used to store strings as well as numbers. For example,

```
    .db "Hello world!\n\x0"
```

can be used to store a string. If the location is labelled, then the label may be used to push the address of the stored string. In Edlinas the allowable strings are exactly like those allowed in the C language except that null termination must be explicitly encoded if it is desired. The C language hex escape sequence `\x` may be used to include a null or any other character into the string.

```
char a = 'A';
main()
{   char *n;
    int i,t;

    n = &a;
    printf("Enter a pointer displacement in hex:");
    scanf("%x",&i);
    printf("Pointer value in hex = %x\n", (n + i));
    printf("Read, write, or skip?  (Enter 0, 1, or 2):");
    scanf("%d", &t);
    if (t == 0)
        printf("Contents there= %x", *(n + i));
    else if (t == 1)
        *(n + i) = 'Y';
    printf("\n");
}
```

Program 8.4

In NASM, non-ASCII characters are coded outside the string using commas.

```
db "Hello world!",0AH,0
```

In order to call scanf() from assembler it is necessary to have a label in a data segment. The scanf() function takes user input and writes it into memory. This memory cannot be in the text segment. It must be in a data segment. Because printf and scanf occur as references to unknown locations, NASM requires the use of an extern directive. NASM will produce an error message if a label is referred to which does not occur in the label field of a line in the program being assembled. Program 8.5 shows how to call printf() and scanf() from a NASM program. A word of warning is in order regarding register usage. Although we might expect C library functions such as printf() and scanf() to save registers on the stack before using them, they don't necessarily. Values stored in registers before a call to printf() need *not* be there after this call. To preserve values from destruction by a library function call, the programmer must assume the responsibility of saving them on the stack. The lines labeled ABC, BCD, and CDE store strings. XYZ is located in the data segment. Consequently, the MOV EAX, [XYZ] instruction can execute without causing a memory violation.

8.5   Other Data Segments

Linux user memory is data space that is internal to the program itself. There are three kinds of data space internal to a program.

```
; This program calculates y = 2 * x + 1
          section .text
          global main
          extern printf
          extern scanf
main:     PUSH ABC
          CALL printf
          ADD ESP, 4
          PUSH XYZ
          PUSH BCD
          CALL scanf
          ADD ESP, 8
          MOV EAX, [XYZ]
          ADD EAX, EAX
          INC EAX
          PUSH EAX
          PUSH CDE
          CALL printf
          ADD ESP, 8
          RET
ABC:      db "Enter a number:   ",0AH,0
BCD:      db "%d \x0" ,0AH,0
CDE:      db "You get %d.\x0" ,0AH,0
          section .data
XYZ:      db 4 * 0
```

Program 8.5

1. Initialized data space. It is space that is internal to the executable file, even when the file is lying idle out on the disk.

2. Uninitialized data space. It is space that is added to the program when the program is loaded.

3. Dynamically Allocated Memory. It is space that is added to the program when it is executing.

8.5.1   Initialized Data Space

In chapter 6, section 6.5.3 the use of the db directive was discussed in connection with the initialization of data. The fact that this data needs to be stored permanently requires that it be a part of the executable file.

If the space which is occupied by this data is ever written to by the program, then it must be in a data segment. The

```
section .data
```

directive is the right tool for this job.

Sometimes stored data is never overwritten. For example, control strings such as "Hello world!" are essentially never written on. This kind of data may just as well be stored in write-protected pages. In the gnu assembler there is a special section label for sections of this kind, .rodata.

8.5.2   Uninitialized Data Space

Space which is needed by the running program, but which does not contain data initially, may be added to the program when it is loaded. An array declared by

```
int x[100000];
```

may well occupy 400,000 bytes of space. Putting such an array into an executable file would be a waste of disk space. To set the space aside at load time, the .bss section label is used.

8.5.3   Dynamically Allocated Memory

Programs get memory at run time using the system call malloc(). System calls are discussed in chapter 9, section 9.5.

8.6   I/O Protection

In section 8.3 we have discussed the use of paging as a way of protecting memory from unregulated user access. We have also noted that I/O addressing is unprocessed. It doesn't use paging, segmentation, or any other kind of tampering with the addresses in the brackets. But there is support for I/O protection in the x86 architecture and Linux does use it.

8.7   Executable Files in ELF Format

In chapter 6, section 6.4 we noted that because programs contain absolute addresses which are not determined until loading time, executable files contain relocation tables which list these locations in the file. These tables need to have some specified format.

In section 8.4 we noted that since programs have segments which are saved on separate pages, depending on whether the segments are writeable or not, the location of these segments within the file must be known to the operating system. If Linux did not have this information, it would not be able to determine which parts of the file to store in writeable pages of memory and which in read-only.

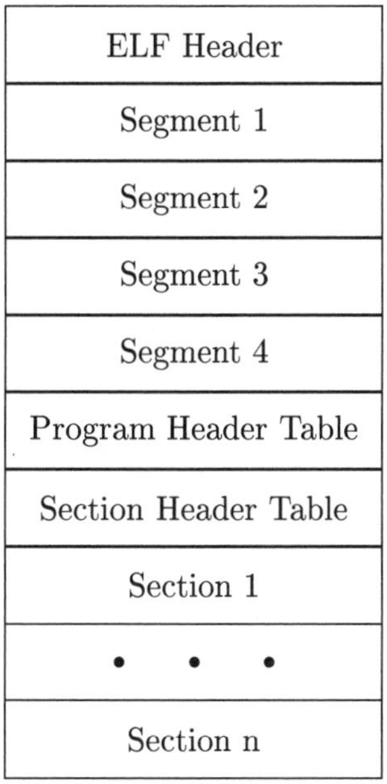

ELF Header
Segment 1
Segment 2
Segment 3
Segment 4
Program Header Table
Section Header Table
Section 1
• • •
Section n

Figure 8-9. ELF Format

For all these reasons, executable files must have some definite format. The format used by Linux, starting with version 2.0, is called ELF (Executable and Linking Format).

Two other Unix executable file formats are COFF (Common Object File Format) and a.out. Although all Unix systems use `a.out` as the name of the executable file produced by the C compiler, it is also the name of one particular format for executable files and object code files. At one time all versions of Unix used the a.out format. Now most versions use ELF. The book *Understanding and Using COFF* presents a thorough description of both COFF and a.out.

Figure 8-9 shows the layout of an executable file in ELF format.

8.7.1   The ELF Header

The ELF header identifies the file as an ELF file and specifies what kind of ELF file it is. It also specifies the size and location of the program header table and the section header table.

- The first entry is an identifier string containing ELF.

- The second entry is a number which is 1 if the file is an object file, 2 if the file is an executable file, 3 if the file is a shared object file, and 4 if it is a core file. Shared object files are discussed in chapter 11. Core files are produced whenever a program crashes. They are created for debugging purposes.

- The third entry number specifies the machine architecture. The number 3 stands for the x86 architecture.

- There are 11 more entries in the ELF header file, including entries for the size and location of the program header table and the section header table.

8.7.2 The Program Header Table

The program header table has one entry for each segment. Each entry in the program header table contains eight items of information:

1. Type. The type is 1 if the segment is to be loaded when the file is executed. Other types are not loaded into memory.

2. File Offset. This offset gives the location of the segment within the file. Like all offsets, it is the number of bytes from the beginning.

3. Virtual Address. This is the address where the first byte of the segment is to be loaded.

4. Physical Address. For x86 Linux systems this entry is a misnomer. It is ignored.

5. File Size. This is the number of bytes in the segment before it is loaded.

6. Memory Size. This is the number of bytes in the segment after it is loaded.

7. Permissions. This code contains the read-write-execute permissions.

8. Alignment. The segment must begin on a multiple of this entry.

As an example, Table 8.1 lists the Program Header table for chmod. Like most Unix commands, the chmod command is actually an executable file. On most systems it is located in /bin. Table 8.1 was produced by running the ob program on this file.

8.7.3 ELF Segments

In Linux 2.0 an executable file typically has five segments. Segment 0 is always the Program Header table. Note that in Table 8.1 the value of the Type field for Segment 0 is 6 for *program header*.

Segments have *read-write-execute* permissions associated with them, just as files in Unix do. The seventh item in each entry of the Program Header table is the permission code for that entry. It is easily understood when written as a binary number. For example, a permission code of 6 means permission to read and write but not to execute.

```
0034:00d4 Program Header Table
     Seg File Virtual Physical File Mem      Align
Num Type Offst Address Address Size Size Perm -ment
00:  0006 0034 8048034 8048034 00a0 00a0 0005 0004
01:  0003 00d4 80480d4 80480d4 0013 0013 0004 0001
02:  0001 0000 8048000 8048000 1d29 1d29 0005 1000
03:  0001 1d30 804ad30 804ad30 011c 01fc 0006 1000
04:  0002 1dc4 804adc4 804adc4 0088 0088 0006 0004

Type 1 = loadable, 2 = dynamic info, 3 = interpreter
     4 = note, 6 = program header
```

Table 8.1. Program Header Table for `chmod`

r	w	x
1	1	0

Note that two of the segments are loadable. These are the code and data segments.

Although the linker combines sections into segments, there are sections which are not part of any segment. The Section Header table lists and describes these sections. These parts of an executable file also occur in an object file and are discussed in section 8.8.

Consider the following C program. Program 8.6 prints out pointers. Pointers are just addresses. Because C is a relatively low-level language, we would expect these pointers to be the same as those occurring in the machine code.

8.8   Object Files in ELF Format

Most programs are not written completely from scratch. They rely on programs which have already been written and are used over and over again, such as `printf()`. Files which need other code in order to run are called *object code files*. It is the job of the *linker* to combine object code from different files into an executable file. The code for `printf()`, for example, is located in `/lib/libc.so`. Typically the programmer creates one or two of these object code files using gcc or an assembler, and the rest are retrieved by the linker from standard libraries stored on the system. This process is not obvious from the command line since the linker is called by gcc.

It is important to realize that the creation of an object code file is the main purpose of an assembler. In section refsdefdir assembler commands for shaping object files will be discussed. But first, object code files themselves need to be described. Just as the format of an executable file is prescribed by ELF, so is the format of an object code file. Figure 8-10 shows the structure of an ELF object code file. The ELF Header in an object file is the same as the ELF header in an

```
int a = 0x55555555, b = 0x66666666;
int c = 0x77777777, d = 0x88888888;

main()
{

/* Store numbers which will be very easy to pick out
from the machine code of the compiled program.  */

    a = 0x11111111;
    b = 0x22222222;
    c = 0x33333333;
    d = 0x44444444;

    printf("Variables:  Addresses:\n")
    printf(" a %x\n", &a);
    printf(" b %x\n", &b);
    printf(" c %x\n", &c);
    printf(" d %x\n", &d);

/* %x means to use "hexadecimal" output.  */

    printf("\n");
}
```

Program 8.6

executable file.

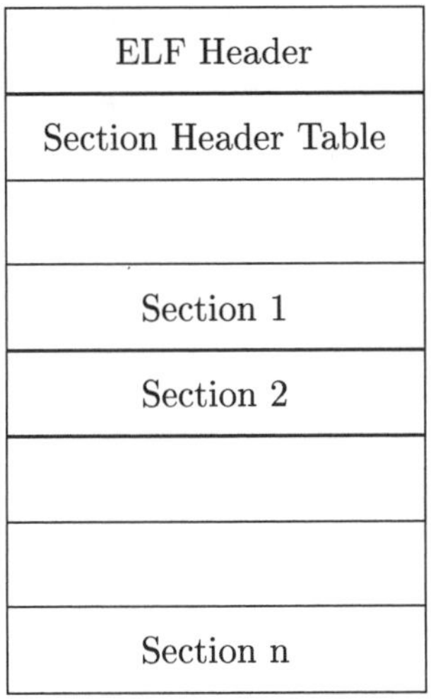

```
┌─────────────────────────────┐
│         ELF Header          │
├─────────────────────────────┤
│    Section Header Table     │
├─────────────────────────────┤
│                             │
├─────────────────────────────┤
│         Section 1           │
├─────────────────────────────┤
│         Section 2           │
├─────────────────────────────┤
│                             │
├─────────────────────────────┤
│                             │
├─────────────────────────────┤
│         Section n           │
└─────────────────────────────┘
```

Figure 8-10. ELF Object File Format

```
01bc:0374 Section Header Table
                    Virtual Off-                   Algn Entry
      Name Type Flgs Address  set  Size Link Info Mod Size
00:   0000 0000 0000 00000000 0000 0000 0000 0000 0000 0000
01:   001b 0001 0006 00000000 0034 0091 0000 0000 0004 0000
02:   0021 0009 0000 00000000 0490 00a0 0009 0001 0004 0008
03:   002b 0001 0003 00000000 00c8 0010 0000 0000 0004 0000
04:   0031 0008 0003 00000000 00d8 0000 0000 0000 0004 0000
05:   0036 0007 0000 00000000 00d8 0014 0000 0000 0001 0000
06:   003c 0001 0002 00000000 00ec 0070 0000 0000 0001 0000
07:   0044 0001 0000 00000000 015c 0012 0000 0000 0001 0000
08:   0011 0003 0000 00000000 016e 004d 0000 0000 0001 0000
09:   0001 0002 0000 00000000 0374 00f0 000a 0009 0004 0010
0a:   0009 0003 0000 00000000 0464 002b 0000 0000 0001 0000

Name:  index into the Section Header String Table (.shstrab)
Type:  1 = Program Bits, 2 = Symbol Table, 3 = String Table
    4 = Relocation Table, 5 = Hash Table, 6 = Dynamic Info
    7 = Note, 8 = No Bits, 9 = Relocation Table
```

Table 8.2. Section Header Table for Program 8.6

8.8.1   Section Header Table

The Section Header table lists all the sections in the object file. The table shown in Table 8.2 was produced by running `ob` on the `.o` file for Program 8.6. The Flags item contains attribute bits, which are somewhat like the permission bits in the program header table of the exectuable file. Bit 2 is 1 if a section is executable. In Table 8.2 the only section with bit 2 set is section 1, which is in fact the text section. Bit 0 is 1 for writeable sections. Only sections 3 and 4 are writeable. Section 3 turns out to be the data section.

8.8.2   Sections

When the linker creates a text segment, it combines the text sections from the object code files. When it creates a data segment, it combines data sections. The linking process involves collating.

When the gnu linker links `.o` files, it needs to designate an address where exececution is to commence. The programmer can designate this by using the label `main` and making sure it is visible to the linker by using the `global` assembler directive.

Further Reading

Understanding ELF Object Files and Debugging Tools, ed. Mary Lou Nohr, Prentice Hall: 1994.

CHAPTER

9

INTERRUPTS

The fetch-execute cycle is a program-driven model of computation. But computers are not totally program driven. To some extent they are hardware driven. CPUs are equipped with input signal pins which allow the fetch-execute cycle to be interrupted. The original purpose of these pins was to increase processor efficiency by reducing the amount of time spent in communication with I/O devices.

In chapter 8 we saw how a device to increase memory efficiency was adopted as a device for controlling memory access. Interrupts have undergone a similar transition. This chapter begins by describing how interrupts economize on processor time. Then, starting with section 9.6, we will see how interrupts are used to control processor access.

9.1 Polling

Without interrupt pins, I/O communication would have to rely on processor instructions such as the IN and OUT commands.

9.1.1 Data Ports

Suppose that a processor is sending characters from a buffer located at ABC to a printer located at port 378H, and that to do this it issues one-byte OUT commands from a loop, as shown in Program 9.1. Then assuming one instruction per machine cycle, each execution of the loop would take five machine cycles. At a clock rate of 100 MHz, all 100,000 characters would be sent to the printer in .005 seconds. This is enough time for the printer to print one or two of them. The printer would be swamped, and most of the output to the printer would be lost.

Printers are slow in comparison to processors. So are most other I/O devices.

9.1.2 Status Ports

To prevent data loss, a printer must have a status port as well as a data port. The processor will then be required to inquire of the status port whether or not the printer is ready to receive another character. The processor will only output another character when the printer is ready.

```
        MOV EDX, 378H   ; Printer Data Port
        MOV ECX, 0      ; Use ECX as the loop counter.
XYZ:    MOV AL, [ABC + ECX]
                        ; ABC is the beginning of the memory area
                        ; that characters are being printed from.
        OUT [DX], AL    ; Send a character to the printer.
        INC ECX
        CMP ECX, 100000 ; Print this many characters.
        JL XYZ
```

Program 9.1

Suppose that the printer with the data port at port 378H also has a status port at port 379H and responds to an inquiry to this port with a 1 when it is ready and with a 0 when it's not. In this case the output loop might look like this: A loop

```
        MOV EDX, 379H   ; Printer status port
        MOV ECX, 0
XYZ:    IN AL, [DX]     ; Ask the printer if it's ready
        CMP AL, 1       ; 1 means it's ready
        JNE XYZ         ; If not try again
        MOV AL, [ABC + ECX]
        DEC EDX         ; Data port is 378H
        OUT [DX], AL    ; Send one byte!
        INC ECX
        INC EDX         ; Put back the status port
        CMP ECX, 100000
        JL XYZ
```

Program 9.2

like this solves the problem of lost data by reducing processor throughput down to the speed of the printer. Most of the processor's time is spent executing the three instructions following the XYZ label.

Successively querying one I/O device after another about its status is called *polling*. Polling makes a modest improvement on this situation by putting an inquiry to all pending I/O devices into one status inquiry loop. But it is still clearly a waste of processor time.

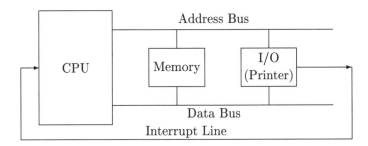

Figure 9-1. A Computer with Only One Interrupt

9.2   External Interrupts

In order to allow programmers to avoid relying on polling, processors have at least one input pin which allows I/O devices to signal the processor when they need the processor to do something. Such a pin is called an *interrupt pin*. An interrupt pin makes it possible for an I/O device to initiate communication with the CPU. A CPU without an interrupt pin has been compared to a telephone without a bell.

Suppose that a printer is connected to an interrupt pin on the CPU, as shown in Figure 9-1. With the printer hooked up to the CPU in this way, the CPU would be able to ignore the printer until it received a signal. It could then process a printer character and return to its main job. There would be relatively little wasted time. This setup would work fine if the printer were the only I/O device which ever needed attention. But of course there are many such devices.

To allow for several I/O devices, one might expect there to be several interrupt pins on the processor. The x86 architecture does not do things this way. It has only one general-purpose interrupt pin. It delegates the arbitration of interrupt signals to an external circuit called the *interrupt controller circuit*, as shown in Figure 9-2. This figure also shows an IRQ bus from the I/O system to the interrupt controller circuit. An IRQ bus consists of wires from various I/O devices. Each device that needs interrupt service is given one of the wires on this bus, assuming that there are enough of them to go around, that is. The IRQ bus wires are numbered IRQ0, IRQ1, etc. IRQ stands for *interrupt request* line. The numbers 0, 1, etc., encountered in this context are called *IRQ numbers*.

The interrupt controller allows several I/O devices to have a signal path to the CPU even though the x86 has only one general-purpose interrupt pin.

9.2.1   x86 Interrupt Handling

When an x86 processor receives an interrupt signal, it first completes the instruction it is currently working on. Then, provided a special flag has not been cleared, it handles the interrupt in three steps.

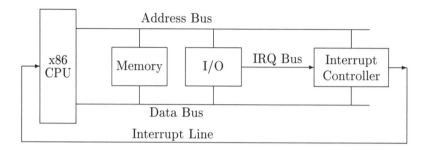

Figure 9-2. A Computer with an Interrupt Controller

1. It reads the number of the interrupt responsible for the interrupt signal from the interrupt controller.

2. It fetches the address of the correct interrupt service routine from the interrupt table in memory.

3. It transfers control to the interrupt service routine.

Once the interrupt has been handled, it resumes processing where it left off. Interrupt service routines are somewhat like ordinary subroutines. One important difference is that they are called on signal from the hardware.

The Interrupt Acknowledge Bus Cycle

Since the x86 receives its general interrupts all via one pin, it cannot tell from a single "knock on the door" which I/O device is signaling for attention. As shown in Figure 9-2, the interrupt controller circuit is connected to the data bus just like memory and I/O. To get the required identification from the interrupt controller, the processor performs a read, which is analogous to a memory or an I/O read. It is called the *interrupt acknowledge bus cycle*. Just as the processor uses the M/IO# pin to indicate whether it is commanding a memory or an I/O read, it uses the D/C# pin to distinguish an I/O controller read from the memory and I/O read cycles. D is for data and C is for code. The complete list of the bus cycles defined by the D/C#, M/IO#, and W/R# pins is given in Table 9.1.

When the processor receives an interrupt, it initiates an interrupt acknowledge bus cycle. Only the interrupt controller may respond to an interrupt acknowledge bus cycle. It responds by depositing a one-byte number on the bottom eight bits of the data bus. This number is called the *interrupt number*. It is not the same as an IRQ number. The processor reads the interrupt number off the data bus.

	D/C#	M/IO#	W/R#
Interrupt Acknowledge	0	0	0
Halt/Special Cycle	0	0	1
Code Read	0	1	0
reserved	0	1	1
I/O Read	1	0	0
I/O Write	1	0	1
Memory Read	1	1	0
Memory Write	1	1	1

Table 9.1. 486 Bus Cycle Definition Pins

ISR Address Fetching

The processor then takes this number and uses it as an index into a table called the Interrupt Descriptor Table. This table contains the addresses of the Interrupt Service Routines. See Figure 9-3. Since the interrupt number is an eight-bit number, the valid interrupt numbers range from 0 to 255.

It is the responsibility of the operating system to create this table. It is also responsible for loading into memory the interrupt service routines whose addresses are listed in this table. These two jobs are done as a part of the system boot. If they have not been done, the system will be unable to respond to interrupts. When Edlinas displays a "Processor halted" message, it is usually because it is trying to respond to an interrupt and no interrupt table has been built.

The Interrupt Descriptor Table

The x86 has a dedicated register which stores the address of the interrupt descriptor table, or IDT. It is called the IDT register. There are special commands for accessing this register. The command

    LIDT mem

loads the register. The command

    SIDT mem

stores the contents of this register. The LIDT command is used in setting up the operating system at boot time. Once an interrupt descriptor table has been created, the LIDT command can point the processor to it.

In responding to an interrupt, the x86 uses the fact that each table entry occupies eight bytes of space. Consequently, if b is the address stored in the IDT register, then in response to the interrupt numbered n, the x86 fetches the eight bytes starting at the address $b + 8 \times n$. These eight-byte entries are called gates.

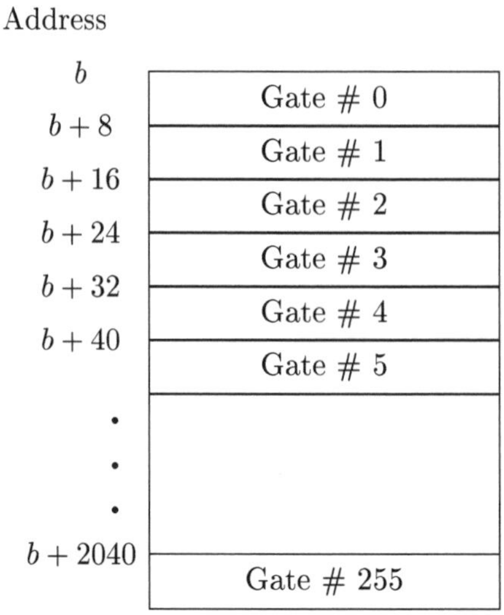

Address

Figure 9-3. Interrupt Descriptor Table, b = IDT register

ISR Execution

Once the address of the interrupt service routine is obtained, it is treated almost like a CALL instruction treats an address. Before jumping to a target address a CALL instruction pushes the next address after its own address onto the stack. This means that the called routine may return to the instruction following the CALL by reading its address off the stack. Since an interrupt service routine also needs to execute a return the address of the instruction which would otherwise have been executed, had the interrupt not arrived, is pushed onto the stack before the ISR is executed. But in the case of an interrupt, the flags register is pushed also. The interrupt service routine does whatever business is demanded by the interrupt. An interrupt service routine should end with an IRET, instruction which is like a RET instruction except that it pops the flags register.

The flags register is a 32-bit register named EFLAGS, which contains all the flags. It is an extension of the 16-bit FLAGS register. Table 9.2 shows the flags in the EFLAGS register on a 486.

The reason for the x86's special flag behavior when responding to interrupts has to do with the problem of interrupt arbitration.

9.2.2   Interrupting an Interrupt

What happens when an interrupt occurs while an ISR is already executing? Can one device interrupt another's ISR? Imagine two devices, each refusing to be pre-empted by the other's ISR. The processor would get bounced back and forth from

Bits	Label	Full Name
18	AC	Alignment Check
17	VM	Virtual 8086 Mode
16	RF	Restart Flag
14	NT	Nested Task
13-12	IOPL	I/O Privilege Level
11	OF	Overflow Flag
10	DF	Direction Flag
9	IF	Interrupt Enable Flag
8	TF	Trap Flag
7	SF	Sign Flag
6	ZF	Zero Flag
4	AF	ASCII Overflow Flag
2	PF	Parity Flag
0	CF	Carry Flag

Table 9.2. EFLAGS Register

one ISR to the other until the accumulation of pending return addresses on the stack overflowed and caused the system to crash.

The Interrupt Enable Flag

The design of the 8086 allows for a very simple way to avoid this situation. The idea would be to enforce a strict "one-at-a-time" interrupt policy. It would work by automatically blocking interrupt signals while an ISR is running, and then unblocking them when it is finished. One of the flags on the x86 processor is called the *interrupt enable flag*. When this flag is cleared, all signals on the general-purpose interrupt pin are ignored. When an 8086 enters an ISR, this flag is automatically cleared. That is why the processor pushes the flags register onto the stack just before entering an ISR. It allows the interrupt enable flag to be restored to its original state when the ISR is done. When the interrupt enable flag is set, interrupts are handled normally.

The one-at-a-time interrupt policy would make life easy for the interrupt controller. The controller could process an incoming interrupt by just passing it along to the processor until it was acknowledged. As soon as the interrupt acknowledge was received, the controller could wash its hands of that interrupt because the processor could be counted upon to work on it nonstop until it was done.

Although the one-at-a-time policy is very easy to implement on an x86 processor, standard PCs do not use it. The problem with it is that interrupts that need a quick response can be kept waiting. If a serial port is getting ready to start trashing data because its buffer is full, then it should not be made to wait while a floppy drive looks for a good sector. A processor with a one-at-a-time interrupt policy can be like a household with a single, occupied bathroom. Unlike the situation with bathrooms, however, interrupting an ISR is not necessarily rude. It sometimes makes good sense to interrupt an ISR.

Nested Interrupts

Most computers prioritize interrupts and then allow higher priority interrupts to interrupt those of lower priority. This kind of policy is called a *nested interrupt* policy. Implementing a nested interrupt policy on an x86 requires that both the interrupt controller and the programmer be given more responsibility. On the x86 the programmer has control over the interrupt enable flag. The

   STI

command sets the interrupt enable flag. The

   CLI

command clears it. By including an STI command at the beginning of an ISR, the programmer can override the default one-at-a-time policy and make an ISR interruptible. Interrupts cannot be nested if they execute with the interrupt enable flag cleared.

There is also more work for the interrupt controller. If the x86 executes ISRs with the interrupt enable flag set, then the interrupt controller has to assume responsibility for enforcing the priority system. Since the processor has its guard down, the interrupt controller must not let every incoming interrupt pass through. Otherwise, as noted above, the ISRs could play ping-pong with the processor. In particular, the controller is responsible for not interrupting an interrupt unless the ISR being interrupted has a lower priority than the one it is allowing through. If the ISR executing has equal or higher priority, then the pending interrupt must wait until the ISR is finished. But in order for the controller to hold off the pending interrupt until then, it needs to know when the ISR gets done. It needs a signal. Without a signal it has no way of knowing. If it doesn't know whether a high priority ISR is finished executing, then it cannot decide whether it is okay to interrupt the CPU with a low priority interrupt or not. Since the interrupt controller has its own read cycle, one might expect a write cycle for this purpose.

The EOI Command

Since the x86 does not have an I/O controller write cycle, it falls to the lot of the programmer to include an "All Done" message to the interrupt controller at the end of each ISR. This message is called an EOI, or *end of interrupt* command.

So that the interrupt controller can receive communications from the processor, it has an I/O address. The programmer can then use an OUT command to issue the EOI. The I/O address is also used when the interrupt controller gets programmed. As noted above, it needs to be programmed so that it knows what interrupt numbers to report.

As a device with an I/O address, the interrupt controller looks like just any other I/O device. But it is special in that it is the only I/O device that can signal the processor directly. All the others must go through the interrupt controller.

9.2.3 The NMI and RESET Interrupts

Besides the general-purpose interrupt pin on the x86, there are two other interrupt pins. They are the NMI and RESET pins.

A signal on the NMI, or *nonmaskable interrupt* pin, is not blocked by clearing the interrupt enable flag. It does not trigger an interrupt acknowledge bus cycle. It is serviced by interrupt service routine number 2. It is used to signal parity errors in memory or power supply problems.

The RESET pin is intended for use in situations where there may be no interrupt descriptor table in memory. For example, when the computer is being turned on. Consequently, there is no point in storing an address for it in the interrupt table. Instead the address is built into the processor. That address is FFFFFFF0H (or FFFF0H on the 8086). It is easily remembered as −16 in two's complement. The read-only memory at this address must contain a jump instruction whose target is the POST, or Power On Self Test, program. This program is located on the ROM chip called the *BIOS*. Read-only BIOS chips are sometimes made by the computer manufacturer, but are more often bought from a third party such as American Megatrends or Phoenix. The POST can be thought of as the ISR for the RESET interrupt. The final act of the POST is to initiate the boot sequence. The RESET pin is connected to the power supply and often to a button on the front of the computer.

9.3 ISA Architecture

The *ISA architecture* is essentially the architecture of the IBM AT   computer. The AT is an 80286-based computer introduced in 1984. The name ISA, or *Industry Standard Architecture*, arose in reaction to the introduction by IBM of a new architecture called *Microchannel* in their PS/2 computers. Microchannel was intended to replace the very popular architecture of the AT. Many third parties manufactured cards which could be inserted into the expansion slots of an AT, or an AT clone. The reaction of these third parties to IBM's new architecture, which would have made all their AT cards obsolete, was to band together and rename the AT architecture the Industry Standard Architecture. As a result, the lifespan of the AT architecture was given a considerable extension. Many important architectural features were standardized in the ISA, including

- the interrupt controller circuit

- many IRQ assignments

- many I/O port assignments

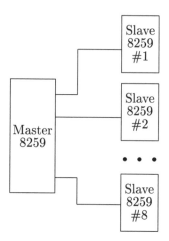

Figure 9-4. General 8259 Configuration

- the signals and connections made available to expansion cards

- the physical connectors used on expansion cards

Many of these features have been retained in all subsequent x86 computers.

9.3.1   The 8259 Interrupt Controller

The ISA interrupt controller circuit is based on the Intel 8259 PIC, or *programmable interrupt controller*. The 8259 is the interrupt controller circuit used in the original IBM PC. 8259s may be used either singly as in the PC or combined into a two-tiered structure with one *master* and anywhere from one to eight *slaves*, as shown in Figure 9-4. In the original PC there was a single 8259. A one master–one slave configuration became fixed as a part of the ISA architecture. The ISA interrupt controller circuit is shown in Figure 9-5. In this configuration there are 15 IRQ lines which feed into the two 8259 circuits.

If the interrupt numbers reported by the 8259 were built in, then the different controllers in this configuration, shown in Figure 9-4, would all report the same set of numbers. This would clearly not be satisfactory. The reason for having a controller circuit is so that different wires on the IRQ bus can generate different interrupt numbers. Consequently, different 8259s need to report different interrupt numbers. The only reasonably easy way to do this was to make the 8259 programmable. An 8259 can be programmed to report any eight consecutive numbers starting at any multiple of 8 less than 256. Programming of the 8259 is done at boot time using OUT commands. The EOI command in 8259 language is 20H. In the ISA architecture the master 8259 is assigned the data port 20H (Could this be geek humor at work?) as well as 21H. The slave is assigned the ports 0A0H and 0A1H.

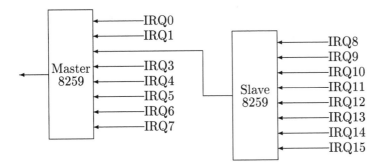

Figure 9-5. ISA Interrupt Controller Circuit

An EOI command in response to an interrupt from the slave controller is sent to both A0H and 20H.

9.3.2 IRQs

Most of these IRQ lines have specified purposes in the ISA architecture. All of them have fixed interrupt numbers. While one interrupt is being serviced or while the interrupt flag is cleared, unserviced interrupts may pile up. The interrupt controller circuit prioritizes these interrupts in the order IRQ0, IRQ1, IRQ8, ..., IRQ15, IRQ3, IRQ4, ..., IRQ7. IRQ0 has the highest priority. IRQ7 has the lowest. The fact that there are only a few IRQ lines available has lead to IRQ conflicts, IRQ sharing, as well as switches on cards which allow an IRQ line to be changed.

Linux maintains a count of the interrupt requests which come in on the IRQ lines. To see this count, you may use the command

```
linuxbox$ cat /proc/interrupts
```

The output of this command should be compared with Table 9.3.

9.4   Internal and Software Interrupts

Interrupts which do not arise as the result of an external signal on an interrupt pin also exist.

9.4.1 Exceptions

Suppose that the fetch-execute cycle encounters the machine code F0FH. This machine code is not defined. Suppose a MOV instruction attempts to access a memory

IRQ	Allocation	Interrupt Number
IRQ0	System Timer	08H
IRQ1	Keyboard	09H
IRQ3	Serial Port #2	0BH
IRQ4	Serial Port #1	0CH
IRQ5	Parallel Port #2	0DH
IRQ6	Floppy Controller	0EH
IRQ7	Parallel Port #1	0FH
IRQ8	Real Time Clock	70H
IRQ9	available	71H
IRQ10	available	72H
IRQ11	available	73H
IRQ12	Mouse	74H
IRQ13	87 ERROR line	75H
IRQ14	Hard Drive Controller	76H
IRQ15	available	77H

Table 9.3. ISA Interrupt Routings

address to which the operating system has not given permission. Suppose that the DIV command produces a quotient which is too big for the destination register. Suppose that the stack overflows. These are situations where the designers of the x86 preferred to delegate to the operating system the decision as to what action should be taken. In fact, they forced the operating system to take over at these points by assigning interrupt numbers to these *exceptions*. These interrupt numbers are built into the x86 processors. Exceptions do not use interrupt acknowledge bus cycles. But they must be handled by numbered ISRs, just as external interrupts are.

Table 9.4 lists the exceptions which are built into the x86 processors. Note that some of these interrupt numbers are the same as the interrupt numbers reported by an ISA interrupt controller. When interrupts are shared like this, the ISR is stuck with the responsibility for distinguishing which situation has caused the interrupt.

9.4.2   Software Interrupts

In order to make the interrupt service routines accessible to programmers, the INT instruction was added to the instruction set. The syntax is simply

    INT imm

where the immediate value is any one-byte number. This instruction can be used to execute any interrupt service routine. It is similar to a CALL instruction.

Allocation	Interrupt Number
Division Overflow	00H
Single Step	01H
NMI	02H
Breakpoint	03H
Interrupt on Overflow	04H
BOUND out of range	05H
Invalid Machine Code	06H
87 Not Available	07H
Double Fault	08H
87 Segment Overrun	09H
Invalid Task State Segment	0AH
Segment Not Present	0BH
Stack Overflow	0CH
General Protection Error	0DH
Page Fault	0EH
reserved	0FH
87 Error	10H

Table 9.4. Built-in Hardware Exceptions

	Ordinary Subroutine	Interrupt Service Routine
Invoke	CALL	INT
Terminate	RET	IRET

Table 9.5. An Interrupt is Like a Subroutine

9.4.3 Faults and Traps

When the service routine for an external interrupt or a software interrupt finishes, control is transferred to the next instruction following the interrupt just as it would be following the completion of a subroutine call. This is usually not the case with hardware exceptions. When the service routines for most exceptions are completed, the instruction giving rise to them is retried. Hardware exceptions for which this is true are called *faults*. A good example of a fault is a page fault. A page fault occurs when a failure to access memory has occurred because it has been paged out to the disk. The interrupt service routine pages it back in again, and then the original instruction is retried.

A few hardware exceptions are like ordinary interrupts, and pass control to the next instruction when they finish. These are called *traps*. An example of a trap is division overflow on an 8086.

9.5   System Calls

One of the basic functions of an operating system is to provide access to hardware
devices, as illustrated in Figure 8-1. In Unix all access to hardware devices is
provided by way of what are called *system calls*. Users ordinarily get access by
using either standard Unix commands, such as `cat`, or `ls`, or by using C library
functions, such as `printf()`, or `scanf()`. But both Unix commands and C library
functions rely on system calls to gain hardware access. See Figure 9-6. `read()`
and `write()` are examples of system calls. The `write()` system call takes three
parameters: a file to be written to, a memory buffer to be written from, and the
number of bytes to be written. It appears to be an ordinary C function and can be
used as though it were. Program 9.3 illustrates a "Hello world" program using the
`write()` system call.

```
main()
{
    char s[] = "Hello world!\n";

    write(1,s,13);
}
```

Program 9.3

But despite appearances, the `write()` system call is not an ordinary C function.
Like all system calls in Linux, it uses INT 80H to transfer control to the kernel. Each
system call in Linux has a number. A list of these calls and their numbers can be
found in `/usr/src/linux/arch/i-386/unistd.h`. In Linux 2.0, `write()` is system
call number 4. To carry out this system call, the number 4 must be stored in the
EAX register before INT 80H is called.

In DOS, many system calls are made using INT 21H. The number stored in the
AH register determines which system call is being made. A list of most of these calls
can be found in standard books on DOS. The book *Undocumented DOS* by Andrew
Schulman, et. al., attempts to list all of them. The existence of undocumented DOS
system calls gave rise to considerable bitterness on the part of developers who could
have put such functions to good use had they but known of them. Needless to say,
programmers at Microsoft did not encounter this obstacle.

To use a system call from assembler, it is necessary to know the parameter
passing conventions. These conventions are established by macros also located
in `unistd.h`. According to the conventions used in Linux 2.2, the parameters
are stored in left to right order in the registers EBX, ECX, EDX, EDI, and ESI
respectively, using as many of these registers as are needed to store the parameters.

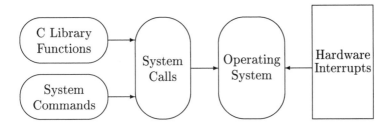

Figure 9-6. System Calls are Just Software Interrupts

The system call, write(1, s, 13), for example, can be completed if 13 is stored in EBX, the string pointer is stored in ECX, and 1 is stored in EDX. Program 9.4 illustrates this. In debugging system calls, the strace utility is invaluable. For example, after getting an a.out from gcc from for Program 9.4 we could use

        linuxbox$ strace a.out

to check on things in the event of difficulty.

```
        ; This program makes a system call.
        ;
        global main
main:
        MOV EAX, 4      ; Write is system call # 4.
        MOV EBX, 1      ; 1 is number for standard output.
        MOV ECX, ABC    ; ABC is the string pointer.
        MOV EDX, 13     ; Writing 13 bytes.
        INT 80H         ; System call interrupt.
        RET
ABC:    db "Hello world!",0AH,0
```

Program 9.4

The resources offered by Linux to the programmer are essentially defined by the capabilities of the system calls. One reason for the success of Linux early on was that it was designed to adhere to the POSIX standard for the programmer's system interface. Linux was one of the first operating systems to achieve POSIX compliance. Windows NT is also POSIX-compliant.

9.6   Privilege Levels

When a system call takes over the processor, it does so because a program needs the kernel to do something which it is unable to do for itself, like read a file or write to the monitor. The program is incapable of these things because the processor itself is blocked from doing them while user code is executing. The difference between kernel code and user code is a difference in *privilege level*. Since the 286, a protection system based on a system of four different privilege levels has been in place. The four levels are

- 0 System level privilege, used by the Linux kernel.

- 1 Unused in Linux.

- 2 Unused in Linux.

- 3 User level privilege, used by Linux user programs.

The privilege level of the currently executing code is called the *current privilege level*. It is stored in a two-bit register called the CPL register.

9.6.1   The CPL Register

The CPL register is one of the most important registers on the machine. Level 0 has the most privilege. Changing the CPL value to 0 is like disengaging the safety catch on the processor. It takes place every time a system call is executed. It is a more drastic step than becoming superuser. From the standpoint of CPL-based privilege, the superuser is just another user. But when the CPL is 0, the processor can do things that *no* user can do. For example, it can modify the page tables or change the interrupt descriptor table.

Of course, given that `root` is the owner of the disk image of the kernel, the file `vmlinuz` in the root directory, `root` can do whatever it wants indirectly by changing this file. `root` can also modify kernel code which is stored in modules. But these changes will only take effect the next time the system is booted or a kernel module is loaded.

9.6.2   Privileged Instructions

The LIDT instruction changes the address stored in the IDT register. This is the address that the processor goes to when it receives an interrupt. This instruction has the effect of changing from one interrupt table to another one. If used by a user, it could be used to take control of all interrupts by sending the processor to a private table for the handling of all interupts. It is a good example of what is called a *privileged instruction*. The processor will not execute a privileged instruction unless the CPL = 0. If this instruction is included in code which is executing while the CPL > 0, for example, in user code where the CPL = 3, it causes an exception called a *general protection error*. See Table 9.4.

The MOV mnemonic names an instruction that can be used to access the control registers. The command

MOV reg, reg

where one **reg** is a control register and the other is a 32-bit general register, can be used to load a value into CR3, for example. CR3 holds the address of the page table table where address translation begins. Loading a new value into CR3 has the effect of changing from one set of page tables to another. If this could be done by a user, the user could take control of physical memory. MOV used with control registers is another good example of a privileged instruction.

9.6.3 Stack Problems

Since the ISR code that the interrupt is jumping to may well use the stack, it is important that the stack not be subject to write access by the user. Even though user code will not function again until the ISR exits, there can still be trouble. For example, suppose that the system call **read()** is being executed. **read()** transfers data from a file to user memory. One of the parameters to this call is the address of some memory that the user has permission to write on. In executing the call, the system will store file data at that address. If the stack being used by the system is the user's stack, then the user has permission to write on it. The user may then supply the stack address as parameter to **read()** and the system will then mess up the stack it is using at the very time it is using it. This would cause a crash.

User code writes where it shouldn't, usually by mistake and not out of malice. But it happens a lot. That's why the Segmentation Fault error message is so gallingly familiar. Code for system calls like **read()** needs to use its own stack. There is a different stack for each value of the CPL. Changing stacks is taken care of by the hardware! Each stack has its own stack pointer. These four stack pointers are stored in a memory area called the *Task State Segment*.

The layout of a gate is built into the x86 processor. Figure 9-7 shows the most important fields in a gate. These fields contain two items that pertain to this

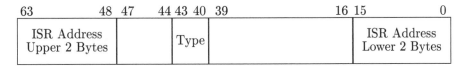

Figure 9-7. Gate Layout

discussion. They are

- A four-bit type value which is stored in bits 40–43.

- The address of the ISR. This 32-bit address is located in bits 48–63 and bits 0–15 of the table entry.

Interrupt gates are used for hardware interrupts. A trap gate is used for the INT 80H system call interrupt.

9.7   Control Transfer

Based on the two items of information gleaned from the gate, the actions discussed in sections 9.7.1 through 9.7.4 are taken.

9.7.1   Clear the Interrupt Enable Flag?

When the x86 loads a descriptor table entry in response to an interrupt, the four-bit type value is checked to see if the interrupt enable flag should be cleared. If the type value is 14, the interrupt enable flag is cleared just as it is on the 8086. Twelve of the 16 possible four-bit values are defined.

Type Value	Gate Type	Clear IE Flag
14	Interrupt Gate	Yes
15	Trap Gate	No

Table 9.6. Interrupt Gates vs. Trap Gates

9.7.2   Store 0 into the CPL

The next step in the processing of an interrupt is that 0 is loaded into the CPL. Confidence in the safety of this step must be based on confidence in the code that is being jumped to.

The original value of the CPL is restored when the IRET instruction executes. The mechanism behind the CPL store and restore is discussed in chapter 13.

9.7.3   Change Stacks

The ESP used by the kernel is waiting in the task state segment. The ESP corresponding to CPL = 0 is loaded from there into ESP when 0 is loaded into the CPL. The current ESP is not stored in the task state segment. It is pushed onto the new stack.

The fact that the task state segment is not changed when 0 is stored into the CPL is sometimes what is meant by saying that the kernel is executing "within" a task or "in behalf of" a task. In other words, there is no task switch involved. The same task is still running.

9.7.4   Jump to the ISR

To do the jump, the return address of the next instruction is pushed onto the new stack. The new EIP is then loaded with the 32-bit address from the gate.

When these four steps have been completed, control has been transferred to kernel code, which runs at CPL = 0. The resources of the processor, which are accessible from this level of privilege, include all the data structures vital to the functioning of the operating system as well as the hardware and the memory.

When the ISR is concluded, then with one exception, control is returned to the user code. Both the old stack and the CPL are restored. The exception is in the case of the timer interrupt.

9.8 Scheduling

In Table 9.3 we see that the maskable interrupt with the highest priority is the timer interrupt. The ISR for this interrupt keeps track of time used by all processes. In particular, it sets a flag called `need_resched` when a process is out of time. When Linux does a return from any interrupt, the timer interrupt included, it checks this flag, and calls the `schedule()` if `need_resched` is set. The `schedule()` system call is the *scheduler*. It is the central program in the operating system. It determines which process gets to run next. When necessary, it initiates a task switch.

So the ultimate computing resource, processor time, also falls under the control of the CPL-based protection system.

Further Reading

ISA System Architecture, Tom Shanley and Don Anderson, Addison-Wesley: 1995.

Interrupt-Driven PC System Design, Joseph McGivern, Annabooks: 1998.

10

BIT MANIPULATIONS

10.1   Bitwise Logic Operations

In chapter 3, section 3.3, circuits and truth tables for the Boolean operations AND, OR, NOT, and XOR were discussed. The truth table for AND is

p	q	(p AND q)
1	1	1
1	0	0
0	1	0
0	0	0

and is implemented using the Boolean circuit

If eight of these Boolean circuits are used in parallel, then two eight-bit numbers,

    1111 0101
    1100 0011

when fed into the eight AND gates, result in one eight-bit output:

    1100 0001

The operation is carried out as shown in Figure 10-1. In hex notation, the bytes F5H and C3H used as inputs to a one-byte AND operation have produced the output C1H. This operation can be applied to any number of bits. The Boolean operations OR, XOR, and NOT can also be applied in bitwise parallel fashion.

10.2   The AND, OR, NOT, and XOR Commands

High-level programming languages include support for Boolean operations such as AND, OR, and NOT. They rely on assembler and machine-level implementation of these operations.

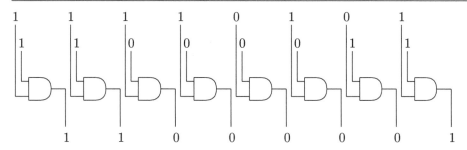

Figure 10-1. Bitwise AND Operation

The AND instruction applies the AND operation to two operands in much the same way that the ADD instruction adds two operands. The following forms are all valid for the AND command:

    AND reg,imm
    AND reg,reg

As with the ADD commands, a memory operand can take the place of one register operand. Also like the ADD command, the two operands must have the same size. For example, suppose that the AL register contains 0F5H and BL contains 0C3H. Then the command

    AND AL, BL

would store the result 0C1H into AL and leave BL unchanged.

Except for the fact that they apply different operations, the OR and XOR commands are the same as the AND command. The NOT instruction takes only one operand, register or memory.

Edlinas can be used to check the results of applying these commands. For example,

    MOV EAX, 0F5H
    MOV EBX, 0C3H
    AND AL, BL

should result in the storage of 0C1H in AL.

All these logic commands clear the overflow and carry flags. They set the sign flag if the most significant bit of the result is 1, and clear it otherwise. They set the zero flag if the result is 0 and clear it otherwise. The zero flag is often used to determine conditional jumps following logic commands.

For example, we can use the AND command to determine whether a number stored in a register is even or odd. A number represented in binary is even when its least significant bit is zero. If we have a one-bye register, then the AND instruction can be applied to it, using the binary number 0000 0001 as the source operand.

Then all the bits of the result will be 0, except possibly the least significant bit. This bit will be 0 if the number being tested is even.

```
MOV BL, AL    ; Prepare to test AL for evenness
AND BL, 1     ; The zero flag is set if BL = 0
JZ EVN        ; Jump if AL is even.
```

The TEST instruction is like the CMP instruction in that it sets flags without storing the result. CMP is an unstored SUB instruction. TEST is an unstored AND instruction. Using TEST, the three instructions used to test the evenness of AL can be shortened to just two.

```
TEST AL, 1
JZ EVN        ; Jump if AL is even.
```

10.3   Bit Setting and Testing

One virtue of logic operations is that they give the programmer control over individual bits of memory or I/O registers.

10.3.1   Turning the Speaker On and Off

The system board speaker is another relatively fixed feature of the standard PC. Its audio signal comes from a 1.19318 MHz square wave. To get control over the speaker's pitch, this signal is divided by the number stored in the two-byte register located at I/O address 42H. This register must be written to using two successive one-byte writes, most significant byte first. Whether the speaker is turned on or not is controlled by the bottom two bits of a very important one-byte register located at I/O address 61H. Some of the bits of this register indicate parity errors in memory. Reports of these errors cause the system to halt! Consequently, we don't want to flip one of them idly or accidentally. The AND and OR instructions are perfectly suited for changing some bits and leaving the others alone. For example, to turn the speaker on, the following three commands are needed:

```
IN AL, [61H]
OR AL, 3
OUT [61H], AL
```

To turn them off,

```
IN AL, [61H]
AND AL, 0FCH
OUT [61H], AL
```

will do.

It should be noted that in Linux, access to I/O ports by users is, by default at least, prohibited. I/O permissions can be given to a process, however, by the system calls `ioperm()` and `iopl()`, which are specially adapted to the x86 architecture.

10.3.2   Edge vs. Level Triggered IRQ Bits

The 8259 programmable interrupt controller discussed in chapter 9, section 9.2 has a register which determines whether the interrupts it receives will be processed as *edge-triggered* or *level-triggered*. There is one bit for each of the eight IRQ lines that it handles. The difference between the two triggering modes is important. If an I/O device uses level-triggered signaling and the 8259 treats its IRQ as edge-triggered, then interrupt signals from the I/O device could be ignored. By using bit manipulation commands, it is possible to single out one bit on this register and change it.

For example, suppose that we are installing a card which sends out edge-triggered interrupt requests on IRQ4. (IRQ4 is the request line conventionally associated with COM1.) On an EISA machine the register which controls this triggering is located at I/O port 4D0H. It is called an ELCR (Edge/Level Control Register). Each 0 bit makes the corresponding IRQ line edge-triggered; each 1 bit causes level triggering. The simplest way to make IRQ4 edge triggered would be to write a 0 to this port.

```
MOV AL,0
MOV EDX, 4D0H; ELCR's address is 4D0H.
OUT [DX], AL ; Store a zero in the ELCR.
```

But this would be a bad idea. It would make all eight bits in the ELCR 0. Any of the IRQs which happened to use level triggering would get fouled up. To set them all correctly, we must know what all the triggerings are for all eight inputs, or we can just leave them as they are except for the fourth bit. To make bit 4 zero, we can OR the contents of the ELCR with the binary number 1110 1111 = EFH. To do that we need to read from the ELCR, do the masking, and then write back to it.

```
MOV EDX, 4D0H   ; ELCR's address is 4D0H.
IN AL, [DX]     ; Read the ELCR register.
AND AL, 0EFH    ; Mask out bit 4.
OUT [DX], AL    ; Write altered byte back out to the ELCR.
```

Program 10.1

10.3.3   Disallowing Non—maskable Interrupts

On ISA machines, non—maskable interrupts can be stopped before they get to the processor. They run through a gate which is controlled by bit 7 of an I/O register located at port 70H. If this bit is 0, NMIs are allowed. Memory problems can cause a nonmaskable interrupt to occur. Suppose that we want to circumvent this safeguard by shutting off NMIs. To make bit 7 equal to 1 we can OR the contents of the I/O register with 1000 0000 = 80H.

```
IN AL, [70H]        ; Read the byte.
OR AL, 80H          ; Mask out bit 4.
OUT [70H], AL       ; Write altered byte back out.
```

Program 10.2

10.4   Shift Instructions

Registers which can shift bits right or left are called *shift registers*. Suppose that a 16-bit shift register contains the binary number

0110 1011 0011 1111

Shifting this number to the right by one bit yields

0011 0101 1001 1111

and sets the carry flag, since the rightmost bit was 1. Shift registers are part of the standard repertoire of microprocessors. In the x86, the bit which is "lost" is generally stored in the carry flag. Hence following the shift just shown, the carry flag would be set. Where the "new" bit comes from depends on which shift command is used. When the new bit is 0, the shift is referred to as a *logical shift*. Notice that shifting the number 6

0110

to the right by one bit in this manner

0011

yields 3. A rightward shift may thus be used to accomplish division by two. The logical shift, however, fails to do this correctly on signed numbers. An eight-bit two's complement value such as -4

1111 1100

when shifted to the right by one using a logical shift

0111 1110

yields 126, not -2. If what we really want is to divide by two, then the new leftmost bit should be copied from the old one. In this case we would get

1111 1110

instead, which actually is -2. This kind of a shift is referred to as an *arithmetic shift*, or sometimes also as a *sign-extended shift*. Since an arithmetic shift produces an erroneous division when a large unsigned value is used, the latter term is a probably better one. The problem does not occur with leftward shifts. The commands for rightward logical and arithmetic shifts are

SHR reg, imm
SHR reg, CL
SAR reg, imm
SAR reg, CL

where the immediate value must be a one-byte number. Leftward shifts use the mnemonics **SHL** and **SAL**. These two mnemonics actually refer to the same opcodes. They have the same valid forms as **SHR** and **SAR**. In all these cases, a memory operand may replace the register operand.

When the "lost" bit is recycled as the "new" bit, the shift is referred to as a *rotate*. **ROL** and **ROR** are mnemonics for rotate left and rotate right. Just as in the logical and arithmetic shifts, the carry flag takes on the value of the rotated bit. But it does not participate in the rotation. To include the carry bit into the cycle, use the **RCR** and **RCL** commands. **RCL** and **RCR** refer to rotate through carry left and rotate through carry right. Table 10.1 illustrates the effect of each of these rotate instructions, assuming that before the rotate instruction is executed AL is 0011 1101 and CF = 1.

Before		Shift	After	
AL Register	CF	Command	AL Register	CF
0011 1101	1	ROR AL,1	1001 1110	1
0011 1101	1	ROL AL,1	0111 1010	0
0011 1101	1	RCR AL,1	1001 1110	1
0011 1101	1	RCL AL,1	0111 1011	0

Table 10.1. Rotate Instructions on AL = 0011 1101, CF = 1

Shift registers are used by the processor to perform multiplication. The 8080 processor does not have a multiplication command. But it does have shift commands. A program like the following can be used to do multiplication using shift commands:

```
              IN EAX, [0]
              MOV ECX, EAX      ; multiplier
              IN EAX, [0]
              MOV EBX, EAX      ; multiplicand
              XOR EAX           ; Initialize the total
AGN:          CMP ECX, 0        ; Is multiplier 0 yet?
              JE DUN
              TEST ECX, 1       ; Is bottom bit of multiplier 1
              JZ SKP            ; If so add the multiplicand
              ADD EAX, EBX      ; Add shifted multiplicand to the total
              JC BAD            ; A carry here is an overflow
SKP:          SHL EBX, 1        ; Multiplicand goes left
              JC BAD            ; Better not overflow here either
              SHR ECX, 1        ; Shift the multiplier to the right
              JMP AGN
DUN:          OUT [1], EAX      ;
BAD:          RET               ; No output if multiplication overflows
```

Program 10.3

11

DEVICE DRIVERS

In chapter 6, the use of memory commands was discussed assuming that the programmer has unrestricted access to memory. In chapter 8, the use of memory commands in user programs where Linux restricts memory access is discussed. In chapter 4, section 4.2, the use of I/O commands is discussed, again assuming that the programmer has unrestricted I/O access. Although there are system commands whose purpose is to grant I/O access to a user, the default situation in Linux disallows the use of IN and OUT instructions in user programs. User access to peripherals takes place only by way of sytem calls. System calls translate user service requests into IN and OUT instructions. Because system calls execute at privilege level zero, these I/O instructions can be executed.

A device driver consists of all the programs needed to translate system calls to a particular device into I/O instructions to that device, plus a program to handle interrupt service requests issued by the device. All the programs in the device driver are incorporated into the Linux kernel. Over half the code in Linux is device driver code.

There is a lot of code involved because there is a lot of variety in the hardware devices being accessed. It is a notable achievement of Unix that this great multiplicity of hardware is brought under the control of a small repertoire of simple commands. An important stage in the development of this repertoire was the concept of a device-independent file.

11.1 Device-Independent Files

To understand what device independence means, it is useful to consider how we might naively begin to program access to an ordinary 1.4 Meg floppy drive, without the aid of this useful concept.

11.1.1 Floppy Drive Controller

A floppy drive includes a motor and a sensing arm and is controlled by a processor called a *floppy drive controller*. See Figure 11-1. Many floppy drive controllers are compatible with the 8272 controller. In the ISA architecture, the 8272-compatible

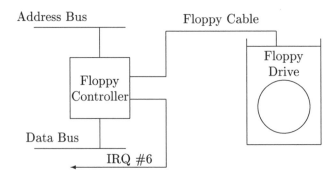

Figure 11-1. The Floppy Drive as an I/O Device

controller is assigned I/O ports 3F0H through 3F7H. Access to the floppy is by way
of these ports.

A 1.4 Meg floppy is carved up into small portions by the floppy drive. Each side
of the floppy has 80 concentric circles, like the rings of a target. These rings are
called *tracks*. Each side is also divided by radii into 18 pieces which are shaped like
pizza slices. Each track moves through all 18 of these pizza slices. Each portion of
one track on one pizza slice is called a *sector*. Each sector contains 512 bytes of
data. The total capacity of the disk is:

$$2 \text{ sides} \times 80 \text{ tracks/side} \times 18 \text{ sectors/track} \times 512 \text{ bytes/sector}$$
$$= 1440 \text{ K bytes.}$$

To get read or write access to the disk, a command must be issued to the 8272.
The command port is at the ISA address 3F4H. 46H is a READ command in
the 8272 language. It must be followed by eight bytes which specify, among other
things, which track, which sector, and which side of the disk will be read. All read
commands read at least one full sector. To read sector number five on cylinder
number six on side number one, for example, the following OUT instructions would
need to be issued:

Although this code accesses 512 bytes, a little arithmetic shows that from a
processor's point of view, it is not accessed all at once. Spinning at 300 rpm, or five
revolutions per second, a floppy drive drive can collect

$$5 \text{ revolutions/second} \times 18 \text{ sectors/revolution} \times 512 \text{ bytes/sector}$$
$$= 46{,}080 \text{ bytes/second}$$

This means bytes are collected every $\frac{1}{46080}$ seconds, or 21.7 microseconds. On a
100MHz machine, this is a wait of 2,170 machine cycles, clearly too much time to
keep the processor idling. This is a good example of a situation where an interrupt
can save time. Each time the 8272 has accumulated one byte of information from

```
MOV AL, 46H        ; Data Read command
OUT [3F4H], AL
MOV AL, 4          ;Side 1, Drive A:
OUT [3F4H], AL
MOV AL, 6          ;The Cylinder number
OUT [3F4H], AL
MOV AL, 1          ;Side 1, (again)
OUT [3F4H], AL
MOV AL, 5          ;The Sector number
OUT [3F4H], AL
MOV AL, 2          ;Sector size code for 512 bytes
OUT [3F4H], AL
MOV AL, 17         ;Last Sector number
OUT [3F4H], AL
MOV AL, 0          ;Gap size
OUT [3F4H], AL
MOV AL, 0FFH       ;Unused special Sector size code
OUT [3F4H], AL
```

Program 11.1

the floppy drive, it signals the system to take the information. It may use IRQ#6 to do this. In section 11.1.3 we will find that another way of handling the input has been developed which is even less wasteful of processor time.

11.1.2 Bad Old Files

The fact that information is handled using absolute addresses, one sector at a time, stands out in our programming of the floppy drive. Space on the disk is used in chunks of 512 bytes. It would be very natural then if all 1.4 Meg floppy disk files had lengths which were multiples of 512 bytes and were referenced using the absolute addresses of the sectors which they occupied. It would also be natural to store the information about which sectors were occupied into the "file," along with the rest of the information. This kind of information constituted what was called a *file control block*. In Unix this kind of information is held by the system in special system memory areas called *inodes* and is not integrated with the data in the file.   When this kind of information is included as a part of the data, elementary operations such as copying a file from one device to another become problematic. File copying programs become device-specific just as programs to convert wordprocessor documents are software package-specific. Copying a file can easily change its length, for example. Residual problems of exactly this nature exist in connection with *text files* in C, where line boundaries may be marked either by system information—the device holding the file may have an intrinsic line structure—or by end of line characters, \n, which are internal to the data file. Copying text files in C is not guaranteed to preserve length. One reason that the C preprocessor concatenates strings is so that intrinsic end of line boundaries can be overcome. *The Standard C Library* by Jim Plauger, its title notwithstanding, contains some fascinating historical asides on these issues.

The point here is that these "bad old files" are shaped by the devices on which they are stored. A device-independent file, on the other hand bears, no imprint of the device on which it is stored. A device-independent file can be copied from one device to another without undergoing change. Device-independent files originated in the Multics operating system, the immediate predecessor of Unix.

11.1.3* Direct Memory Access

The reader interested in getting on to device drivers may skip ahead to section 11.2. The reader curious about what keeps the floppy drive, or other peripherals for that matter, from interrupting the processor after every fetched byte should read the next two paragraphs.

In addition to the IRQ line, the 8272 also has an output line called DMARQ, for *DMA request*. DMA stands for *direct memory access*. Instead of using the IRQ line, the 8272 may be programmed to use the DMARQ line instead. The DMARQ line runs from the 8272 to a processor called a *DMA controller* which is equipped to issue , bus control signals and thus initiate Memory Write bus cycles. It can therefore relieve the CPU of the task of transferring bytes one at a time from the floppy drive into memory. In order that the use of the bus cycle machinery by the DMA controller not interfere with the CPU, which is constantly using the buses to fetch instructions, there is a HOLD line running from the DMA controller to the CPU and a HOLDA (hold acknowledge) line running from the CPU to the DMA controller. To use the buses, the DMA controller must ask for permission using the HOLD line and receive it on the HOLDA line. Incidentally, the programmer may instruct the CPU to withhold permission by using the LOCK prefix.

Setting up a DMA transfer requires more work on the part of the programmer than setting up a 512-byte read. Commands must be issued to both the DMA controller and the floppy controller, but it results in saving a great deal of CPU time.

Since any device which transfers blocks of data to and from memory can take advantage of DMA service to avoid placing unnecessary demands on the processor, a DMA handling circuit, very similar to the interrupt handling circuit shown in Figure 9-5, with a Master and a Slave DMA controller exists in the ISA architecture. There is a DMARQ line for each device which gets DMA service. These DMA lines are called *DMA channels*.

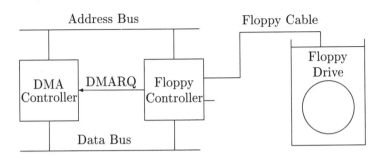

Figure 11-2. Floppy Controller Using DMA instead of an Interrupt

11.2   Devices as Files

A device-independent file is a list of bytes with a name, and that's all it is. As such, it is an abstraction. It soon proved to be a very useful abstraction. Immediately in the wake of the device-independent file concept followed another innovation of the Multics operating system. This was the idea that it should be possible for a programmer to treat I/O devices (printers, terminals, etc.) as device-independent files. This idea is the basis of the Unix device driver. Inputting data from a device can then be done just as you would "read" from a file. Outputing data to a device can be done just as you would "write" to a file. Turning file operations into generic device operations makes using devices easy for the applications programmer and also clarifies the role of the device driver. Its role is to provide the kernel with device specific versions of `read()`, `write()`, `open()`, etc., that can be accessed when it is processing those generic system calls which come from user programs.

For example, in section 11.3 where a Morse code speaker device is defined, the function `cq_write()` is defined. This function is called by the kernel when the system call `write()` is used to access the Morse Code speaker. This might happen, for example, when a user sends a string of text to the speaker.

```
linuxbox$ echo "Hello world" > /dev/cq
```

Because most devices are idiosyncratic in at least some respect or other, there must be room left over for features that do not fit into the generic read and write type system calls. The system call `ioctl()` is designed to take care of these leftovers. Each idiosyncratic feature is assigned a unique number called a *magic number*. An idiosyncratic feature of the speaker, for example, is its pitch. When `ioctl()` calls the speaker function cq_ioctl() using the correct magic number, the pitch-setting function is called.

The connotations of the term *magic number* are unfortunate, putting as they do an aura of mystery around a mere detail and value on privileged information where a value on openness would be more socially responsible. *Stupid number* would be better. But, be that as it may, magic numbers are at least not hard to find. They are, by convention, given in #define statements where their usage is explained. POSIX conventions require that magic numbers be not only unique for a device, but systemwide unique.

In the following sections, two examples of device drivers are presented. The purpose of these examples is to show what is involved in writing a device driver which incorporates some assembly code. The first driver is a toy. Its reason for existence is to serve as an example of a device driver. The second driver was written in response to a request from a friend who needed to input data from an external device as part of a research project involving the measurement of lizard metabolic rates. The goal of the research is a better understanding the mechanism by which environmental variations bring about lizard speciation (and also extinctions). So, although it is not a big program, it is not just a toy. The main feature the second driver has that the first one does not have is that it installs its own interrupt handler. The Morse Code driver merely adds some chores to those of an already installed handler.

11.3   Morse Code Speaker Driver

The basic structure which is used to connect device specific functions, such as cq_write(), with their generic counterparts, such as write() is the file operations structure.

11.3.1   The file_operations Structure

The definition of this structure is in /usr/src/linux/include/linux/fs.h. A simplified version of it is given here.

```
struct file_operations
{
    long long * llseek();
    int * read();
    int * write();
    int * readdir ();
    int * poll();
    int * ioctl();
    int * mmap();
    int * open();
    int * flush();
    int * release();
    int * fsync();
    int * fasync();
    int * check_media_change();
    int * revalidate();
```

```
    int * lock();
};
```

All the components of this structure are pointers to functions. The function names are given exactly, but their parameter declarations are omitted and the return types are given using a familiar but nonportable x86 version, e.g. `int` instead of the more portable `ssize_t`. The use of types such as `ssize_t`, however valuable for the sake of getting the same code to compile and run on different architectures, has a serious downside when it comes to reading the code. For example to chase down the definition of `ssize_t`, we need to find

```
    typedef __kernel_ssize_t ssize_t;
```

in `/usr/src/linux/include/linux/types.h` and then

```
    typedef int __kernel_ssize_t;
```

in `/usr/src/linux/include/asm-i386/posix_types.h`. Learning an operating system should not turn into an exercise in using the `grep` command.

The creation of an instance of `struct file_operations` for a particular device is the key to writing a device driver. The biggest part of writing the driver is defining the functions in this structure. These functions handle the system calls which result in calls from the system to the device. Handling calls from the device to the system requires setting up an interrupt handler, or as in the case of the Morse Code speaker driver, piggy-backing off of an existing interrupt handler. Not all of the functions named in the `struct file_operations` structure are needed in every device. Unneeded components may simply be defined as NULL. For the Morse Code driver, the following declaration sets up the needed file operations structure.

```
static struct file_operations cq_fops =
{
    cq_lseek,
    NULL,    /* cq_read */
    cq_write,
    NULL,    /* cq_readdir */
    NULL,    /* cq_poll */
    cq_ioctl,
    NULL,    /* cq_mmap */
    cq_open,
    NULL,    /* cq_flush */
    cq_release
};
```

The coding for these component functions is given in section 11.3.10. The omitted components following `cq_release` may be safely left to gcc which fills them in with the value NULL.

```
void delay(int i)
{
    /* VERY roughly:  delay by i hundredths of a second.  */

    i = i * 1000000; /* Multiply by a million.  */
    while(i > 0) i = i - 1; /* Could be just one instruction.  */

/* Many instructions take just one clock cycle.  * /
/* On a 100 MHz machine one million clock cycles take .01 sec.  */
}
```

Program 11.2

11.3.2   Timing Using Delay Loops

Before getting into the details of the individual functions, however, it would be worth while to take an overview of how the whole thing works. In an unprotected single user system such as in DOS, for example, we could turn the speaker on and off at will using IN and OUT instructions. The timing of the ons and offs could be managed using delay loops as shown in Program 11.2. The time spent in these delay loops would not be a big problem since, as a single user system, the machine would probably not be doing anything else anyway.

We could also use this technique in a Linux device driver. There is nothing to stop us. Program 11.3 shows the result. However, in a Linux device driver this code would be terrible. Linux does not interrupt kernel code. Since device drivers are part of the kernel, this code would never get timed out. It would monopolize the system.

Instead of strangling the computer, the driver needs to let go of the CPU and reschedule itself for execution at a later time. The driver can do this by taking advantage of existing Linux system resources, in this case the system timer. The system timer is a clock which interrupts the processor every .01 second. It uses IRQ #0. In Linux, all interrupts are counted and the counts are displayed in the /proc/interrupts directory. The counter for the timer interrupt is called `jiffies` and its value is displayed along with the other interrupt counts. When the ISR for this interrupt executes, it checks a queue of jobs which have a scheduled execution time. This queue is called the *timer queue*.

11.3.3   The Timer Queue

Using the timer queue is not difficult. Each timer queue entry is like a handy little order form. It has structure shown in Figure 11-3. When submitting an order, you fill in the last three items and leave the first two blank.

```
while(<Code not done>)
{
    if(<Dot starts>)
    {
        speaker_on();
        dtime = 20;
    }
    else if(<Dash starts>)
    {
        speaker_on();
        dtime = 40;
    }
    else if(<Dot or Dash stops>)
    {
        speaker_off();
        dtime = 30;
    }
    delay(dtime);
        /* dtime is how long to run the delay loop.   */
}
```

Program 11.3

- next and prev are typical doubly-linked list pointers. On a submitted job, they should be set to NULL. They are reset later by Linux when the entry is linked into the timer queue.

- expires is the time in jiffies when the job is supposed to begin executing.

- The function component is the job to be done. As its name implies, it is

```
struct timer_list
{
    struct timer_list * next;
    struct timer_list * prev;
    unsigned long expires;
    unsigned long data;
    void * function();
};
```

Figure 11-3. Definition of the Timer Queue

just a pointer to a function. When the time specified in `expires` arrives, the function pointed at by `function` gets called.

- The `data` component is the argument passed to the function pointed at by `function`.

To submit one of these order forms to Linux, you call the add_timer() function on a pointer to it. That's all there is to using the timer queue.

```
void cq_timer_handler(unsigned long x)
{
    unsigned long dtime;
            /* dtime is how long to wait on the timer queue.

    if(<Code not done>)
    {
        if(<Dot starts>)
        {
            speaker_on();
            dtime = 20;
        }
        else if(<Dash starts>)
        {
            speaker_on();
            dtime = 40;
        }
        else if(<Dot or Dash stops>)
        {
            speaker_off();
            dtime = 30;
        }
        (cq_timer -> expires) = jiffies + dtime;
        (cq_timer -> function) = cq_timer_handler;
                /* Here cq_timer_handler is adding its
                    own name to the timer queue entry form.  */
        add_timer(&cq_timer);
                /* Now submit the queue entry.  */
    }
}
```

Program 11.4

If we use the timer queue to fix Program 11.3, Program 11.4 results. It is essentially the same as Program 11.3, except that it exits promptly after it turns

the speaker on or off instead of hogging the CPU. It relies on the timer interrupt
to get itself called again later. The `data` component of the `struct timer_list`
structure is not used. Once this code is called, it uses the timer to call itself back
again. It is a little like recursion, except that it does not call itself directly, but
indirectly, by sending its name to the timer queue. Since any function can add this
entry to the timer queue, there is no problem getting it started. In fact, this is done
by `cq_write()`.

11.3.4 Device Memory

The next problem we face in writing this driver is memory access. The memory
labels (variable names and function names) used in Program 11.4 are referenced
when the ISR for interrupt #0 is executed. This interrupt may occur during the
running of any process. The page tables in effect at that time are those belonging
to whatever process happens to be running at that time. It need not be the process
that is sending text to the speaker.

Note that in the uncoded portions of Program 11.4, such as <Dot starts> or
<Code not done>, there must be references to the text being sent to the speaker.
This text is located in memory belonging to the process which originally called the
device driver. However, getting access to this memory is a problem. The problem
is not access rights; it is finding a usable address. The only address we have for this
text is defined relative to a set of page tables that are pointed at by a CR3 value
that is not loaded into CR3. Kernel privileges do not solve this problem. Doing
a task switch back to the calling process would restore the CR3 value needed to
access the page tables, but if all we need to do is to turn the speaker on or off, then
this would be a ridiculous waste of time.

```
struct cq_struct
{
    int flags;
    unsigned int timerdiv;   /* Timer divisor determines pitch */
    unsigned int wholenote;  /* Duration in centiseconds */
    char * mcode;    /* Pointer into current Morse Code string.*/
    char buffer[CQ_BUFFER_SIZE];
    unsigned int buffer_offset;  /* Current character */
    unsigned int buffer_end;    /* End of buffer.  */
    struct wait_queue *cq_wait_q;
}cq_area;
```

Figure 11-4. Device Memory for Speaker

A good solution to this problem is to set aside some kernel memory for the device
and have `cq_write()` copy from the user's memory into the device's memory. Unlike
`cq_timer_handler()`, `cq_write()` is called in response to a user's system call and

executes while the user's page tables are still in effect. At that time, locating the text is not a problem. But like cq_timer_handler(), it executes with kernel privilege so it has the rights needed to access kernel memory.

Since kernel addresses are shared systemwide, they are valid no matter what process is running. For example, we can look up the address of jiffies or add_timer any time we want by doing a grep such as

```
linuxbox$ grep jiffies /System.map
```

Essentially, all devices need some memory of their own in order to function. The structure whose definition is shown in Figure 11-4 sets aside device memory needed for the speaker driver. The components of this structure are

- flags: The bits of the flags carry information about the state of the device.

```
#define CQ_EXIST    0x0001
#define CQ_BUSY     0x0002
#define CQ_OFF      0x0004
```

The CQ_EXIST bit merely indicates that the device driver is installed. The CQ_BUSY bit is used to keep more than one process from using the device at the same time. This bit is checked when open() is called on the device. Blocking other processes from using /dev/cq does not block them from using the speaker. A ctrl-G (a beep) sent to the terminal will still get through. A true speaker device driver would not let this happen. All kernel code accessing the speaker would be rerouted through the speaker driver. But since emergency code needs direct access to the speaker, this would not be desirable. The CQ_OFF bit indicates that the device driver has the speaker turned off at the moment. This bit is checked every time cq_timer_handler() is called. These definitions are always inserted into a header file associated with the device. In this case, the file name cq.h is more or less inevitable.

- timerdiv: The timerdiv component holds the value of the timer divisor which determines the pitch of the speaker. Putting this number into device memory allows the pitch to be reset every time the Morse speaker is used, thus protecting it from being changed by a ctrl-G from some other process, and still be modifiable using ioctl().

- wholenote: Similarly, the wholenote component holds a unit time value that is used as the basis for calculating all the other time values in the program. Altering this value changes the overall rate at which the Morse Code comes out of the speaker. It is given in terms of the duration of one musical "whole note. "

- buffer[CQ_BUFFER_SIZE]: The buffer, buffer[CQ_BUFFER_SIZE], holds the text from the calling process. This is the text which is in the process of being sent to the speaker. The fact that text is stored here in kernel memory is what makes it unnecessary to do a task switch every time the speaker is ready for another letter.

- **mcode:** The pointer, **mcode**, keeps track of where in the string of dots and dashes for the current character we are.

- **buffer_offset:** The **buffer_offset** component picks out which character in the buffer the speaker is currently working on.

- **buffer_end:** The **buffer_end** marks the end of the current buffer load. It is usually just the same as **CQ_BUFFER_SIZE**. But in case the buffer is given only a partial load, **buffer_end** allows the driver to quit on time without running all the way to the end of the buffer.

- **cq_wait_q:** The last component, **cq_wait_q**, is there because although the text buffer, **buffer[CQ_BUFFER_SIZE]**, is a good idea, it does not completely solve the problem of accessing the user's text. When all the text in the buffer has been sent to the speaker and there is more to go, then we're back where we were before when we had no buffer, trying to get ahold of user's text when the user's process is not running (and hence the user's address space is not functional).

The buffer in device memory does not eliminate the need to do task switches. It can only reduce the number of the them. It can do this by making the buffer larger. The bigger the buffer, the less often a task switch is needed. But a bigger buffer increases the size of kernel memory. We have here a typical time vs. space trade off.

The user-called process, which fills the buffer, and the timer-handler, which empties the buffer, are an example of what is called a producer-consumer pair.

11.3.5   Wait Queues

Wait queues were designed to allow processes to suspend operation is such a way that they can be easily reactivated when needed. For example, a producer can suspend operation when it has produced a surplus and be reactivated by a consumer when the supply is exhausted.

A process may suspend its own operation by calling **sleep_on()**. It can be reactivated using **wake_on()**.

In the case of our speaker driver, the producer **cq_write()** fills **cq_area.buffer**, the speaker's text buffer, and could call **sleep_on()** as soon as it was done. When the timer handler **cq_timer_handler()** has used up a buffer load by sending it off to the speaker, it could call the function **wake_up()** to get **cq_write()** to fill the buffer back up again.

From the name **wake_up()** we might get the idea that an immediate task switch would be initiated. In fact what happens is that the process running **cq_write()** gets put back on a queue called the *run queue*, which consists of all processes which

```
cq_write(<File>, u, n)
{
/* This program puts itself to sleep
            after it fills device memory.  */
    int k, total = 0;

    while(total < n)
    {
        k = CQ_BUFFER_SIZE;
        copy_from_user(cq_area.buffer, k, u);
        add_timer(&cq_timer);/* Start timer handler */
        total = total + k;
        sleep_on(&(cq_area.wait_q));
    }
}
cq_timer_handle(unsigned int x)
{
/* This program wakes up the user
            process when device memory is empty.  */

    <Turn speaker on or off>
    if(<Character done>))
    {
        cq_area.buffer_offset = cq_area.buffer_offset + 1;
        if(cq_area.buffer_offset == cq_area.buffer_end)
        {
            cq_area.buffer_offset = 0;
            wake_up(&(cq_area.wait_q));
            return; /* No future scheduling done here!  */
        }
        add_timer(&cq_timer);/* Continue calling timer handler */
    }
}
```

Program 11.5

are currently taking turns using the processor. Each time another process on the run queue takes its turn on the processor, there has to be a task switch, of course.

Both sleep_on() and wake_up() must be called on an argument whose type is (struct wait_queue **), a pointer to to a pointer to a wait queue structure. Although this sounds horrible, it is really no problem to set up one of these things. The definition of a struct wait_queue is in /usr/src/linux/include/linux/wait.h.

But, actually, to use a wait queue, we don't need to know anything about its internals. As long as we call wake_up() on the same pointer that we give to sleep_on(), we're all set. The wait_q component of our struct cq_struct gives us a (single) pointer to a wait queue structure. Since cq_write() uses sleep_on() and cq_timer_handler() uses wake_up(), then the wait queue double pointer must be located in a place where both functions can address it. This is another example where device memory comes in handy. That is why the wait queue pointer is located there. A pointer to this pointer then gives us the argument that we need: &(cq_area.wait_q).

Program 11.5 shows how the sleep_on() and wake_up() calls work together. In Program 11.5, cq_write() calls sleep_on() as soon as it has filled the device buffer in kernel memory. cq_timer_handle() wakes up the sleeping cq_write() process when it has emptied the device buffer.

Now that we can program the necessary task switches, we are in a position to write a workable driver. Unfortunately, the driver as outlined so far would have a serious failing. It would not respond to what are called *signals*.

11.3.6 Signals

Processes in Unix have a handful of different mechanisms available to communicate with each other. One of these is the sending of *signals*. When a process is killed with a ctrl-C or a kill command, the process has received a signal. To explain what a signal is, we need to expand a little on the notion of a task. We have described the task state segment as a region of memory where registers get saved when a task switch occurs. The task state segment is maintained by the hardware. But it is only a part of the contextual information that is maintained by Linux for each process. There is a structure called a struct task_struct defined in /usr/src/linux/include/linux/sched.h which keeps all the information Linux needs on a process. This information is available to the device driver when it is executing in behalf of a process because there is a global variable in kernel memory called current whose value is always the task structure for the current process. In the driver for /dev/cq, for example, it makes sense to access this variable from cq_write() but not from cq_timer_handle(). One of the components of struct task_struct is tss, the hardware's task state segment. The pid component is the Process ID number which shows up when ps is run. It is needed when killing jobs from the command line. Another component of struct task_struct is signal. This component is currently typed as an array of integers. Each bit on each integer in the array can carry a signal. With two 32-bit integers in the array, Linux is configured for a maximum of 64 signals. Whatever the subtle distinctions are between all of these different signals, receiving a signal means just one thing to a device driver: it's time to quit.

Drivers that Can't Be Killed

The signal_pending() call checks the **signal** component of the process for non-zero bits. It is the responsibility of the writer of the device driver to make sure this is done and to go ahead and quit if such bits are found. Failure to do so results in a device driver that can't be killed. This is an easy mistake to make and a serious one. Multitasking in Linux is sometimes called *cooperative multitasking*. User tasks which execute with kernel privilege, such as **cq_write()**, are expected to yield to the processor voluntarily. If they don't, the scheduler won't force them to do so. In order to fulfill this responsibility, the driver must include code such as

```
if(signal_pending(current))
        return value;
```

at points in the code which will be encountered frequently enough so that waiting for the device driver to arrive at these points as it executes will not cause undue delay.

One more detail needs fixing in order to make sure the driver responds to signals.

11.3.7   States of a Process

A very important component of **struct task_struct** is **state**. Its most important values are assigned in **/usr/src/linux/include/linux/sched.h**:

```
#define TASK_RUNNING 0
#define TASK_INTERRUPTIBLE 1
#define TASK_UNINTERRUPTIBLE 2
#define TASK_ZOMBIE 4
#define TASK_STOPPED 8
```

Tasks which are on the run-queue, i.e. those which are now taking turns using the processor, have **TASK_RUNNING** as the value of their **state** component. When a task puts itself onto a wait queue, **state** may take either **TASK_INTERRUPTIBLE** or **TASK_UNINTERRUPTIBLE** as values. And it makes a big difference. Although we might reasonably suppose that the difference has to do with interrupts, it doesn't. It has to do with signals.

If **state** has the value **TASK_UNINTERRUPTIBLE**, then its **signal** component will not be altered by a Ctrl-C or a **kill**. Unfortunately, this is the value assigned to **state** by the **sleep_on()** function. Fortunately, there is a closely related function called **sleep_on_interruptible()** which assigns the value **TASK_INTERRUPTIBLE** to **state**. Hence in Program 11.5, the calls to **sleep_on()** and **wake_up()** need to be replaced by their interruptible counterparts. Otherwise we would have the same problem that we would get if we omitted the signal_pending() check. The definitions of two sleep_on functions are defined in **/usr/src/linux/kernel/sched.c** as well as the main part of **wake_up()**. The two wake_up macros are defined in **/usr/src/linux/include/linux/sched.h**.

In the digitizer driver in section 11.4, `wake_up_interruptible()` macro definition must be consulted to find out the actual function call since the gcc preprocessor isn't used by NASM.

The main features of the Morse Code speaker driver are now in place, so we can do the fun part next.

11.3.8 Timing the Morse Code

The timing of dots and dashes is an art, not a science. A Morse Code driver has good timing if it sounds right to a Morse Code practitioner. Time values in this driver are based on the following rules:

- All time values are based on the duration of the `wholenote` component of `cq_area`, which is given in hundredths of a second, or `jiffies`.

- A dash is one-fourth of a `wholenote`.

- A dot is one-sixteenth of a `wholenote`.

- Quiet intervals between dots and dashes of a lettter are one-eighth of a `wholenote`.

- Quiet intervals between letters are three-eighths of a `wholenote`.

- A character not included in the Morse Code get a silent interval of one-quarter of a `wholenote`.

11.3.9 Assembly Language Speaker Code

To turn the speaker on and off, the two little assembler routines shown in Program 11.6 are used. Although the bulk of the device driver is written in C, this is often the case. Many times, small routines are coded in assembly language and the rest is coded in a higher-level language.

If the file containing Program 11.6 is called `speak.asm`, it can then by assembled using NASM:

```
linuxbox$ nasm -f elf speak.asm
```

The `-f elf` switch determines the format of the resulting object code file called `speak.o`. It should be stored in `/usr/src/linux/drivers/char`.

```
        global speaker_on
        global speaker_off
        extern cq_area
SYSP    equ 61H ; System port for controlling speaker feed
DIVREG  equ 42H ; Port for timer divisor
speaker_off:
        IN AL,[SYSP]
        AND AL, 0FCH
        OUT [SYSP], AL
        MOV EAX, [cq_area]
        OR EAX, 4
        MOV [cq_area],EAX
        RET
speaker_on:
        MOV EAX,[cq_area + 4]
; timerdiv is offset by 4
        OUT [DIVREG], AL
        SHR EAX, 8
        OUT [DIVREG], AL
        IN AL,[SYSP]
        OR AL,3
        OUT [SYSP], AL
        MOV EAX, [cq_area]
        AND EAX, 0FFFFFFFBH
        MOV [cq_area], EAX
        RET
```

Program 11.6

11.3.10   C Language Driver Code

```c
#include <linux/errno.h>     /* Need this for ENODEV, etc.  */
#include <linux/kernel.h>    /* Need this for printk() */
#include <linux/major.h>     /* Need this for CQ_MAJOR */
#include <linux/sched.h>     /* Need this for sleeping and waking */
#include <asm/uaccess.h>     /* Need this for copy_from_user() */

#include <linux/cq.h>        /* Note the cq file.  */

void cq_timer_handler(unsigned long);
static void cq_set_pitch(unsigned long);
static void cq_set_tempo(unsigned long);

void speaker_on(void);
void speaker_off(void);

char * morse_code[40] ={"",
  ".-","-...","-.-.","-..",".","..-.","--.","....","..",".---","-.-","-..",
  ".-..","--","-.","---",".--.","--.-",".-.","...","-","..-","...-",".--","-..-",
  "-.--","--..",".----","..---","...--","....-",".....","-....","--...",
  "---..","----.","-----","--..--","-.-.-.","..--.."};

/* The empty string, followed by the 26 letter codes,
followed by the 10 numeral codes, followed by the comma,
period, and question mark.  */

struct cq_struct cq_area = {0, 0, 0, {0}, 0, 0, "", NULL};

struct timer_list cq_timer = {NULL, NULL, 0, 0, &cq_timer_handler};

inline char * mcodestring(int asciicode)
{
    char * mc;
    /* This is the mapping from the ASCII code
        into the mcode array of strings.  */

    if(asciicode > 122) /* Past 'z' */
        mc = morse_code[CQ_DEFAULT];
    else if(asciicode > 96) /* Upper case */
        mc = morse_code[asciicode - 96];
    else if(asciicode > 90) /* Uncoded punctuation */
        mc = morse_code[CQ_DEFAULT];
    else if (asciicode > 64) /* Lower case */
```

```
            mc = morse_code[asciicode - 64];
        else if (asciicode == 63) /* Question Mark */
            mc = morse_code[39]; /* 36 + 3 */
        else if(asciicode > 57) /* Uncoded punctuation */
            mc = morse_code[CQ_DEFAULT];
        else if (asciicode > 47) /* Numerals */
            mc = morse_code[asciicode - 21]; /* 27 + (asciicode - 48) */
        else if (asciicode == 46) /* Period */
            mc = morse_code[38]; /* 36 + 2 */
        else if (asciicode == 44) /* Comma */
            mc = morse_code[37]; /* 36 + 1 */
        else
            mc = morse_code[CQ_DEFAULT];
        return mc;
}


static int cq_reset(void)
{
    speaker_off();
    cq_set_pitch(CQ_DEF_PITCH); /* Pitch in Hz */
    cq_set_tempo(CQ_DEF_TEMPO); /* Quarter note equals this */

    return 0;
}


void cq_timer_handler(unsigned long x)
{
    /* This is the function which is called because
        its name is submitted to the timer queue.  */

    int status;
    unsigned int time_value;

    time_value = jiffies + 1; /* Mollify gcc */

    status = cq_area.flags ;

    if ((*(cq_area.mcode) == 0) && (status & CQ_OFF)
        && (cq_area.buffer_offset + 1 == cq_area.buffer_end))
        /* This buffer load is done */
    {
        wake_up_interruptible(&(cq_area.cq_wait_q));
        return;
    }
```

```
    if ((*(cq_area.mcode) == 0) && (status & CQ_OFF))
        /* This character is done.  Reset mcode. */
    {
        cq_area.buffer_offset = cq_area.buffer_offset + 1;
        x = cq_area.buffer[cq_area.buffer_offset];
        cq_area.mcode = mcodestring(x);
    }
    if ((*(cq_area.mcode) == 0) && (status & CQ_OFF))
        /* Preceding if-block put in the empty string. */
        /* Empty string gets a quarter note. */
    {
        time_value = cq_area.wholenote >> 2;
    }
    else if (status & CQ_OFF)
        /* Speaker is off.  Begin another dot or dash */
    {
        if(*(cq_area.mcode) == '_')
            time_value = cq_area.wholenote >> 2;
        else if (*(cq_area.mcode) == '.')
            time_value = cq_area.wholenote >> 4;
        (cq_area.mcode) = (cq_area.mcode) + 1;
        speaker_on();
    }
    else if(*(cq_area.mcode) == 0)
        /* Speaker is on.  End of character. */
    {
        time_value =
            (cq_area.wholenote >> 3) + (cq_area.wholenote >> 2);
            /* inter-letter rest */
        speaker_off();
    }
    else /* Speaker is on.  In the midst of a character. */
    {
        time_value = (cq_area.wholenote >> 3);
            /* Short intra-letter rest */
        speaker_off();
    }
    cq_timer.expires = jiffies + time_value;
/*
    cq_timer.expires = jiffies;
            In case you have seen this elsewhere,
            it does Not Work!
*/
    add_timer(&cq_timer);
```

```
        return;
}

static ssize_t cq_write(struct file * file, const char * buf,
                        size_t count, loff_t *ppos )
{
    /* This function fills the buffer and then goes to sleep.  */
    unsigned long copy_size;
    unsigned int time_value;
    ssize_t total_bytes_written = 0;
    time_value = 1;

    total_bytes_written = 0;
    do
    {
        if(signal_pending(current))
            return total_bytes_written;
        copy_size = (count <= CQ_BUFFER_SIZE ? count :  CQ_BUFFER_SIZE);
        cq_area.buffer_offset = 0;
        cq_area.buffer_end = copy_size;
        copy_from_user(cq_area.buffer, buf, copy_size);
        cq_area.mcode = mcodestring(cq_area.buffer[0]);

        time_value = cq_area.wholenote>> 4;
        cq_timer.expires = jiffies + time_value;
        add_timer(&cq_timer);
        speaker_off();
        interruptible_sleep_on(&(cq_area.cq_wait_q));
        total_bytes_written = total_bytes_written + copy_size;
        count = count - copy_size;
        buf = buf + copy_size;
    } while (count > 0);
    del_timer(&cq_timer);
    return total_bytes_written;
}


static long long cq_lseek(struct file * file,
                long long offset, int origin)
{
    return -ESPIPE;
}

static int cq_open(struct inode * inode, struct file * file)
```

```
{
    unsigned int minor = MINOR(inode->i_rdev);

    if (minor > 0 ) /* Stereo No */
        return -ENXIO;
    if ((cq_area.flags & CQ_EXIST) == 0)
        return -ENXIO;
    if (cq_area.flags & CQ_BUSY)
        return -EBUSY;

    cq_area.flags = (cq_area.flags | CQ_BUSY);
        return 0;
}

static int cq_release(struct inode * inode, struct file * file)
{
    cq_area.flags = (cq_area.flags & ~ CQ_BUSY);
    return 0;
}

static void cq_set_pitch(unsigned long cps)
{
    cq_area.timerdiv = 1193180 / cps;

        /* Frequency of the OSC signal on the AT bus */
}

static void cq_set_tempo(unsigned long beats_per_minute)
{
        /* Quarter note = 1 beat, timer works in centiseconds */

    cq_area.wholenote = 24000 / beats_per_minute;
}

static int cq_ioctl(struct inode *inode, struct file *file,
                unsigned int cmd, unsigned long arg)
{
    unsigned int minor = MINOR(inode->i_rdev);
    int retval = 0;

    if (minor > 0)
        return -ENODEV;
    if (((cq_area.flags) & CQ_EXIST) == 0)
        return -ENODEV;
```

```
    switch ( cmd )
    {
    case CQABORT:
        if (arg)
            cq_area.flags = (cq_area.flags | CQ_ABORT);
        else
            cq_area.flags = (cq_area.flags & ~ CQ_ABORT);
        break;
    case CQSETPITCH:
        if (arg)
            cq_set_pitch(arg);
        else
            retval = -EINVAL;
        break;
    case CQSETTEMPO:
        if (arg)
            cq_set_tempo(arg);
        else
            retval = -EINVAL;
        break;
    case CQRESET:
        cq_reset();
        break;
    case CQGETFLAGS:
        retval = verify_area(VERIFY_WRITE,
                             (void *) arg, sizeof(int));
        if (retval)
            return retval;
        else
        {
            int status = cq_area.flags;
            copy_to_user((int *) arg, &status, sizeof(int));
        }
        break;
    default:
        retval = -EINVAL;
    }
    return retval;
}

int cq_init(void)
{
    /* Initialization code like this can be called
        if a call to it is placed in mem.c */
```

```
    if (register_chrdev(CQ_MAJOR,"cq",&cq_fops))
    {
        printk(KERN_INFO "cq:  unable to get major %d\n", CQ_MAJOR);
        return -EIO;
    }
    cq_area.flags = (CQ_OFF | CQ_EXIST);
    cq_reset();
    return 0;
}
```

Program 11.7

It is customary to include definitions of parameters used in the C program in an include file. An include file for the Morse Code driver follows.

```
#define CQ_EXIST      0x0001
#define CQ_BUSY       0x0002
#define CQ_OFF        0x0004
#define CQ_ABORT      0x0008

/* IOCTL numbers */

#define CQABORT       0x0714
#define CQSETTEMPO    0x0716  /* Store whole note int cq_area. */
#define CQSETPITCH    0x0719  /* Store a timer divisor into cq_area.  */
#define CQRESET       0x071c  /* reset speaker */
#define CQGETFLAGS    0x071e  /* get status flags */

#define CQ_BUFFER_SIZE
#define CQ_DEF_CHAR        0   /* Default character */
#define CQ_DEF_PITCH     440   /* Default pitch */
#define CQ_DEF_TEMPO     160   /* Default tempo */
/*
function prototypes
*/
extern int cq_init(void);
```

The functions defined in **struct cq_struct** take care of the response by the driver to requests that the kernel makes in executing a system call which is asking for service from the driver. The **cq_timer_handler()** function takes care of the driver's response to a timer interrupt. These are the main things that need to be done. But when the device driver works, commands such as

```
    linuxbox$ cat file > /dev/cq
```

will start the speaker beeping. In order for this to happen, there has to be an entry named cq in the /dev directory, which has a connection with the programs such as cq_write().

11.3.11   Loose Ends

To finish the device driver, it is only necessary to

- Add a major number for the device to the /usr/include/linux/major.h file.

- Create an entry for the device in the /dev directory using the mknod command.

- Write a cq_init() function and include a call to it in the mem.c file.

- Modify the Makefile for the directory containing the driver, in this case /usr/src/linux/drivers/char, and recompile the kernel.

The /dev directory contains a list of a great many files, most of which are not actually files. The ls -l command distinguishes different types of files in the very first character of each line. Files which really are files are listed beginning with a -, directories are listed with a d, hard links with an l, etc. Devices are listed with either a b or a c, depending on whether they are *block devices* or *character devices*. Block devices transfer data in blocks, i.e., big uniformly-sized chunks. To do this, they interact with the kernel's *buffer cache*. Block devices can be *mounted*, i.e., incorporated into Unix's tree-structured file heirarchy. A hard drive is a good example of a block device. Character devices don't use blocks and they don't get mounted. Our little speaker driver is a character device. Each device listing, whether for a block or a character device, also lists a *major number* and a *minor number*. The major number is used as an index into chrdevs, a kernel array of character device drivers.

        struct device_struct chrdevs[MAX_CHRDEV]

Each device driver is just a

```
struct device_struct
{
        const char * name;
        const struct file_operations * fops;
};
```

The device is entered into the array by the function register_chrdev() which is defined in /usr/src/linux/fs/devices.c. The most important lines of this definition are as follows.

```
int register_chrdev(unsigned int major,
                    const char * name,
                    struct file_operations *fops)
{
        chrdevs[major].name = name;
        chrdevs[major].fops = fops;
        return 0;
}
```

Program 11.8

When this function is called, the major number is connected to the file operations structure set up by the device driver. The call is made by the device driver in the cq_init() function. The only other task performed by cq_init() is the initialization of some of the values in cq_area. In order to get the call performed during boot time, a call to it may be placed in the mem.c program near the end near the call to lp_init(). The command

```
linuxbox$ mknod /dev/cq c 102 0
```

creates an entry in file system for the cq device, giving it a major number of 102 and a minor number of 0. This entry in the /dev directory is then used to translate references to /dev/cq into calls to the functions listed in the file operations structure.

11.4 Serial Port Digitizer Driver

The Scalex device is a hand-held measuring device for reading distances off of a flat surface. It inputs data at a rate of 600 baud through the serial port. Since it has no handshaking hardware it does not respond to software which treats it as a modem or a terminal. It also handles data in a special format which packs two four-bit characters into each byte sent or received. For both of these reasons it is useful to write a special driver for it.

One important element of a typical device driver, which was not needed in the Morse Code device driver, was the installation of an interrupt handler. The Morse Code driver simply took advantage of the services of the existing interrupt handler for the timer interrupt.

11.4.1 Setting Up a New Interrupt Handler

Most device drivers need an ISR to handle interrupts which come from the device. The Linux function request_irq() takes care of the installation of a new handler. Its definition is located in /usr/src/linux/arch/i386/kernel/irq.c.

```
int request_irq(unsigned int irq,
```

0	Ctrl-@	32	\<SPC\>	64	@	96	`
1	Ctrl-A	33	!	65	A	97	a
2	Ctrl-B	34	"	66	B	98	b
3	Ctrl-C	35	#	67	C	99	c
4	Ctrl-D	36	$	68	D	100	d
5	Ctrl-E	37	%	69	E	101	e
6	Ctrl-F	38	&	70	F	102	f
7	Ctrl-G	39	'	71	G	103	g
8	Ctrl-H	40	(	72	H	104	h
9	Ctrl-I	41	)	73	I	105	i
10	Ctrl-J	42	*	74	J	106	j
11	Ctrl-K	43	+	75	K	107	k
12	Ctrl-L	44	,	76	L	108	l
13	Ctrl-M	45	-	77	M	109	m
14	Ctrl-N	46	.	78	N	110	n
15	Ctrl-O	47	\	79	O	111	o
16	Ctrl-P	48	0	80	P	112	p
17	Ctrl-Q	49	1	81	Q	113	q
18	Ctrl-R	50	2	82	R	114	r
19	Ctrl-S	51	3	83	S	115	s
20	Ctrl-T	52	4	84	T	116	t
21	Ctrl-U	53	5	85	U	117	u
22	Ctrl-V	54	6	86	V	118	v
23	Ctrl-W	55	7	87	W	119	w
24	Ctrl-X	56	8	88	X	120	x
25	Ctrl-Y	57	9	89	Y	121	y
26	Ctrl-Z	58	:	90	Z	122	z
27	Ctrl- [	59	;	91	[	123	{
28	Ctrl- \	60	<	92	\	124		
29	Ctrl-]	61	=	93	]	125	}
30	Ctrl-ˆ	62	>	94	^	126	~
31	Ctrl- _	63	?	95	_	127	\<DEL\>

Table 11.1. ASCII Code Chart

```
void (*handler)(int, void *, struct pt_regs *),
unsigned long irqflags,
const char * devname,
void *dev_id);
```

11.4.2   Scalex Interrupt Handler

One vital link between the interrupt handler, which is written in assembler, and the rest of the program is the definition of the scalex device memory area. Since the assembly code does not have access to the labels used in the C compiler, it is important to count off the offset bytes from the beginning of the structure. These are used to access the device memory. Hence `scalex_area + 4` is used instead of `scalex_area.readin`. Since all the components of this structure are four bytes in size, there are no tricks in the counting.

```
struct cq_struct
{
    unsigned long flags; /* 0 */
    unsigned int readin; /* 4 */
    unsigned int readout; /* 8 */
    unsigned int writein; /* 12 */
    unsigned int writeout; /* 16 */
    char *read_buffer; /* 20 */
    char *write_buffer; /* 24 */
    struct wait_queue *rdwait_q; /* 28 */
    struct wait_queue *wrwait_q; /* 32 */
};
```

```
 global scalex_interrupt
```
RBS equ 256 ; This must be a power of 2.
COM1 equ 3F8H ; COM1 Base I/O Address and Data Port
```
extern scalex_area
extern printk
extern __wake_up
;
scalex_interrupt:
```
; Push all the registers that get used, except EAX
```
        PUSH ECX
        PUSH EDX
        PUSH EBX
        PUSH ESI
        PUSH EDI
        MOV EDX, COM1 + 5 ; Line Status Register
        IN AL, DX        ;
        TEST AL, 1       ; See if Data Has Arrived
        JZ NEAR WRD      ; No? Then Need to Write Data?
;
; Process Incoming Data
;
        MOV ESI, [scalex_area + 4] ; readin component of structure
```

```
          ADD ESI, RBS + 2; Read Buffer Size + 2
          SUB ESI, [scalex_area + 8] ; readout component of structure
          AND ESI, RBS - 2  ; Read Buffer Size - 2
          JZ NEAR RBF        ; Read Buffer Full
;
; These lines test the condition:
```

; readin + 1 = readout OR readin + 2 = readout (mod 2^n)
; If it is true then the circular buffer has overflowed. Note RBS = 2^n.
;

```
          MOV EDX, COM1  ; Data Port has zero offset.
          IN AL, DX          ; This is the data byte right here!
          MOV CL, AL         ; Keep whole byte in AL
          AND ECX, 15        ; Clear ECX and look at halves in CL

          MOV DL, [OKC + ECX]; Translate incoming half byte
          MOV EBX, [scalex_area + 28]; Get address of Read Buffer
          MOV ESI, [scalex_area + 4] ; readin component of structure
          MOV [EBX + ESI], DL; Store translated byte in Read Buffer
          INC ESI            ; Increment readin
          AND ESI, RBS - 1  ; mod 2ⁿ of course
          MOV [scalex_area; + 4], ESI
          CMP DL, 10         ; Was that a terminal signal?
          JZ NEAR RQW        ; If so wake up the reading process.

          MOV CL, AL         ; Now do the other half byte
          SHR CL, 4
          MOV DL, [OKC + ECX]; Translate incoming half byte
          MOV [EBX + ESI], DL ; Store translated byte in Read Buffer
          INC ESI            ; Increment readin
          AND ESI, RBS - 1  ; mod 2ⁿ of course
          MOV [scalex_area + 4], ESI ;
          CMP DL, 10         ; Was that a terminal signal?
          JZ NEAR RQW        ; If so wake up the reading process.
;
; Process Outgoing Data
;
WRD:
          MOV EDX, COM1 + 2 ; Interrupt Identification Register
          IN AL, DX
          TEST AL, 2         ; Check the Data Has Been Sent Bit
          JZ NEAR LEV        ; No? Then quit.
;
; See if the end of the write buffer has been reached.
          MOV EDI, [scalex_area + 16] ; writeout component of structure
```

```
            CMP EDI, [scalex_area + 12]; writein component of structure
            JZ WQW            ; If done then wake up writing process.
POL:
            MOV EDX, COM1 + 5 ; Line Status Register
            IN AL, DX         ;
            TEST AL, 64       ; Data Has Been Sent Bit
            JZ POL            ; Should be just a short wait
            MOV EBX, [scalex_area + 24] ; Get address of Write Buffer
            MOV AL, [EBX + ESI]
            MOV EDX, COM1  ; Data Port
            OUT DX, AL        ; Here is the outgoing byte!
            INC ESI
            MOV [scalex_area + 16], ESI; writeout
            JMP LEV
```

```
WQW:; Write Queue Wake-up
; Since __wake_up() looks like a function we should expect
; to push the arguments as shown on the next two lines.
;          PUSH dword 1;TASK_INTERRUPTIBLE
;          PUSH dword scalex_area + 32; Wake up
;                         This is the double pointer!
; However __wake_up() actually wants its arguments passed
; in registers EDX and EAX!
            MOV EDX, 1;TASK_INTERRUPTIBLE
            MOV EAX, scalex_area + 32; Write wait queue
            CALL __wake_up
            JMP LEV
```

```
RQW:; Read Queue Wake-up
; Test flags component for the Read Pending Bit
            TEST dword [scalex_area], 8
            JZ NEAR LEV       ; No? False alarm, just quit.
            MOV EDX, 1;TASK_INTERRUPTIBLE
            MOV EAX, scalex_area + 28; Read wait queue
            CALL __wake_up
            JMP LEV
```

```
RBF: ; Read Buffer Full
            PUSH dword OVR  ; Overflow
            CALL printk
            ADD ESP, 4
            JMP LEV
```

; Error message:

OVR: db "Read buffer overflow!",0AH,0
;
; Half-byte to Byte Translation table:
OKC: db "0123456789AB-",0AH,".F"

LEV:

```
        POP EDI
        POP ESI
        POP EBX
        POP EDX
        POP ECX
        RET
```

Program 11.9

11.4.3   Scalex System Call Handlers

Here are the functions which are pointed at in the file operations structure.

```c
#include <linux/errno.h>
#include <linux/kernel.h>
#include <linux/major.h>
#include <linux/sched.h>
#include <linux/malloc.h>
#include <linux/delay.h>
#include <linux/scalex.h>
#include <asm/io.h>
#include <asm/irq.h>
#include <asm/uaccess.h>

struct scalex_struct scalex_area =
            {0, 0, 0, 0, 0, NULL, NULL, NULL, NULL};
static int scalex_reset(void)
{
    int retval = 0;
    scalex_area.flags = SCALEX_EXIST;
    scalex_area.readin = 0;
    scalex_area.readout = 0;
    scalex_area.writein = 0;
    scalex_area.writeout = 0;
    return retval;
}

static inline char cut(char x)
```

```
{
    char y;
    if (x == '.')  y = 14;
    else if (x == '-') y = 12;
    else if (x >= 'A' && x <= 'F') y = (x - 'A') + 10;
    else if (x >= 'a' && x <= 'f') y = (x - 'a') + 10;
    else if (x >= '0' && x <= '9') y = x - '0';
    else if (x == 0) y = 13;
    else if (x == 10) y = 13;
    else if (x == 13) y = 13;
    else y = -1;

    return y;
}
static inline char char_fill( char x)
{
/* Convert four-bit code into a C character */

    char y;

    if (x == 15) y = 'F';
    else if (x == 14) y = '.';
    else if (x == 13) y = 0; /* Termination flag!!  */
    else if (x == 12) y = '-';
    else if (x == 11) y = 'B';
    else if (x == 10) y = 'A'; /* Not used. */
    else if (x < 10) y = x + '0';
    else y = 0; /* Keep the compiler happy.  */

    return y;
}


static inline int ok_ascii_char( char x)
{
    /* Just a validity check on the to see if x
is one of the characters codeable in the four-bit scalex code */

    return((x >= 'A' && x <= 'F') ||
        (x >= 'a' && x <= 'f') ||
        (x >= '0' && x <= '9') ||
        (x == '.')  || (x == '-')||(x == '\n') || (x == 0));
}
```

```
static inline void write_byte(char x)
{
    while(!(inb_p(SCALEX_COM_BASE + 5) & SCALEX_LSR_DATA_OUT_EMPTY))
        udelay(100); /* Check Line Status Regsiter until its okay */

    outb_p(x,SCALEX_COM_BASE);
}


static ssize_t scalex_write(struct file * file, const char * buf,
            size_t count, loff_t *ppos)
{
    ssize_t retv;
    unsigned long copy_size;
    int j, k, lsr_reg;
    char c, d;
    struct scalex_struct *scalex = &scalex_area;

    /* Scalex takes short command strings.
        Characters following termination will be discarded.
        Termination will be added to all strings.
    */

    k = 0;
    while(buf[k] != 0 && k < SCALEX_WRITE_SIZE &&
            k < count) k = k + 1;

    if ( k == SCALEX_WRITE_SIZE)
        return -EINVAL;
    if (k == 0) return count;

    /* Since count <= SCALEX_WRITE_BUFSIZE */
    copy_size = k;

    for(k = 0; k < copy_size; k = k + 1)
    {
        c = buf[k];
        if(!(ok_ascii_char(c)))
            return -EFAULT;
    }

    if (copy_from_user(scalex->write_buffer, buf, copy_size))
    {
        return -EFAULT;
```

```
    }
    k = copy_size;
/* Pack each two bytes from the user's buffer into one byte
of the scalex buffer.  */
    for(k = 0, j = 0; k <= copy_size; k = k + 2,j = j + 1)
        if (k == copy_size)
        {
            scalex->write_buffer[j] = 0xfd;
        }
        else if (k + 1 == copy_size)
        {
            c = cut(buf[k]);
            scalex->write_buffer[j] = (0xd0 | c);
        }
        else
        {
            c = cut(buf[k]);
            d = cut(buf[k+1]) << 4;
            scalex->write_buffer[j] = (d|c);
        }

    scalex->writein = j; /* Number of bytes into scalex buffer */
    while(!(inb_p(SCALEX_COM_BASE + 5) & SCALEX_LSR_DATA_OUT_EMPTY));
    scalex->writeout = 1; /* Next byte to be transmitted */
    lsr_reg = inb_p(SCALEX_COM_BASE + 5);
    if(lsr_reg & 1)
    {
/* Read this damn byte.  It shouldn't be here but it is.  */
        c = inb_p(SCALEX_COM_BASE);
        d = char_fill(c & 0xf);

    if ((scalex -> readout == /* Circular buffer is full.  */
        ((scalex -> readin + 1) % SCALEX_READ_BUFFER_SIZE))||
        (scalex -> readout ==
        ((scalex -> readin + 2) % SCALEX_READ_BUFFER_SIZE)))
    {
        scalex -> flags =
        (scalex -> flags | SCALEX_ERR | SCALEX_RFULL);
        printk("The read buffer overflowed!\n");
        return -EFAULT;
    }
    if (d == 0) /* Other half byte should be just filler.  */
    {
/* Don't store this.  It might get the read stuck.  */
```

```
    }
    else
    {

        scalex -> read_buffer[scalex -> readin] = d;
        scalex -> readin =
            ((scalex -> readin + 1) % SCALEX_READ_BUFFER_SIZE);

        d = char_fill(c >> 4);
        if (d == 0)
        {
/* Don't store this either.  */
        }
        else
        {
            scalex -> read_buffer[scalex -> readin] = d;
            scalex -> readin =
            ((scalex -> readin + 1) % SCALEX_READ_BUFFER_SIZE);
        }
    }
    }
        outb_p(scalex->write_buffer[0], SCALEX_COM_BASE );
    interruptible_sleep_on(&scalex->wrwait_q);
    if (signal_pending(current))
            return -EINTR;
        retv = count;
        return retv;
}


static long long scalex_lseek(struct file * file,
                long long offset, int origin)
{
    return -ESPIPE;
}



static ssize_t scalex_read(struct file * file, char * buf,
size_t length, loff_t *ppos)
{
    struct scalex_struct * scalex = &scalex_area;
    ssize_t count ;
    int k = 0;
/*
    Read from ascii_read buffer.
```

```
      Make the interrupt handler do the translating.
          see if char is waiting in buffer
          if so read it.
          if not set READ PENDING bit and go to sleep
/
      scalex->flags = (scalex->flags | SCALEX_RPEND);
      count = length;
      do
      {
          if(scalex->readin == scalex->readout)
              interruptible_sleep_on(&scalex->rdwait_q);
          if(scalex->readin != scalex->readout)
      {
          buf[k] = scalex->read_buffer[ scalex->readout];
          scalex->readout
              = (scalex->readout + 1) % SCALEX_READ_BUFFER_SIZE;
              k = k + 1;
          if(buf[k -1] == SCALEX_READ_STRING_TERMINAL)
          return k;
/*
Whether the TERMINAL string is counted as one of the bytes read
or not has a drastic effect.  Scanf hangs on EOLs if it is
but on ordinary strings if it is not.
It is probably better to count it.
/
      }
      count = count - 1;
}
      while(count > 0);

      count = k;
/* Interrupt handler should check READ_PENDING bit
and issue a wake up if its set.  */

      scalex->flags = (scalex->flags &   SCALEX_RPEND);
      return count;
}

static int scalex_open(struct inode * inode, struct file * file)
{
      char c;
      if ((scalex_area.flags & SCALEX_EXIST) == 0)
          return -ENXIO;
      if (scalex_area.flags & SCALEX_BUSY)
```

```
        return -EBUSY;

    scalex_area.read_buffer =
        (char *) kmalloc(SCALEX_READ_BUFFER_SIZE, GFP_KERNEL);

    scalex_area.write_buffer =
        (char *) kmalloc(SCALEX_WRITE_BUFFER_SIZE, GFP_KERNEL);

    if (!scalex_area.read_buffer ||!scalex_area.write_buffer)
    {
        scalex_area.flags = (scalex_area.flags &  SCALEX_BUSY);
        return -ENOMEM;
    }
/*
Initialize the Scalex Area
/
    scalex_area.readin = 0;
    scalex_area.readout = 0;
    scalex_area.writein = 0;
    scalex_area.writeout = 0;


/*

    Initialize the COM port
/


    c = inb_p(SCALEX_COM_BASE + 3); /* Line Control Register.  */
    c = c | 0x80; /* Bit 7 allows Baud Rate Setting */
    outb_p(c, SCALEX_COM_BASE + 3);
    outb_p(0, SCALEX_COM_BASE + 1);/* Baud Rate Divisor,Upper Byte */
    outb_p(0xc0, SCALEX_COM_BASE); /* 600 Baud, BRD, Lower Byte */
    outb_p(3, SCALEX_COM_BASE + 3);
            /* Put back bit 7 and make parity 8,N,1 */
    c = inb_p(SCALEX_COM_BASE + 4); /* Modem Control Register */
;
    outb_p(3, SCALEX_COM_BASE + 1); /* Interrupt Enable Register */
/* Transmit and Receive Ready Only */
    c = (c | 8);
    outb_p(c, SCALEX_COM_BASE + 4); /* Enable interrupts */


    return 0;
}


static int scalex_release(struct inode * inode, struct file * file)
```

```
{
    unsigned int minor = MINOR(inode->i_rdev);
    char c;

    if (minor > 0)
        return -ENODEV;
    kfree_s(scalex_area.read_buffer, SCALEX_READ_BUFFER_SIZE);
    kfree_s(scalex_area.write_buffer, SCALEX_WRITE_BUFFER_SIZE);
    scalex_area.read_buffer = NULL;
    scalex_area.write_buffer = NULL;
    scalex_area.flags = (scalex_area.flags &  SCALEX_BUSY);
    c = inb_p(SCALEX_COM_BASE + 4); /* Disable interrupts */
    c = (c & 0xf7);
    outb_p(c, SCALEX_COM_BASE + 4);
    return 0;
}

static int scalex_ioctl(struct inode *inode, struct file *file,
        unsigned int cmd, unsigned long arg)
{
    unsigned int minor = MINOR(inode->i_rdev);
    int status;
    int retval = 0;


    if (minor > 0)
        return -ENODEV;
    if ((scalex_area.flags & SCALEX_EXIST) == 0)
        return -ENODEV;
    switch ( cmd ) {
        case SCALEXRESET:
            scalex_reset();
            break;
        case SCALEXGETFLAGS:
            status = scalex_area.flags ;
            if (copy_to_user((int *) arg, &status, sizeof(int)))
            return -EFAULT;
            break;
        default:
            retval = -EINVAL;
    }
    return retval;
}
```

```
static struct file_operations scalex_fops = {
    scalex_lseek,
    scalex_read,
    scalex_write,
    NULL, /* scalex_readdir */
    NULL, /* scalex_poll */
    scalex_ioctl,
    NULL, /* scalex_mmap */
    scalex_open,
    NULL, /* flush */
    scalex_release
};


int scalex_init(void)
{

    if (register_chrdev(SCALEX_MAJOR, "scalex", &scalex_fops))
    {
        printk("scalex: unable to get major %d\n", SCALEX_MAJOR);
        return -EIO;
    }
    if (request_irq(4, scalex_interrupt, 0, "scalex", NULL))
    {
        printk("scalex: unable to get irq %d\n", 4);
        return -EIO;
    }
    scalex_area.flags = SCALEX_EXIST;
    return 0;
}
```

Program 11.10

```
#define SCALEX_EXIST       0x0001
#define SCALEX_BUSY        0x0004
#define SCALEX_RPEND       0x0008
#define SCALEX_RFULL       0x0010
#define SCALEX_RERR        0x0020

#define SCALEX_COM_BASE  0x3F8
#define SCALEX_IIR_DATA_IN_FULL       4
#define SCALEX_IIR_DATA_OUT_EMPTY     2
#define SCALEX_LSR_DATA_IN_FULL       1
#define SCALEX_LSR_DATA_OUT_EMPTY     64
```

```
#define SCALEX_WRITE_SIZE          20
#define SCALEX_WRITE_BUFFER_SIZE   256
#define SCALEX_READ_BUFFER_SIZE    1024
#define SCALEX_READ_STRING_TERMINAL 10

/* IOCTL numbers */

#define SCALEXRESET 0x072c /* reset scalex */
#define SCALEXGETFLAGS 0x072e /* get status flags */

#define SCALEX_WRITE_BUFFER_SIZE 256
#define SCALEX_READ_BUFFER_SIZE 1024

/*
function prototypes
*/
extern int scalex_init(void);
```

Program 11.11

Further Reading

Writing Unix Device Drivers, George Pajari, Addison Wesley: 1992.

Linux Device Drivers, Alessandro Rubini, O'Reilly: 1998.

12

DOS PROGRAMS

Linux was written for the 386. The 386 retains many of the features of the 8086. Since DOS was written for the 8086, there is much to be learned about the 386 from the study of DOS programs.

The environment in which a DOS program operates is very different from the environment of a Unix user program. It is remarkable that one and the same processor can sustain both of these environments. Three main differences between the DOS environment and the Unix user program environment are

1. Memory referencing. In Unix, memory access is controlled using a virtual memory system. In Linux, virtual memory is based on paging. The applications programmer has no direct access to physical memory. In DOS, there is no paging. Knowing the physical address of a memory location enables the programmer to write directly to that location. It requires manipulation of the segmentation process, as is explained in chapter 12, section 12.1. In Unix, the applications programmer may ignore the segmentation process since, for users, there is just one big segment and it is always the same.

2. Privilege level. In Unix, only system programs have system-level privilege. User programs do not. Strictly speaking, DOS has no privilege levels. But

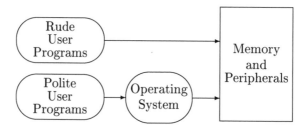

Figure 12-1. Unprotected Operating System such as DOS

actually, when DOS is running, all programs execute at effectively system-level privilege. Linux user programs do not carry system-level privilege. One consequence of this is that they do not have direct I/O access. That is, they are not allowed to use either the IN or the OUT instructions. Privilege levels are discussed in chapter 9, section 9.6.

3. Coding default. x86 Linux programs execute with a 32-bit coding default. DOS programs execute with a 16-bit coding default. Coding defaults are discussed in chapter 5, section 5.5.

When x86 processors, starting with the 80286, create a DOS environment, they are said to be operating in *real mode*. When not in real mode, they are said to be in *protected mode*. In Linux, user programs and most kernel programs run in protected mode. Linux only uses real mode for booting and this is necessary since the only way an x86 processor can boot is in real mode.

Privilege levels and coding defaults have already been discussed, but segmentation has been totally ignored to this point. However, DOS programs require it. We begin our discussion of segmentation with real mode segmentation. Segmentation in protected mode is discussed in chapter 13, section 13.2.

12.1   Real Mode Segmentation

The terms *segment* and *segmentation* are used in many overlapping and conflicting ways. Consequently, it would be well to make a preliminary attempt at clarifying terminology. In DOS, code and data segments of a program may be stored in code and data segments of memory, but aren't necessarily. In Linux, they never are. Text and data segments of a program are stored on separate pages of memory, not separate segments of memory. In x86 Linux, the error message "Segmentation Fault" does not refer to a segmentation fault; it refers a page protection fault. Worst of all is the term *logical segment* which accurately specifies nothing at all.

To avoid wantonly muddying things further, this book will doggedly adhere to the following distinctions between program segments, memory segments, and segmentation.

Segments and Segmentation

- Program segment. Since chapter 8, we have applied the term *segment* to a chunk of an executable file. This is standard usage. Programs typically have text and data segments.

- Segmentation process. In this book, the term *segmentation* is applied only to an address processing mechanism which has the effect of dividing memory into chunks.

- Memory segment. It is customary to apply the term *segment* to the chunks of memory produced by the segmentation process. In this book, memory segments will always be referred to in connection with a special kind of register called *segment register*.

On an x86 processor, segmentation is controlled by segment registers.

12.1.1 Segment Registers

On the 8086, four of the general registers can be used for addresses: BX, BP, SI, and DI. That is, they can be used in brackets to refer to memory. For example, the commands

```
MOV BX, 1234H
MOV AL, [BX]
```

would copy the contents of one memory location into the AL register. But BX, BP, SI, and DI are 16-bit registers and the 8086 has a 20-bit address bus. So an address register can only address 64K of the available 1 Meg of memory! To get around this problem, the designers of the 8086 created special 16-bit registers called *segment registers* which, on the 8086, specify the first address, or *base address*, of a 64K chunk of memory. On the 8086, a 64K chunk of memory specified by a segment register is called a *memory segment*. An 8086 memory segment may begin on any five-digit hex address which ends in a zero. The first four digits of this address are stored in the associated segment register. The 8086 segment registers are CS, DS, ES, and SS. The memory segment specified by the CS register, for example, is called the CS segment (code segment). On an x86 processor, code is always fetched from the CS segment. Likewise the stack is always located in the SS segment (stack segment). The 80386 and subsequent x86 processors have two additional segment registers: FS and GS.

Segment registers may be accessed using the command

```
MOV reg,reg
```

where one register is any 16-bit general register, and the other may be any segment register. An exception is that CS may not be used as the destination register. Since instructions are fetched from the CS segment, storing a new value in CS would have the drastic effect of changing the segment that code is being fetched from. A jump to a different segment is called a *far jump*. Carrying out a far jump requires a special command. Intrasegment jumps are called *near jumps*.

There is no load immediate command for segment registers. The following command, for example, is illegal.

```
MOV DS, 1234H
```

Suppose that DS, ES, and SS have values stored in them via the following commands:

```
MOV AX, 2000H
MOV DS, AX
```

```
MOV AX, 5000H
MOV ES, AX
MOV AX, 0C800H
MOV SS, AX
```

So then DS holds 2000H, ES holds 5000H, and SS holds C800H. Figure 12-2 shows the three segments which are enabled by these three register loads. The entire memory consists of the addresses from 0 through FFFFFH. The DS segment consists of the addresses from 20000H through 2FFFFH. The ES segment ranges from 50000H through 5FFFFH. The SS segment goes from C8000H through D7FFFH.

12.1.2 Segment:Offset Notation

Suppose now that we would like to refer to the memory whose address is 23456H in an assembler command. This address lies in the DS segment. (This is because 2000H was just stored in the DS register.) It is 3456H bytes from the base address. This difference, the address minus the base address, is called the *offset*. The segment:offset pair is often used in the assembly language as follows:

```
MOV BL, DS:[3456H]
```

In NASM the syntax is

```
MOV BL, [DS:3456H]
```

This command loads the contents of memory location 23456H into BL. 23456H = 20000H + 3456H. Note that the base address itself is a five-digit hex number, even though DS only holds four digits, in this case 2000H.

The address 23456H is a physical address, not a virtual address. The bits which the processor pumps out onto the address bus may be read off the binary number

```
0010 0011 0100 0101 0110
```

The same memory read could be accomplished using a 16-bit address register as follows:

```
MOV BX, 3456H
MOV BL, [DS:BX]
```

BX, BP, SI, and DI may be used for addressing in this way, but SP, AX, CX, and DX may not.

12.1.3 Default Segments

Segment designations may be omitted. There is always a default segment. Referring to Table 12.1, we see that the default segment for an immediate address is the DS segment. Hence the command

```
MOV BL, [3456H]
```

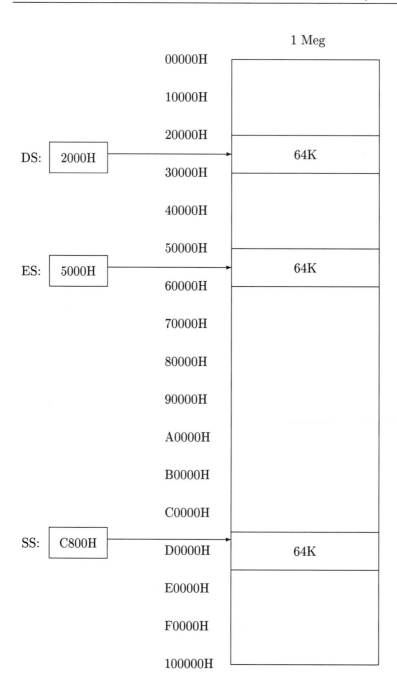

Figure 12-2. 8086 Memory with Three Distinguished Segments

32-bit address		16-bit address	
[imm]	DS	[imm]	DS
[EAX]	DS	[AX]	illegal!
[EBX]	DS	[BX]	DS
[ECX]	DS	[CX]	illegal!
[EDX]	DS	[DX]	illegal!
[ESI]	DS	[SI]	DS
[EDI]	DS*	[DI]	DS*
[ESP]	SS	[SP]	SS
[EBP]	SS	[BP]	SS

Table 12.1. Default Segments

* ES with string instructions

also accomplishes the same load as the MOV BL, [DS:BX] instruction. So do the commands

    MOV BX, 3456H
    MOV BL, [BX]

The default segment for both immediate addresses and for addresses stored in the BX register is the DS segment.

Default segments exist in 32-bit code as well. In fact, that is what makes it possible to do programming without reference to segments, as is done in chapter 8. The Linux programs there all make use of a default segment. It is actually a 4 Gig segment. Setting up big segments like this is discussed in chapter 13. In x86 Linux, the CS, DS, ES, and SS segments all refer to the same 4 Gig segment. So the programmer has no options, and the default segment is always okay.

12.2 Edlinas Environment Variables

Many assemblers have directives which allow variables to be defined and then used in subsequent expressions. In NASM, the syntax for such a directive is

    var equ value

In Edlinas, it is

    var .= value

In Edlinas, there are built-in variables whose values control the behavior of the assembler and the simulator. One of these is USE, which determines whether the assembler uses 16-bit or 32-bit coding. The default is 32. DOS programs require 16.

NASM uses a directive called BITS. For example, to specify 16-bit code in NASM, the line

    BITS 16

does the trick. Another environment variable is DOTO. It determines the format of .o files saved by Edlinas. The default is ELF. DOS needs the COM format.

NASM governs the format of the output file using a command line switch. To get a COM format in NASM, the -f bin switch works. It is also the default so that no switch at all will do the same thing. A file with this format has essentially no extra code at all. It is just a plain binary file.

Edlinas environment variables may also be defined in an EDL.INI file or from the > prompt.

12.3   Fixed Memory Areas

Real mode allows the programmer to use physical memory addresses. Memory addresses specified in real mode are used on the address bus, just like I/O addresses. This gives the programmer unimpeded access to memory. In this section, as an exercise in the use of real mode addresses, we consider two areas of memory which are defined by fixed physical addresses: the video buffer and the keyboard buffer. The location of the video buffer is fixed in the hardware. But the keyboard buffer is only fixed by DOS, and hence it can be moved. Referring to Figure 12-1, programs which access these physical memory areas directly are definitely "rude" programs as opposed to "polite" programs.

12.3.1   Video Buffer

On standard PCs, there is a region of memory starting at the address B8000H called the *video buffer*. In the most commonly used video text mode, the video buffer holds the text information which is displayed on the screen. A very simple, but somewhat tedious, way to output information on a PC is to store ASCII codes in this buffer. (See Table 11.1.)

The address B8000H is the actually address of the ASCII code for the character in the upper left-hand corner of the screen. See Figure 12-3. The next byte, which is at B8001H, contains the *attribute* information for this same character. Table 12.2 shows how the eight bits of an attribute byte are used. B8002H is the ASCII code of the second character in the first row; B8003H is its attribute byte, and so on. The top row consists of 80 characters, or 160 bytes, since each character takes two bytes of storage. One screenful is 25 rows × 80 columns × 2 bytes per character = 4000 bytes. The buffer actually contains 4096 bytes = 1000H.

Program 12.1 prints "Hello" on the screen by storing five ASCII codes into the video buffer. Figuring the address of the thirty-seventh character on line 13 in hex,

$$B8000H + D \times A0 + 24H \times 2 = B8000H + 820H + 48H = B8868H$$

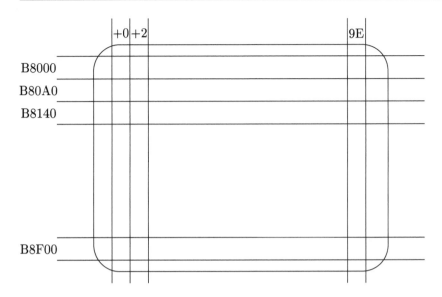

Figure 12-3. Upper Left at B8000 through Lower Right at B8F9E

Program 12.2 is a little 17-byte program which colors the screen yellow on blue by writing to all the attribute bytes in the video buffer. It begins at FFFH and counts down by twos.

12.3.2 Keyboard Buffer

When a key is either pressed or released, an interrupt is generated. On an ISA machine this interrupt is allotted, IRQ #1, which in turn is reported by the interrupt controller as interrupt number 9. (See Table 9.3.)

The DOS interrupt service routine 9 interrogates the keyboard at I/O port 64H and deposits characters it receives from there in a tiny buffer located at 41EH. The

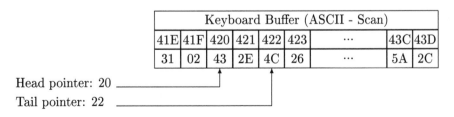

Figure 12-4. DOS Keyboard Buffer

characters come in from the keyboard as *scan codes*. The ISR converts each scan code to an ASCII character and stores both a scan code and an ASCII code in the

```
USE     .= 16
DOTO    .= COM
;
; Write Hello by storing ASCII codes into the video buffer.
;
        MOV AX, 0B886H  ; First 4 digits of B8868H
        MOV DS, AX
        MOV DI, 8       ; Last digit of B8868H
        MOV AH, 72      ; ASCII for H
        MOV [DI], AH    ; Store the character.
        ADD DI,2        ; Next odd address
        MOV AH, 101     ; ASCII for e
        MOV [DI], AH    ; Store the character.
        ADD DI,2        ;
        MOV AH, 108     ; ASCII for l
        MOV [DI], AH    ; Store the character.
        ADD DI,2        ;
        MOV AH, 108     ; ASCII for l
        MOV [DI], AH    ; Store the character.
        ADD DI,2        ;
        MOV AH, 111     ; ASCII for o
        MOV [DI], AH    ; Store the character.
        RET             ; Return to DOS
```

Program 12.1

buffer. From this buffer, the keys are picked up by the application program or the command line interpreter. The two bytes stored at 41A point to the next departing bytes. In Figure 12-4, there is one key waiting to be picked up. It is the letter C, whose ASCII code is 43H. 2E is its scan code. The two bytes stored at 41C point to the location where the next arriving bytes will be stored. Since the departing pointer is only two bytes behind the arrival pointer, this means there is only one character in the buffer, C in this case. Both pointers wrap around when they reach 43E. For this reason, the buffer is called a *circular buffer*.

Program 12.3 stores the string DIR into the keyboard buffer.

12.4 Real Mode Interrupts

When "polite" user programs want access to peripherals, they call the operating system. In a protected operating system, there is no choice about this. In an unprotected operating system like DOS, the call to the operating system is optional. (See Figure 12-1.) Just as the programs in section 12.3 accessed peripherals by barging

```
USE     .= 16
DOTO    .= COM
        MOV AX, 0B800H  ; Video buffer begins at B8000H
        MOV DS, AX
        MOV BX, 0FFFH   ; Odd address ending the 4K buffer.
        MOV AH, 1EH     ; Yellow on blue.
AGN:    MOV [BX], AH    ; Attribute goes into odd address
        DEC BX          ; Get next
        DEC BX          ; odd address
        JNS AGN         ; Continue till the beginning of the buffer
        RET             ; Return to DOS
```

Program 12.2

Bit	Usage	Example
7	Blinking	0
6	Background Red	0
5	Background Green	0
4	Background Blue	1
3	Foreground Intensity	1
2	Foreground Red	1
1	Foreground Green	1
0	Foreground Blue	0

Table 12.2. Attribute Byte: Yellow on Blue is 1EH

in on their private memory space, "rude" programs can also access peripherals by using using IN and OUT instructions.

Like Linux, the DOS operating system is accessed using software interrupts. The interrupt most used for access to DOS is INT 21H. To call one of the *functions* available under INT 21H, its number is stored in the AH register before the interrupt is called.

12.4.1 DOS Interrupts

To call the DOS function which outputs a character to the cursor location on the screen, the function number 2 is stored in the AH register and the ASCII code of the character to be printed is stored in the DL register. (Table 11.1 shows the ASCII code.) For example, the following code would print the letter H.

```
MOV AH, 2
MOV DL,72 ; ASCII code for H.
INT 21H
```

```
USE     .= 16
DOTO    .= COM
        MOV AX, 40H      ; Make 400H the base address
        MOV DS, AX       ; of the DS segment.
        MOV DL, 44h      ; ASCII code for 'D'
        CALL CST         ;
        MOV DL, 49H      ; ASCII code for 'I'
        CALL CST         ;
        MOV DL, 52H      ; ASCII code for 'R'
        CALL CST         ;
        RET
CST:    MOV SI,[1CH]     ; Pointer to end of keyboard buffer
        MOV [SI], DL     ; Store the character into the buffer.
        SUB SI, 1CH
        AND SI, 15       ; Add 2 (mod 16) to SI - 1EH
        ADD SI, 1EH      ;
        MOV [1CH], SI    ; Store the revised pointer.
        RET
```

Program 12.3

A related DOS function which outputs a string of characters can be called using AH = 9. The segment:offset address of the string is stored in DS:DX. The string must be terminated by a dollar sign character, ASCII 24H.

Many of these DOS functions call programs stored in ROM. They are often called BIOS programs. Many BIOS interrupts are accessed using INT 16H or INT 10H.

12.4.2   BIOS Interrupts

To call the BIOS function to output a character to the cursor location on the screen, the function number 0AH is stored in the AH register, and the ASCII code of the character to be printed is stored in DL. The number of times the character is to be written is stored in CX.

```
MOV AH, 10
MOV DL,72 ; ASCII code for H
MOV CX, 1 ; Number of times H is printed
MOV BH, 0 ; Current page
INT 10H
```

The BH register needs a 0 in order to send the output to the video buffer described in section 12.3. There is usually another 4K video buffer starting at B9000H. To access this buffer, a 1 should be stored in BH. Each of these buffers is called a *page*.

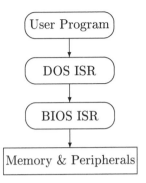

Figure 12-5. DOS Memory and Peripheral Access

These pages make it possible to flip from one screen to another without copying 4K of memory. The DOS function call takes responsibility for accessing the current page; the BIOS call does not.

Figure 12-5 illustrates the typical sequence of function calls. The fact that DOS programs call BIOS programs and not directly to the hardware leaves hardware designers free to make at least minor changes in their hardware without the necessity for changes in DOS. By revising the BIOS programs so as to maintain the same functionality of BIOS interrupts, changes in DOS become unnecessary. Similarly, changes in DOS can be accomplished without disrupting applications programs, provided that the DOS interrupt is rewritten so that it affords the same functionality to the applications program. These layers afford applications programmers, systems programmers, and hardware designers a modest degree of independence from one another.

User programs which bypass one or more of these layers risk a loss in portability. A program which calls directly to the hardware may not run on a machine with different hardware. The strongest reason a software developer has for sacrificing portability is that bypassing software layers reduces execution time. Execution time is still a problem in connection with video processing. That is one reason that the video buffer became standardized. So much software wrote to it directly that moving it would have made the graphics hardware with the old video buffer missing difficult to sell.

12.4.3   The Real Mode Interrupt Table

When an interrupt occurs, the interrupt number is used as an index into the interrupt table. The interrupt table contains the locations of all the service routines. The first entry in the table is for interrupt number 0, the second is for interrupt number 1, etc. The Linux interrupt table is described briefly in chapter 9, section 9.2.1. The real mode interrupt table differs from the protected mode interrupt

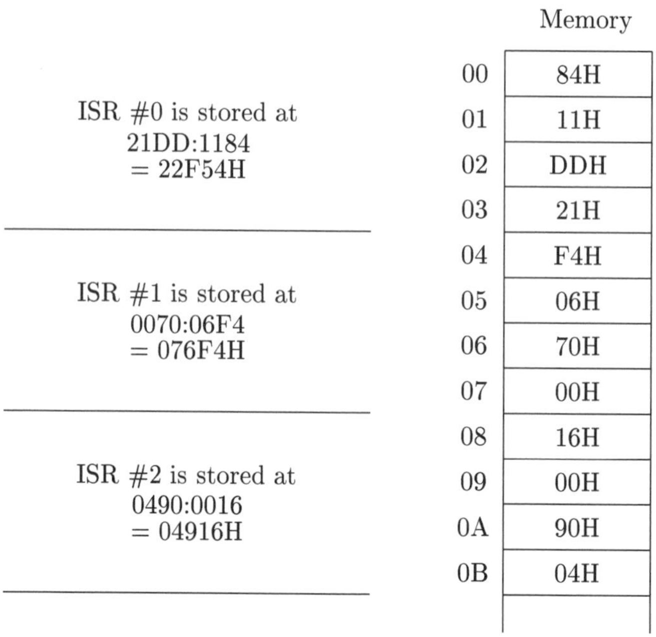

Memory

00	84H
01	11H
02	DDH
03	21H
04	F4H
05	06H
06	70H
07	00H
08	16H
09	00H
0A	90H
0B	04H

ISR #0 is stored at
21DD:1184
= 22F54H

ISR #1 is stored at
0070:06F4
= 076F4H

ISR #2 is stored at
0490:0016
= 04916H

Figure 12-6. Real Mode Interrupt Table

table used by Linux in several respects.

Every entry in the real mode interrupt table occupies four bytes. The first two bytes are a little endian offset value and the next two are a little endian segment value designation.

In real mode, the table is customarily located starting at address zero in memory. So the address of the interrupt service routine for interrupt 0 is stored in bytes 0 through 3. The address of the routine for interrupt 1 is stored in bytes 4 through 7. In general, if n is the number of an interrupt, then the address of the entry number n in the interrupt table is $4 \times n$. For example, if the interrupt number is 33H then the address of the ISR #33 is to be found in bytes CCH to CFH. The largest valid interrupt number is 255. The address for that routine is stored in bytes 1020 through 1023, or 3FCH through 3FFH. $4 \times 255 = 1020$.

Interrupt Vectors

The term *interrupt vector* is often used in connection with this table. Unfortunately, many conflicting meanings of the term are in use. The term has been used to mean

- the interrupt table itself

- one of the 256 entries contained in the table

- a memory location containing an entry in the table

- a number in the range 0–255 used as an index into the table

The term has been damaged beyond repair and it is best to just not use it any more.

Knowledge of this table makes it possible to write a program which supercedes a DOS or BIOS interrupt. By changing the stored ISR address from that of the DOS or BIOS interrupt, the new program can take the place of the old one. A new program can also insert itself as a layer by calling the old program after it has done whatever it wants with the original function call.

12.5   Checking DOS Memory

One simple but useful application of the shift commands is the conversion of the contents of a register into a four-digit sequence of hex characters. For example, to print out the first digit of the number stored in BX, say 3C4DH, we can make a copy of BX and shift it 12 bits to the right and get 0003H. The ASCII code for 3 is 30H + 3 = 33H. We can then send this code to the screen either directly using the video buffer, as in section 12.3, or as an interrupt, as in section 12.4. To get the second digit, we can shift a copy of BX eight bits to the right and get 003CH. To mask out all but the bottom four bits, we can AND with 000FH.

Program 12.4 uses this simple register conversion to display the regions of the 1 Meg DOS memory which are ROM. It works by checking every 16th byte in memory. The fact that the program sweeps through the entire memory means that at some point it becomes self-modifying code. The critical lines where code is modified in Program 12.4 span from the instructions MOV [DI], DL to the DEC BYTE [DI] instruction. The value stored in DI at the beginning must be chosen so that the modified bytes skip over this critical section of code. It so happens that 0 works with this code. To see why you can check the hex code to find the addresses of this critical section of code. You can use Edlinas to do this, or the DOS program DEBUG, or a hex editor. Both Emacs and the the elvis clone of vi can be used as hex editors. In this case the addresses are from 11H to 1BH, so 0 works fine.

Program 12.4 prints out ROM and RAM one letter at a time. They can also be printed out as strings. DOS interrupt 21H, using AH = 9, will print out a string which ends in a $ character and whose starting address is stored in DX. Instead of using

```
MOV DX, ABC
...
ABC: db 'RAM$'
```

to store a pointer to the string, we need to add the offset of the beginning of the program to DX. DOS loads .COM programs at an offset of 100H. So the code shown works if the MOV instruction is followed by

```
        ADD DX, 100H
```

A sample run of Program 12.4 produces an output such as

```
        RAM  00000
        ROM  A0000
        RAM  B8000
        ROM  C8000
```

```
; Map RAM vs. ROM in DOS's 1 Meg
;
                BITS 16             ; DOS programs use a 16-bit coding default
                MOV AH, 2           ; AH = 2 for DOS video output interrupt
                XOR BL, BL          ; BL = RAM/ROM check, 1 = RAM, 0 = ROM
                MOV DI, 0           ; DI is which byte out of each 16 to check
                XOR SI, SI          ; SI = 0 Start at the beginning of memory
TOP:            MOV DS, SI
                MOV BH, BL          ; Save previous RAM/ROM indication in BH
                XOR BL, BL          ; BL = 0 unless incremented below
                MOV DL, [DI]        ; Get memory value
                INC DL              ; Change it
                MOV [DI], DL        ; Try storing the changed value
                CMP [DI], DL        ; See if it worked
                JNE ROM             ; If they're not equal it's ROM
                DEC BYTE [DI]       ; Quick! Put back original value
                INC BL              ; 1 = RAM, 0 = ROM
ROM:            CMP BH, BL          ; Compare old with new value
                JG PRO              ; Changed from RAM to ROM, so print ROM
                JL PRA              ; Changed from ROM to RAM, so print RAM
                INC SI              ; Increment main loop counter
BOT:            JNZ TOP
DUN:            RET                 ; All done
;
PRO:            MOV DL, 'R'         ; 'R'. Print start of ROM
                INT 21H
                MOV DL, 'O'         ;
                INT 21H
                JMP MRG
PRA:            MOV DL, 'R'         ; 'R'. Print start of RAM
                INT 21H
                MOV DL, 'A'         ; 'A'
                INT 21H
MRG:            MOV DL, 'M'         ; 'M'
                INT 21H
```

```
               MOV DL, 32        ; <space>
               INT 21H
               MOV CL, 12        ; Prepare to print four digits
PRL:           MOV DX, DI        ;
               SHR DX, CL        ;
               AND DX, 15        ; Mask everything except hex one's digit
               CMP DL, 10        ; Does this print as a numeral or as a letter?
               JL NML
               ADD DL, 7         ; Letters need an extra seven
NML:           ADD DL, 30H
               INT 21H           ; Print hex digit
               SUB CL, 4
               JGE PRL           ;
               MOV DL, '0'       ; Fifth digit is 0
               INT 21H
               MOV DL, 13        ; Carriage return
               INT 21H
               MOV DL, 10        ; Need an EOL too
               INT 21H
               RET
```

Program 12.4

Further Reading

Advanced Assembly Language Programming, Allen Wyatt, Sr., Que: 1992.

13

LINUX BOOT TIME PROGRAMS

In chapter 12, we discussed the main differences between the environment provided to user programs which run under Linux and the environment under which DOS programs run. We saw how very different these two environments are. Much of the difference between these two environments is due to the fact that a different operating system is running in each. But there is also a difference at the hardware level. DOS was written for the 8086 processor. In order for DOS to run on a machine, that machine must act like an 8086. Linux is a multitasking system. In order for it to run on a machine, that machine must have hardware support for the protection of one task from another. The x86 processors, from the 80386 on, support both of these operating systems by running in two distinct operating modes, *real mode* which emulates an 8086 and *protected mode*, which has multitasking support.

13.1 Changing to Protected Mode

Whether an x86 processor runs in real or protected mode is determined by the bottom bit of the CR0 register. This register is a 32-bit extension of the 16-bit Machine Status Word register on the 80286. The least significant bit in this register is actually the most significant bit on the entire processor. If it is cleared, the processor operates in real mode. If it is set, the processor operates in protected mode.

Table 13.1 shows the bit allocations of the CR0 register in the 486.

To change to protected mode from DOS is easy.

```
MOV EAX, CR0
OR EAX, 1        ; Make the least significant bit 1.
MOV CR0, EAX     ; Here goes!
```

Program 13.1

But changing to protected mode should not be attempted without preparation. The

Bits	Label	Full Name
31	PG	Paging Enable
30	CD	Cache Disable
29	NW	No Write Through
18	AM	Alignment Mask
15	WP	Write Protect
5	NE	Numeric Error Enable
4	ET	Extension Type (287 vs. 387)
3	TS	Task Switched
2	EM	Emulate Math Chip
1	MP	Math Chip Present
0	PE	Protected Mode Enable

Table 13.1. 486 CR0 Register

machine will promptly crash if Program 13.1 is run before the following steps are taken.

1. In protected mode, all memory references depend on memory segment descriptor tables, particularly on the *global descriptor table*. Memory references, including those used in code fetching, will not work until these tables are set up. These tables are discussed in section 13.2.

2. In protected mode, the use of a radically different addressing system means that instructions will be fetched from a different CS segment. Code must be stored in the new CS segment.

3. In protected mode, each entry in the interrupt table is a specially formatted eight-byte entry. So the DOS interrupt table where each entry is just a four-byte address will not work. Before going into protected mode, a new interrupt table must be created.

This is why all x86 processors boot in real mode.

Note that switching to protected mode does not start paging. As checking Table 13.1 shows, paging is turned on using the top bit of CR0.

13.2 Protected Mode Segmentation

An assembler programmer working on an 8086 has access to whatever memory the machine has. All addresses are accessible. To get around problems caused by the misfit of the 20-bit addresses and 16-bit addresss registers, addressing on the 8086 uses 64K memory segments. The location of these memory segments is specified by the segment registers. Once a segment register is loaded, one can read to or write from the specified memory segment. Since on an 8086 the programmer can write to

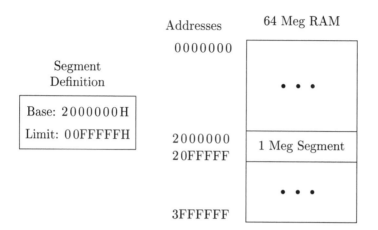

Figure 13-1. A Protected Mode Memory Segment

any segment register at will, a programmer can read from or write to any location in memory, (except for physically read-only memory). This means that memory protection on an 8086 is impossible.

Beginning with the 80286, the segmentation mechanism was completely re-designed for the purpose of turning it into a memory protection mechanism. Memory segments on a 286 have access permissions somewhat like Unix file permissions. They also have an access privilege level. Memory segments are no longer required to be 64K in length, but can be whatever length the operating systems programmer decides upon. Memory segments are defined by eight-byte data structures called a *segment descriptors* or sometimes just a *descriptors*. These descriptors are stored in tables called *descriptor tables*. Descriptor tables are located in memory just like the interrupt table. (See chapter 9, section 9.2.)

Segment registers are used to store pointers into these descriptor tables. These pointers are called *selectors*. They select segment descriptors from the descriptor tables. See Figure 13-2.

13.2.1 Protected Mode Memory Segments

The most important characteristics of a protected mode memory segment are its *base address* and its *limit*. See Figure 13-1 for an example of a 1 Meg segment situated at the halfway point of a 64 Meg memory. Suppose that the DS register contains a selector selecting a descriptor for this memory segment. Then the command

    MOV EAX, [DS:80000H]

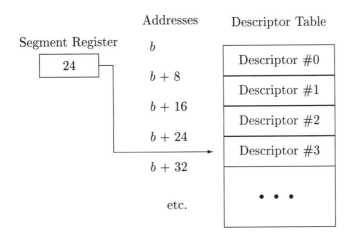

Figure 13-2. Selector Picks Segment Descriptor from the Descriptor Table

would access the four bytes located at the addresses 2080000H through 2080003H. On the other hand, the command

    MOV EAX, [DS:180000H]

would cause a general protection fault, a hardware exception which generates interrupt number 13. See chapter 9, section 9.4. This is because the all four offset addresses referenced by the command exceed the limit. For example,

    180003H > FFFFFH

The command is trying to read from a location 1.5 Meg from the beginning of a segment which is only 1 Meg in length. Because the hardware enforces these segment boundaries, the segmentation system can be used to protect one task's memory from another's. It was used to protect kernel memory from user processes in versions of Linux before version 2.1.39, but is no longer used for memory protection in Linux. Segments in Linux now use a base address of 0 and a limit of FFFFFFFFH, i.e. all 4 Gig.

A more complete list of the characteristics of a protected mode memory segment is as follows:

1. Base. This is the address of the first byte of the segment. It is the address corresponding to the offset of zero, [0]. In real mode, the base address is obtained by just appending a zero to the four hex digits stored in the segment register.

2. Limit. This is the last valid offset address. It is one less than the number of bytes in the segment. It is thanks to this parameter that segments are not

necessarily 64K any more. The limit needed to specify a 1 Meg segment, for example, is FFFFFH.

3. Access Permissions. Permissions to read, write, and execute can be specified.

4. Access Privilege Level. This privilege level is the least privileged value the CPL may have in order for access to be granted.

5. Miscellaneous. There are four or five functional bits in the descriptor unused by items 1 through 4. In the case of executable segments, one of these bits determines whether the code stored in the segment will be executed using a 16-bit or a 32-bit default, (see section 5.5).

In order to carry out base plus offset computations and offset versus limit comparisons without the delay which would be caused by a memory access, each segment register has associated with it base and limit registers which are reloaded every time the segment register is changed to reference a different segment. Figure 13-3 shows these registers. Although Figure 13-3 shows only base address and limit registers, there are also registers for all the other permission and privilege bits defined by the segment descriptor.

13.2.2   Special Memory Segments, the GDT and the IDT

Shown in Figure 13-3 are registers for the task state segment, the local and global descriptor tables, and the interrrupt descriptor table, the TSS, LDTS, GDT, and IDT. None of these are memory segments in the sense that they can be used in an ordinary memory access command. For example,

    MOV EAX, [TSS:10H]

is not valid code. But they are chunks of memory that have base addresses and limits. Since the GDT and the IDT are not accessed via selectors, they are not called memory segments. The TSS and the LDT are referred to as *special memory segments*.

The task state segment is used in task switches. The task being exited saves its registers in its task state segment. The base address and limit of the TSS is defined by a segment descriptor, just like other memory segments.

The local descriptor table (segment), LDTS, is used to store descriptors of segments which are not shared with all other tasks on the system.

The global descriptor table is used for storing descriptors of memory segments which are accessed by all tasks on the system, as well as all LDTS and TSS descriptors.

As we can see from Figure 13-3, there can be only one global and one local descriptor table in effect at any given time. When a task switch occurs, the local descriptor table is changed, just like the page tables are changed. But the global descriptor table stays the same.

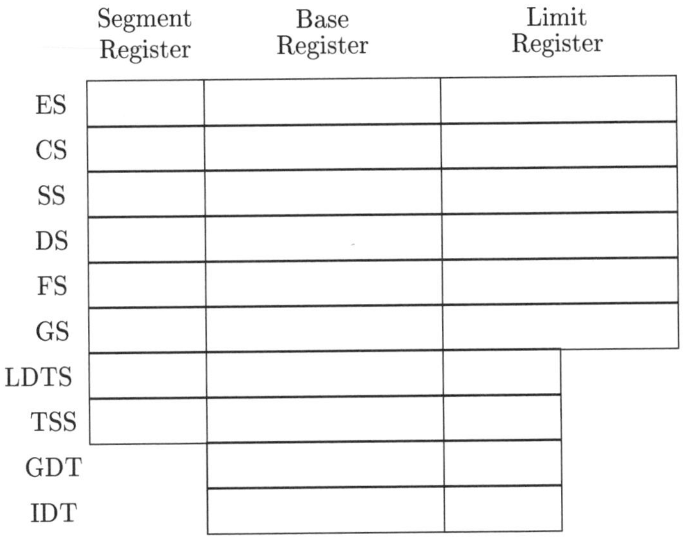

	Segment Register	Base Register	Limit Register
ES			
CS			
SS			
DS			
FS			
GS			
LDTS			
TSS			
GDT			
IDT			

Figure 13-3. Selector, Base, and Limit Registers

The IDT, the interrupt descriptor table, and its entries are described in chapter 9.

The global descriptor table and interrupt descriptor table also have base addresses and limits, and hence, there are registers for them. But these addresses are never coded into descriptors, so there is no point in having selectors for them. Intel does not consider the global descriptor table or the interrupt descriptor table to be segments because they are not accessed using selectors.

13.2.3 Selectors

In real mode, segment registers such as DS specify segments by holding the first four hex digits of the base address of the segment. In protected mode segment, registers specify segments by holding pointers to their descriptors. Each descriptor consists of a complete definition of the segment. The pointer points into a descriptor table. The table may either be the global descriptor table or the local descriptor table.

A very simple way to implement a pointer like this would be to use the offset from the beginning of the descriptor table. This is what is shown in Figure 13-2. Although the value 24 shown in the figure would work just as illustrated, it is not the case that the selector is simply an offset.

Suppose that a descriptor we want to point to were located 48 bytes from the beginning of a descriptor table. In that case, the offset 48 would make a very good pointer to that descriptor, assuming we know which table the descriptor is located in. Since each descriptor occupies eight bytes of storage, all such offsets are multiples of 8. Hence in binary, the three least significant bits of each offset are zero. The x86 takes advantage of this fact and puts those three bits of the selector to work carrying other information. Bits 0 and 1 carry a privilege level. Bit 2 is the table indicator bit which determines whether the selector is a pointer into the global table or the local table, 1 = local, 0 = global. To recover the offset from the selector, the bottom three bits must be zeroed back out again. Figure 13-4 illustrates the example where DS contains 51, or 33H. As a 16-bit binary number, it is The pointer into the descriptor table is the table offset, 48 in this case, or 30H.

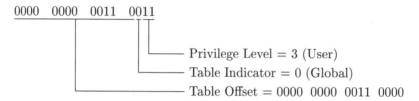

Figure 13-4. Selector Encoding

The three least significant bits are zeroed out. To locate the descriptor for the DS segment, we would get the address of the global descriptor table from the GDT base address register and add 30H.

There is one selector which does not use the format just described.

It is desirable that one selector value be a null-value. That makes it possible to shut down unused segments. A selector which points to offset zero in the global table is by definition a null selector. Storing a null selector in a segment register disallows the use of that segment. All attempts to access a segment marked with a null selector cause a general protection fault. This, incidentally, makes it impossible for any selector to actually point to the first entry in the global table. (So it doesn't matter what this entry contains.)

13.2.4   Segment Operations

The GDT has to be there for memory references to work in protected mode and the IDT has to be there for interrupts to work. The load commands for these tables are

>   LGDT mem

and

>   LIDT mem

where mem points to six bytes of memory containing a two-byte limit, followed by a four byte base address. These commands would ordinarily be executed just once while the system was booting in real mode.

	Load	Store	MOV Load	MOV Store
ES	LES		X	X
CS				X
SS	LSS		X	X
DS	LDS		X	X
FS	LFS		X	X
GS	LGS		X	X
LDTS	LLDT	SLDT		
TSS	LTR	STR		
GDT	LGDT	SGDT		
IDT	LIDT	SIDT		

Figure 13-5. Segment Load and Store Commands

Other segment registers are loaded using selectors. Figure 13-5 shows the commands for loading and saving segment registers, as well as the commands for loading and saving the GDT and IDT base and limit registers. When segment registers are loaded, all the other registers associated with them are loaded as well, unless the null selector is used or unless some access violation occurs.

These eight bytes would include the base address and size of the DS segment. These eight bytes would also include a privilege level. Since the privilege carried in DS is only a 3, the privilege level in the segment descriptor would need to be a 3, or the processor would nail us with an error. In protected mode, a command such as

MOV DS, AX

will cause a protection fault whenever the privilege level carried by the two least significant bits of the selector in AX is inferior to the privilege level written into the descriptor of the segment. Because the local descriptor table is implemented as a segment, access to it requires that a selector for it be loaded into a segment register. Since the local descriptor table is a special segment, not just any segment register will do. There is a segment register dedicated to the local descriptor table, the LDT register. To load the LDT register, the following command is used,

LLDT rm2

where **rm2** must be a two-byte register or memory location containing a selector referencing an entry in the global descriptor table. This entry should be a descriptor for a local descriptor table. Because the command uses the global table, it only works in protected mode. For example, if AX contains a selector which points at a descriptor located in the global descriptor table and this descriptor describes a local table, then

> LLDT AX

Suppose we have a computer with 64 Meg of memory and we want a 1 Meg segment starting at the beginning at the halfway point, i.e., at the address 32 Meg.

> Base: 02000000H (Start at 32 Meg)
> Limit: 000FFFFFH (1 Meg Segment)
> Permissions: Read and Write
> Privilege Level: User

This information can be coded into an eight-byte descriptor. This descriptor can then be added to a descriptor table. For a user program to access this segment, it must have the index or *selector* of this descriptor stored in a segment register such as DS. The offset address used in accessing the segment must be less than the limit defined in the descriptor.

13.2.5   Descriptor Encoding

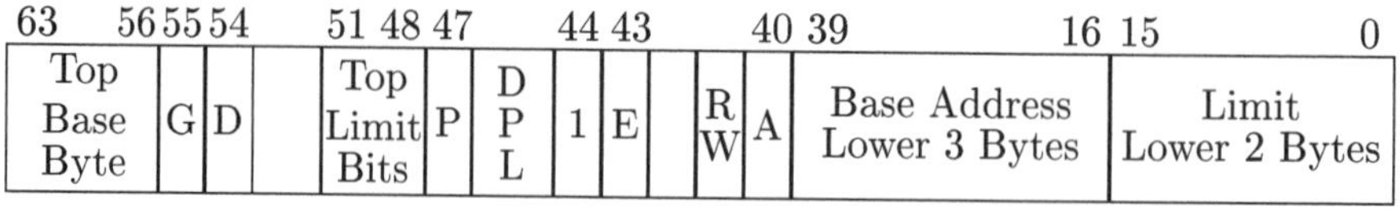

Figure 13-6. Segment Descriptor Layout

The two main items that need to be encoded into the memory segment descriptor are the base and the limit. Since these are both four-byte numbers and the descriptor is an eight-byte structure, it would appear that the space available is all used up by just these two items. By squeezing on the limit encoding, however, extra bits are freed up. Instead of allowing all eight hex digits of the four-byte limit value to be configurable, the segment designer is allowed only five digits to play with. This saves three hex digits or 12 bits. These three hex digits are allowed to be either 0s tacked on at the front or Fs tacked on at the end. The first is called *byte granularity* and the second is called *page granularity*. Specifying which of these two granularities is used costs one more bit. This bit is called the *granularity bit*. As an example of how this descriptor format is used, let us encode the sample 1 Meg segment just described. The four-byte base value 02000000H would be stored in bits 16–39 and 56–63, 24 bits plus eight bits. (This odd fracture is a vestige of the 24-bit addressing used on the 80286.) Displaying all eight bytes as a 16-digit hex number, using X for undetermined digits yields

> 02 XX XX 00 00 00 XX XX

The 32-bit limit values are coded into 21 bits by restricting the number of allowable limit values. The 20 bits from 0–15 and 48–51 encode five hex digits. Bit 55, G for granularity, determines whether the three remaining hex digits will be 0s added to the top end or Fs added to the bottom. The value 000FFFFFH may be encoded using either scheme. If we use G = 0 for byte granularity, then inserting the 20 limit bits, FFFFFH, gives us:

> 02 XF XX 00 00 00 FF FF

In the CS segments, the D bit is extremely important. In x86 code, there is a coding default which may either be for 16-bit code or 32-bit code. See chapter 5, section 5.5 for details on how this works. In protected mode, the default is determined by the D bit of the CS segment descriptor. D = 1 means that the default is 32-bit code, D = 0 means it is 16. In real mode, the default is always 16-bit code. With G = 0, D = 1 and bits 52 and 53 as 0, we get

> 02 4F XX 00 00 00 FF FF

Bit 51, P for present, should be marked 1. If this is to be a user accessible segment, then the DPL bits must be 3. DPL stands for *descriptor privilege level*. If this is a data segment, then E = 0, i.e., it is not executeable, and W = 1, i.e., it is writeable. Making the remaining two bits, 40 and 42, 0 yields

> 02 4F F2 00 00 00 FF FF

13.2.6 Task Isolation via Local Descriptor Tables

A process can only access memory segments that are listed in two tables, its own table called the *local descriptor table*, and another table called the *global descriptor table*. The system has only one global descriptor table. All processes have access to the global table, but local tables need not be shared. Consequently one method the operating system could use to isolate tasks from one another would be to hand out different local descriptor tables to different processes. If a segment is not listed in either the global descriptor table or the process's own local descriptor table, then the process can't get to it. Before discussing protection further, we need to look at some of the details of descriptors, selectors, and the descriptor tables.

Segmentation on the 80286 was designed to allow different tasks to have their own memory segments to which other tasks would not have access. Each task can have its own local descriptor table. Descriptors of private memory segments can be stored in these local tables. The x86 architecture implements local descriptor tables as segments, complete with descriptors in the global table. In the memory shown

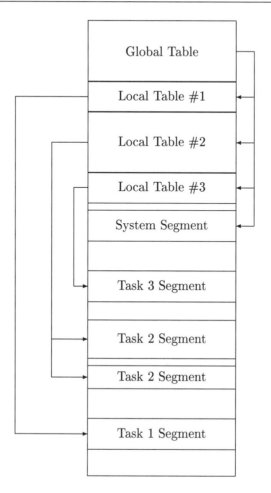

Figure 13-7. Memory with Protected Segments

in Figure 13-7, there are eight memory segments. Each of these memory segments is defined by a descriptor situated in a descriptor table. Although the global table is like a segment, it is not a segment. There is no descriptor for it anywhere in memory and no selector for it anywhere in the processor.

Reviewing briefly, the operating system protects the memory belonging to one task from access by another task by using local descriptor tables. A new task would receive a local descriptor table containing descriptors of all the segments to which that task is allowed access. So long as the operating system did not put the same descriptor in the local table belonging to some other task, that segment would then be private. A task can only access a segment if a descriptor for that segment is in the global table or its own local table.

This system of protection is incomplete, however. Locking the front door to your house doesn't lock the house if the back door is unlocked. Since all tasks can access the global table, there must be something to prevent a rogue task from reading the descriptors defining the local descriptor tables belonging to other tasks.

Consider this code:

```
        MOV AX, 0       ;
                        ; AX is a 16-bit selector.
                        ; Bit 2 is 0. ; We're pointing into the global table.
                        ; Bits 0 and 1 are 0
                        ; That's system level privilege.
HAK:    LLDT AX         ;
                        ; AX is pointing at some descriptor
                        ; It could be a local table descriptor
                        ; If so it's probably not our own local table.
                        ; And in that case we have just borrowed someone
                        ; else's private descriptor table and we can
                        ; access anything listed in there.
        ADD AX, 8       ; Maybe not.
                        ; Go to the next descriptor
        JMP HAK         ; The local tables are in here.
                        ; We'll find them.
```

Program 13.2

Memory protection by itself doesn't work. User processes must not be allowed to execute code like the above code.

13.3   Setting Up the Global Descriptor Table

When an x86 processor is turned on or restarted, it does not create a global descriptor table automatically. Hence (unless a manufacturer puts one in ROM), none exists at boot time. Since the processor can't use memory in protected mode without a global table, the processor must boot up in real mode. The processor can subsequently be switched into protected mode, but only after the global table has been set up.

The processor has base address and limit registers for the global descriptor table (GDT). These registers are loaded using the command

```
    LGDT mem
```

where **mem** points to six bytes of memory containing a two-byte limit and a four-byte base address for the global table. Although a register MOV command might have been a more convenient way of doing this, there are no six-byte registers available.

As an example of how we might use the **LGDT** command, suppose that ten descriptors that we want to use as our global table have been stored starting at address 10000H. Our global table will therefore be eighty bytes long and start at 10000H. The limit is one less than eighty, or 4FH. In order to use the LGDT command, we need to store these values in memory somewhere. Suppose we set up a "scratch" memory area at 20000H and put our GDT values there. After this code

```
MOV AX, 2000H    ; Set up a segment for the scratch area.
MOV DS, AX       ;
MOV AX, 4FH      ; GDT's limit is a 2 byte value.
MOV [DS:0], AX   ; Store 79 into the first 2 bytes of
                 ; scratch.
MOV EAX, 10000H  ; GDT's base address is a 4 byte value.
MOV [DS:2], EAX  ; Store this 4 byte address
                 ; 2 bytes into the scratch.
                 ; (Don't overwrite the first two bytes.)
LGDT [DS:0]      ;
; This loads the both the GDT base address register
                 ; and the GDT limit register
                 ; i.e., load all 6 bytes.
```

Program 13.3

has executed, the GDT bases address and limit registers will be loaded. The global table has not been used for anything yet. In fact, we could even run this code first and then store those eighty bytes next. The global table will not go into operation until the processor is switched into protected mode.

13.4   Closing

The surface has barely been scratched. But the way forward is open.

INDEX

LICENSE AGREEMENT AND LIMITED WARRANTY

READ THE FOLLOWING TERMS AND CONDITIONS CAREFULLY BEFORE OPENING THIS SOFTWARE MEDIA PACKAGE. THIS LEGAL DOCUMENT IS AN AGREEMENT BETWEEN YOU AND PRENTICE-HALL, INC. (THE "COMPANY"). BY OPENING THIS SEALED SOFTWARE MEDIA PACKAGE, YOU ARE AGREEING TO BE BOUND BY THESE TERMS AND CONDITIONS. IF YOU DO NOT AGREE WITH THESE TERMS AND CONDITIONS, DO NOT OPEN THE SOFTWARE MEDIA PACKAGE. PROMPTLY RETURN THE UNOPENED SOFTWARE MEDIA PACKAGE AND ALL ACCOMPANYING ITEMS TO THE PLACE YOU OBTAINED THEM FOR A FULL REFUND OF ANY SUMS YOU HAVE PAID.

1.　　　**GRANT OF LICENSE:** In consideration of your payment of the license fee, which is part of the price you paid for this product, and your agreement to abide by the terms and conditions of this Agreement, the Company grants to you a nonexclusive right to use and display the copy of the enclosed software program (hereinafter the "SOFTWARE") on a single computer (i.e., with a single CPU) at a single location so long as you comply with the terms of this Agreement. The Company reserves all rights not expressly granted to you under this Agreement.

2.　　　**OWNERSHIP OF SOFTWARE:** You own only the magnetic or physical media (the enclosed software media) on which the SOFTWARE is recorded or fixed, but the Company retains all the rights, title, and ownership to the SOFTWARE recorded on the original software media copy(ies) and all subsequent copies of the SOFTWARE, regardless of the form or media on which the original or other copies may exist. This license is not a sale of the original SOFTWARE or any copy to you.

3.　　　**COPY RESTRICTIONS:** This SOFTWARE and the accompanying printed materials and user manual (the "Documentation") are the subject of copyright. You may not copy the Documentation or the SOFTWARE, except that you may make a single copy of the SOFTWARE for backup or archival purposes only. You may be held legally responsible for any copying or copyright infringement which is caused or encouraged by your failure to abide by the terms of this restriction.

4.　　　**USE RESTRICTIONS:** You may not network the SOFTWARE or otherwise use it on more than one computer or computer terminal at the same time. You may physically transfer the SOFTWARE from one computer to another provided that the SOFTWARE is used on only one computer at a time. You may not distribute copies of the SOFTWARE or Documentation to others. You may not reverse engineer, disassemble, decompile, modify, adapt, translate, or create derivative works based on the SOFTWARE or the Documentation without the prior written consent of the Company.

5.　　　**TRANSFER RESTRICTIONS:** The enclosed SOFTWARE is licensed only to you and may not be transferred to any one else without the prior written consent of the Company. Any unauthorized transfer of the SOFTWARE shall result in the immediate termination of this Agreement.

6.　　　**TERMINATION:** This license is effective until terminated. This license will terminate automatically without notice from the Company and become null and void if you fail to comply with any provisions or limitations of this license. Upon termination, you shall destroy the Documentation and all copies of the SOFTWARE. All provisions of this Agreement as to warranties, limitation of liability, remedies or damages, and our ownership rights shall survive termination.

7.　　　**MISCELLANEOUS:** This Agreement shall be construed in accordance with the laws of the United States of America and the State of New York and shall benefit the Company, its affiliates, and assignees.

8.　　　**LIMITED WARRANTY AND DISCLAIMER OF WARRANTY:** The Company warrants that the SOFTWARE, when properly used in accordance with the Documentation, will operate in substantial conformity with the description of the SOFTWARE set forth in the Documentation. The Company does not warrant that the SOFTWARE will meet your requirements or that the operation of the SOFTWARE will be uninterrupted or error-free. The Company warrants that the media on which the SOFTWARE is delivered shall be free from defects in materials and workmanship under normal use for a period of thirty (30) days from the date of your purchase. Your only remedy and the Company's only obligation under these limited warranties is, at the Company's option, return of the warranted item for a refund of any amounts paid by you or replacement of the item. Any replacement of SOFTWARE or media under the warranties shall not extend the original warranty period. The limited warranty set forth above shall not apply to any SOFTWARE which the Company determines in good faith has been subject to misuse, neglect, improper installation, repair, alteration, or damage by you. EXCEPT FOR THE EXPRESSED WARRANTIES SET FORTH ABOVE, THE COMPANY DISCLAIMS ALL WARRANTIES, EXPRESS OR IMPLIED, INCLUDING WITHOUT LIMITATION, THE IMPLIED WARRANTIES OF MERCHANTABILITY AND FITNESS FOR A PAR-TICULAR PURPOSE. EXCEPT FOR THE EXPRESS WARRANTY SET FORTH ABOVE, THE COM-PANY DOES NOT WARRANT, GUARANTEE, OR MAKE ANY REPRESENTATION REGARDING THE USE OR THE RESULTS OF THE USE OF THE SOFTWARE IN TERMS OF ITS CORRECTNESS, ACCURACY, RELIABILITY, CURRENTNESS, OR OTHERWISE.

IN NO EVENT, SHALL THE COMPANY OR ITS EMPLOYEES, AGENTS, SUPPLIERS, OR CONTRACTORS BE LIABLE FOR ANY INCIDENTAL, INDIRECT, SPECIAL, OR CONSEQUEN-TIAL DAMAGES ARISING OUT OF OR IN CONNECTION WITH THE LICENSE GRANTED UNDER THIS AGREEMENT, OR FOR LOSS OF USE, LOSS OF DATA, LOSS OF INCOME OR PROFIT, OR OTHER LOSSES, SUSTAINED AS A RESULT OF INJURY TO ANY PERSON, OR LOSS OF OR DAM-AGE TO PROPERTY, OR CLAIMS OF THIRD PARTIES, EVEN IF THE COMPANY OR AN AUTHO-RIZED REPRESENTATIVE OF THE COMPANY HAS BEEN ADVISED OF THE POSSIBILITY OF SUCH DAMAGES. IN NO EVENT SHALL LIABILITY OF THE COMPANY FOR DAMAGES WITH RESPECT TO THE SOFTWARE EXCEED THE AMOUNTS ACTUALLY PAID BY YOU, IF ANY, FOR THE SOFTWARE.

SOME JURISDICTIONS DO NOT ALLOW THE LIMITATION OF IMPLIED WARRAN-TIES OR LIABILITY FOR INCIDENTAL, INDIRECT, SPECIAL, OR CONSEQUENTIAL DAMAGES, SO THE ABOVE LIMITATIONS MAY NOT ALWAYS APPLY. THE WARRANTIES IN THIS AGREE-MENT GIVE YOU SPECIFIC LEGAL RIGHTS AND YOU MAY ALSO HAVE OTHER RIGHTS WHICH VARY IN ACCORDANCE WITH LOCAL LAW.

ACKNOWLEDGMENT

YOU ACKNOWLEDGE THAT YOU HAVE READ THIS AGREEMENT, UNDERSTAND IT, AND AGREE TO BE BOUND BY ITS TERMS AND CONDITIONS. YOU ALSO AGREE THAT THIS AGREEMENT IS THE COMPLETE AND EXCLUSIVE STATEMENT OF THE AGREEMENT BETWEEN YOU AND THE COMPANY AND SUPERSEDES ALL PROPOSALS OR PRIOR AGREE-MENTS, ORAL, OR WRITTEN, AND ANY OTHER COMMUNICATIONS BETWEEN YOU AND THE COMPANY OR ANY REPRESENTATIVE OF THE COMPANY RELATING TO THE SUBJECT MAT-TER OF THIS AGREEMENT.

Should you have any questions concerning this Agreement or if you wish to contact the Com-pany for any reason, please contact in writing at the address below.

Robin Short
Prentice Hall PTR
One Lake Street
Upper Saddle River, New Jersey 07458

ABOUT THE CD

The CD-ROM accompanying this book contains six directories:

1. The cq directory contains the device driver files for theMorse code speaker driver.
2. The dosemu directory contains a distribution of the dosemu program. It can also be obtained from www.dosemu.org.
3. The edlinas directory contains the DOS executable EDL.EXE and another file X86.DAT, which is required for Edlinas to execute. Subdirectories of this directory contain source code, compiling information, and sample programs.
4. The nasm directory contains the compressed download of the NASM program as well as a copy of the license governing its use. It can also be obtained from www.cryogen.com/nasm.
5. The ob directory contains the source code for the object code parser, ob.
6. The scalex directory contains the device driver files for the Scalexdevice driver.

TECHNICAL SUPPORT

Prentice Hall does not offer technical support for this CD-ROM. However, if there is a problem with the media, you may obtain a replacement copy by emailing us with your problem at:

disc_exchange@prenhall.com